Middle East

lonely planet

phrasebooks

Middle East phrasebook
1st edition – September 2007

Published by
Lonely Planet Publications Pty Ltd ABN 36 005 607 983
90 Maribyrnong St, Footscray, Victoria 3011, Australia

Lonely Planet Offices
Australia Locked Bag 1, Footscray, Victoria 3011
USA 150 Linden St, Oakland CA 94607
UK 72–82 Rosebery Ave, London, EC1R 4RW

Cover illustration
Middle Eastern Marriage by Wendy Wright

ISBN 978 1 86450 261 9

text © Lonely Planet Publications Pty Ltd 2007
cover illustration © Lonely Planet Publications Pty Ltd 2007

 10 9 8 7 6 5 4 3 2

Printed through the Bookmaker International Ltd
Printed in Hong Kong

acknowledgments

This book is based on existing editions of Lonely Planet's phrasebooks as well as new content. It was developed with the help of the following people:

- Shalome Knoll for the Modern Standard and Levantine Arabic chapters
- Siona Jenkins for the Egyptian Arabic chapter
- Kathryn Stapley for the Gulf and Tunisian Arabic chapters
- Yavar Dehghani for the Farsi chapter
- Mimoon Abu Ata for the Hebrew chapter
- Arzu Kürklü for the Turkish chapter

Special thanks to Shalome Knoll for proofing and additional translations for the Egyptian, Gulf and Tunisian Arabic chapters.

.onely Planet Language Products

ublishing Manager: Chris Rennie
ommissioning Editors: Karin Vidstrup Monk & Rachel Williams
ditors: Vanessa Battersby & Branislava Vladisavljevic
ssisting Editor: Emma Koch
anaging Editor: Annelies Mertens

Layout Designers: Jacqueline McLeod & Jacqui Saunders
Managing Layout Designer: Sally Darmody
Cartographer: Wayne Murphy
Series Designer & Illustrations: Yukiyoshi Kamimura

contents

CONTENTS

5

Middle East

- ■ Arabic (Modern Standard)
- ▨ Egyptian Arabic
- ▨ Gulf Arabic
- ▨ Levantine Arabic
- ▨ Tunisian Arabic

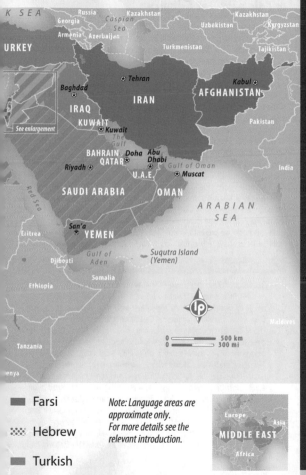

Farsi

Hebrew

Turkish

Note: Language areas are
approximate only.
For more details see the
relevant introduction.

MIDDLE EAST

middle east – at a glance

The use of the term 'Middle East' is almost as complex as the history of the region itself. The expression first appeared in English at the start of the 20th century and had replaced the term 'Near East' by the middle of the century. In some languages, such as German or Russian, the region is still referred to as the 'Near East'. In a cultural sense, the name 'Middle East' can be used only in relation to the Arab world, but it's generally also applied to the non-Arabic lands of Israel, Turkey and Iran. In terms of geography, 'Middle East' means primarily the Levant (the eastern shore of the Mediterranean) and the Persian Gulf States (the Arabian Peninsula, Iran and Iraq). Broader geographical definitions, however, also include the Maghreb (Northern Africa) and even parts of Central Asia.

Along with a wealth of religions and cultures, the Middle East boasts great linguistic diversity. Its languages belong to three large families – Afro-Asiatic, Indo-European and Ural-Altaic. Arabic is truly the lingua franca of the region, with official status in all Middle Eastern countries except for Iran and Turkey. Many of these countries have several minority languages as well – the Berber dialects in North Africa, or Kurdish and Armenian in Iraq and Turkey, for example. European languages are often widely used too – English throughout the Arabian Peninsula and the Persian Gulf, and French in North Africa and the Levant.

In this book, we present Modern Standard Arabic and the four main colloquial Arabic varieties in one section, followed by the Farsi, Hebrew and Turkish languages.

did you know?

- The League of Arab States (more informally called the Arab League) was formed by seven Arab states on 22 March 1945 with the Alexandria Protocol. Today, it has 22 member states from the Middle East and Africa. Its headquarters are in Cairo, Egypt. The official language of the League is Modern Standard Arabic.
- The Middle Eastern countries use an array of currencies. The main ones are: dinar, dirham, lira, pound, riyal, shekel and shilling. Their official names always include the country name (eg 'Egyptian pound', 'Saudi riyal').
- Al-Jazeera, the famous satellite television network, is headquartered in Doha, Qatar. It was launched in 1996 with a news and current affairs program in Arabic. Since then, several other specialty channels have been founded within the network, including an English-language current affairs channel.
- Five of the Seven Wonders of the Ancient World belong to the Middle East: Pharos of Alexandria and the Pyramids of Giza (Egypt); the Hanging Gardens of Babylon (Iraq); the Mausoleum of Halicarnassus and the Temple of Artemis (Turkey). The two exceptions are the Colossus of Rhodes and the Statue of Zeus (both in Greece).

introduction to arabic

The Arabic language is characterised by a number of colloquial varieties. Here, we introduce you to Modern Standard Arabic (MSA) – the lingua franca of all Arabic countries – alongside the four most common Arabic varieties spoken across the Middle East: Egyptian, Gulf, Levantine and Tunisian.

Muslims say that Arabic is the most perfect language of all, as it's the language in which the Quran was revealed. Religious beliefs aside, the international status of Arabic is impressive: it's one of the world's 10 most widely spoken languages, with over 200 million speakers. Arabic is spoken as the first language across the Middle East and North Africa and is widely used as a second language throughout the Islamic world. It has official status in 25 countries, the Arab League and the African Union, and it's one of the six official languages of the United Nations.

As a member of the Afro-Asiatic language family's Semitic branch, Arabic is related to Hebrew and Amharic, and to the ancient Aramaic and Phoenician languages. It's a bit misleading to speak just of 'Arabic', however, as there are many varieties of this language. It's often given as an example of 'diglossia' – two varieties of the same language used in different contexts. Classical Arabic (اللغة العربية الفصحى al·lu·gha·tul 'a·ra·bee·ya·tul fus·ha), the highly respected language of the Quran and classical literature, is used mainly for literary and religious purposes. Modern Standard Arabic or MSA (اللغة العربية الحديثة al·lu·gha·tul 'a·ra·bee·ya·tul ha·dee·tha) is the modernised version of Classical Arabic, used in schools, administration and the media – the official lingua franca of the Arab world. The colloquial language, ie everyday spoken version of modern Arabic (اللغة العامية al·lu·gha·tul 'aa·mee·ya), has many regional dialects, sometimes mutually unintelligible and with no official written form. Each dialect is strongly influenced by the indigenous or colonial languages of the area in which it's spoken (eg Berber or French in North Africa). Of all the dialects, Egyptian Arabic (اللهجة المصرية al·lah·ja·tul mis·ree·ya) is probably the most familiar to all Arabic speakers, thanks to the popularity of Egyptian television and cinema. Gulf, Levantine and Tunisian Arabic are other spoken varieties that cover broad parts of the Middle East.

Take one look at the elegant Arabic script and it's obvious why calligraphy is an art form in the Arab world. The Arabic alphabet evolved from the Aramaic script in the 4th century, and its earliest written record dates from AD 512. Arabic is written from right to left and the form of each letter changes depending on whether it's at the start, in the middle or at the end of a word or whether it stands alone.

The huge impact of Arabic on English and many other languages is easily visible, although it often came by way of other languages, for example Spanish or Hindi. It's the source of many common English words – *alcohol, candle, coffee, cotton, jar, mattress* and *syrup*, to name only a few – and is also responsible for a few more esoteric terms like *assassin, elixir, genie, harem, zenith* ...

pronunciation

The sounds of Modern Standard Arabic are the basis for the pronunciation of other Arabic varieties. However, there are a few variations in pronunciation, as shown in the following tables. The regional differences between the varieties of Arabic are indicated in brackets – the other sounds are common to all versions of Arabic included in this phrasebook. If you follow our coloured pronunciation guides, you won't have problems being understood.

vowel sounds

symbol	english equivalent	arabic example	transliteration
a	act	أَنْتَ	an·ta
aa	father	الآن	al·aan
ae (Levantine)	air	جامعة	jae·mi·'a
ai (Egyptian, Gulf, Tunisian)	aisle	أَيْنَ	ai·na
aw	law	يَوْم	yawm
ay	say	بَيْتْ	bayt
e (Egyptian, Levantine, Tunisian)	bet	بنزين	ben·zeen
ee	see	فِيْلْ	feel
i	hit	كِتَابْ	ki·taab
o (Egyptian, Tunisian)	pot	نوم	nom
oo	zoo	فُوْلْ	fool
u	put	ثُمَّ	thum·ma
'	like the pause in the middle of 'uh-oh'	الْعَرَبِيَّة	al·'a·ra·bee·ya

word stress

Stress usually falls on the first syllable of a word or the one with a long vowel. Just follow our pronunciation guides, in which the stressed syllable is always in italics.

consonant sounds

symbol	english equivalent	arabic example	transliteration
b	bed	بَيْت	bait
ch (Gulf)	cheat	كَتف	chatf
d	dog	دَار	daar
dh (not in Egyptian)	that	ذَاكِرَة، ظَهْر	dhaa·ki·ra, dhahr
f	fun	فَمّ	fam
g (not in MSA)	go	جَدِيدٌ، قَدِيمٌ	ga·deed, ga·deem
gh	a guttural sound, like the Parisian French 'r'	غَادِر	ghaa·dir
h	hat	حُلْوَة، هُوَ	hal·wa, hu·wa
j (not in Egyptian)	jar	جِدِيدٌ	ja·deed
k	kit	كِتَاب، قَدِيمٌ	ki·taab, ka·deem
kh	as the 'ch' in the Scottish *loch*	خَرِيطَة	kha·ree·ta
l	lot	لَيْل	lail
m	man	مَطْحَف	mat·haf
n	not	نَظِيفٌ	na·dheef
r	run (rolled)	رِيَال	ri·yaal
s	sun	سَبْعَة، صَيْف	sab·'a, saif
sh	shot	شِتَاء	shi·taa'
t	top	تِسْعَة، طَائِرَة	tis·'a, taa·'i·ra
th (not in Egyptian)	thin	ثَقِيل	tha·keel
w	win	وَسِيلَة	wa·see·la
y	yes	يَمِين	ya·meen
z	zero	زَمَان	za·maan
zh (Egyptian)	pleasure	جراج	ga·raazh
'	like the pause in the middle of 'uh-oh'	عَيْن، سَأَلَ، سُؤَالٌ، سَائِل، شِتَاء	'ain, sa·'a·la, su·'aal, saa·'il, shi·taa'

arabic alphabet

word-final	word-medial	word-initial	alone	letter
ـا	ـا	ا	ا	alef'
ـب	ـبـ	بـ	ب	'ba
ـت	ـتـ	تـ	ت	'ta
ـث	ـثـ	ثـ	ث	'tha
ـج	ـجـ	جـ	ج	jeem
ـح	ـحـ	حـ	ح	'ha
ـخ	ـخـ	خـ	خ	'kha
ـد	ـدـ	دـ	د	daal
ـذ	ـذـ	ذـ	ذ	dhaal
ـر	ـرـ	رـ	ر	'ra
ـز	ـزـ	زـ	ز	'za
ـس	ـسـ	سـ	س	seen
ـش	ـشـ	شـ	ش	sheen
ـص	ـصـ	صـ	ص	saad
ـض	ـضـ	ضـ	ض	daad
ـط	ـطـ	طـ	ط	'ta
ـظ	ـظـ	ظـ	ظ	'dha
ـع	ـعـ	عـ	ع	ain'
ـغ	ـغـ	غـ	غ	ghain
ـف	ـفـ	فـ	ف	'fa
ـق	ـقـ	قـ	ق	kuf
ـك	ـكـ	كـ	ك	kaf
ـل	ـلـ	لـ	ل	lam
ـم	ـمـ	مـ	م	mim
ـن	ـنـ	نـ	ن	nun
ـه	ـهـ	هـ	ه	'ha
ـو	ـوـ	وـ	و	waw
ـي	ـيـ	يـ	ي	'ya
			ء	hamza
ـَا	ـَـوَ	أَ	أَ	a
ـا	ـُـوُ	أُ	أُ	u
ـِا	ـِـوَ	إِ	إِ	i
ـْا	ـْـوَّ	أْ	أْ	' (glottal stop)
ـا	ـاـ	آ	آ	aa
ـُو	ـُو-	أُو	أُو	oo
ـِيّ	ـِيـ	إِيّ	إِيّ	ee
ـَوّ	ـَوْ-	آوّ	آوّ	aw
ـَي	ـَيـ	أَي	أَي	ay

12

Modern
Standard
Arabic

language difficulties

Do you speak English?

هل تتكلّم/تتكلّمين
الإنجليزية؟

hal ta·ta·*kal*·la·mu/ta·ta·kal·la·*mee*·na
al·'inj·lee·*zee*·ya m/f

Do you understand?

هل تفهَم/تفهمين؟   hal *taf*·ha·mu/taf·ha·*mee*·na m/f

I (don't) understand.

أنا (لا) أفهم.   'a·naa (laa) 'af·ham

Could you please …?	لو سمحتَ يمكنكَ أن ...؟	law sa·*mah*·ta yum·*ki*·nu·ka 'an … m
	لو سمحتِ يمكنكِ أن ...؟	law sa·*mah*·ti yum·*ki*·nu·ki 'an … f
repeat that	تكرر/تكرري ذلك	tu·*ka*·ri·ra/tu·*ka*·ri·ree *dhaa*·lik m/f
speak more slowly	تتكلّم/تتكلّمي ببطء	ta·ta·*kal*·la·ma/ta·ta·*kal*·la·mee bi·*but'* m/f
write it down	تكتبَه/تكتبيه على الورقة	tak·*tu*·ba·hu/tak·*tu*·bee·hi 'a·laa al·*wa*·ra·ka m/f

numbers

0	٠	صفر	sifr	20	٢٠	عشرون	'ish·*roon*
1	١	واحد	*waa*·hid	30	٣٠	ثلاثون	tha·laa·*thoon*
2	٢	اثنان	'ith·*naan*	40	٤٠	أربعون	'ar·ba·*'oon*
3	٣	ثلاثة	tha·*laa*·tha	50	٥٠	خمسون	kham·*soon*
4	٤	أربعة	'ar·ba·*'a*	60	٦٠	ستون	sit·*toon*
5	٥	خمسة	*kham*·sa	70	٧٠	سبعون	sab·*'oon*
6	٦	ستة	*sit*·ta	80	٨٠	ثمانون	tha·maa·*noon*
7	٧	سبعة	*sab*·'a	90	٩٠	تسعون	tis·*'oon*
8	٨	ثمانية	tha·*maa*·ni·ya	100	١٠٠	مائة	*mi*·'a
9	٩	تسعة	*tis*·'a	1000	١٠٠٠	ألف	'alf
10	١٠	عشرة	*'a*·sha·ra	1,000,000		مليون	mal·*yoon*

Note that Arabic numerals, unlike letters, are read from left to right.

time & dates

What time is it?	كم الساعة الآن؟	kam as-*saa*-'a-tul 'aan
It's one o'clock.	الساعة الواحدة.	as-*saa*-'a-tul *waa*-hi-da
It's (two) o'clock.	الساعة (الثانية).	as-*saa*-'a tu (ath-thaa-*nee*-ya)
Quarter past (two).	(الثانية) والربع.	(ath-thaa-*nee*-ya-tu) war-*rub*.'u
Half past (two).	(الثانية) والنصف.	(ath-thaa-*nee*-ya-tu) wan-*nus*-fu
Quarter to (two).	(الثانية) إلا الربع.	(ath-thaa-*nee*-ya-tu) 'il-la ar-*rub*-'u
At what time ...?	في أيّ ساعةٍ ...؟	fee *'ay*-yee *saa*-'a-tin ...
At ...	في ...	fee ...
am	صباحاً	sa-*baa*-han
pm	مساءً	ma-*saa*-'an
Monday	يوم الاثنين	yawm al-*'ith*-*nayn*
Tuesday	يوم الثلاثاء	yawm ath-thu-*laa*-*thaa'*
Wednesday	يوم الأربعاء	yawm al-'ar-bi-*'aa*
Thursday	يوم الخميس	yawm al-kha-*mees*
Friday	يوم الجمعة	yawm al-*jum*-'a
Saturday	يوم السبت	yawm as-*sabt*
Sunday	يوم الأحد	yawm al-*'a*-had
yesterday	أمس	*'am*-si
today	اليوم	al-*yawm*
tomorrow	غداً	*gha*-dan
last/next ...	الماضي/القادم ...	al-*maa*-dee/al-*kaa*-dim ...
night	الليل	al-*layl*
week	الأسبوع	al-'us-*boo*'
month	الشهر	ash-*shahr*
year	العام	al-*'aam*
yesterday/tomorrow ...	أمس/غداً ...	*'am*-si/*gha*-dan ...
morning	صباح	sa-*baah*
afternoon	بعد الظهر	*ba*-'da adh-*dhuh*-ri
evening	مساء	ma-*saa*'

What date is it today?

ما تاريخ اليوم؟   maa taa-*ree*-khul yawm

It's (15 December).

'in-na-hu (al-*khaa*-mis *'a*-shar min   اّنه (الخامس عشر من
dee-*sem*-bir)   ديسمبر).

border crossing

I'm here ...	... غرض زيارتي هو	gha·ra·du zee·*yaa*·ra·tee *hu*·wa ...
in transit	العبور	al-'u·*boo*·ru
on business	التجارة	at·ti·*jaa*·ra
on holiday	السياحة	as·see·*yaa*·ha

I'm here for ...	... مدّة إقامتي هنا	*mud*·da·tu 'i·*kaa*·ma·tee *hu*·na ...
(10) days	(عشرة) أيّام	('a·sha·ra·tu) 'ay·*yaam*
(three) weeks	(ثلاثة) أسابيع	(tha·*laa*·tha·tu) 'a·sa·*bee*
(four) months	(أربعة) أشهر	('ar·*ba*·'a·tu) *ash*·hur

I'm going to (Jerash).
سأسافر إلى (جرش). sa·'u·*saa*·fi·ru 'i·*laa* (*ja*·rash)

I'm staying at the (Hilton).
سأقيم بـ(فندق الهلتون). sa·'u·*kee*·mu bi·(*fun*·du·kil hil·*toon*)

I have nothing to declare.
ليس لدي ما يستوجب الإقرار. *lay*·sa la·*day*·yi ma yas·*taw*·ji·bu al·'ik·*raar*

I have something to declare.
لديّ ما يستوجب الإقرار. la·*day*·yi ma yas·*taw*·ji·bu al·'ik·*raar*

I didn't know I had to declare it.
لم أعرف بأنها من الواجب lam 'a·ri·fu bi·'an·na·haa min al·*waa*·ji·bi
أن أقرره. 'an 'u·kar·*ri*·ra·hu

That's (not) mine.
ذلك (ليس) لي. *dhaa*·li·ka (*lay*·sa) lee

tickets & luggage

Where can I buy a ticket?
من أين أشتري تذكرة؟ min 'ay·na 'ash·ta·ree tadh·ka·ra

Do I need to book a seat?
هل يلزمني أن أحجز مقعد؟ hal yal·zi·mu·nee 'an 'ah·ji·za mak·'ad

One ... ticket	تذكرة ... واحدة	tadh·ka·ra·tu ... *waa*·hi·da
(to Amman),	(إلى عمّان),	('i·*laa* am·*maan*)
please.	لو سمحت.	law sa·*mah*·ta
one-way	ذهاب فقط	dha·*haa*·bu *fa*·kat
return	ذهاب وإياب	dha·*haa*·bu wa·'ee·*yaab*

I'd like to ... my	... أن أريد	'u·*ree*·du 'an ...
my ticket, please.	تذكرتي، لو سمحت.	tadh·*ki*·ra·tee law sa·*mah*·ta
cancel	ألغي	'ul·*ghi*·ya
change	أغيّر	'u·*ghay*·yi·ra
collect	أجمعَ	'aj·*ma*·a

I'd like a ... seat,	... مقعداً أريد	'u·*ree*·du mak·'a·dan ...
please.	لو سمحت.	law sa·*mah*·ta
nonsmoking	في قسم غير	fee *kis*·mi *ghay*·ril
	المدخّنين	mu·dakh·khi·*neen*
smoking	في قسم	fee *kis*·mil
	المدخّنين	mu·dakh·khi·*neen*

Is there air conditioning?

هل يوجد مكيف الهواء؟ hal *yoo*·ja·du mu·*kay*·ya·ful ha·*waa*'

Is there a toilet?

هل يوجد دورات المياه؟ hal *yoo*·ja·du daw·*raa*·tul mee·*yaah*

How long does the trip take?

كم مدّة الرحلة؟ kam *mud*·da·ti ar·*rih*·la

Is it a direct route?

هل الطريق مباشر؟ hal at·ta·*reek* mu·*baa*·shir

My luggage has been ...	... حقائبي	ha·*kaa*·'i·bee ...
damaged	متضررة	mu·ta·*dar*·ri·ra
lost	ضائعة	*daa*·'i·'a
stolen	مسروقة	mas·*roo*·ka

transport

Where does flight (CL58) arrive/depart?

من أين تغادر/تصل رحلة min '*ay*·na tu·*ghaa*·di·ru/ta·si·lu *rih*·la
(سي ال ثمانية وخمسون)؟ (see el tha·*maa*·ni·ya wa kham·*soon*)

Is this the ...	... الـ هذا هل	hal *haa*·dhaa al ...
to (Dubai)?	إلى (دبي)؟	'*i*·laa (*du*·ba·yee)
boat	سفينة	sa·*fee*·na
bus	باص	baas
plane	طائرة	*taa*·'i·ra
train	قطار	ki·*taar*

What time's the ... bus?	في أيِّ ساعةٍ يغادرُ الباص الـ ...؟	fee 'ay·yee saa·'a·tin yu·ghaa·di·ru al·baas al ...
first	أوّل	'aw·wal
last	آخِر	'aa·khir
next	قادِم	kaa·dim

How long will it be delayed?

كم ساعةٍ سيتأخّر؟   kam saa·'a·tin sa·ya·ta·'akh·khir

What station/stop is this?

أيّ محطةٍ/موقفٍ هذا؟   'ay·yee ma·hat·ta/maw·kif haa·dhaa

Please tell me when we get to (Jerusalem).

| لو سمحتَ، خبّرني عندما نصلُ إلى (القدس). | law sa·mah·ta khab·bir·nee 'an·da·maa na·si·lu 'i·laa (al·kuds) m |
| لو سمحتِ، خبّريني عندما نصلُ لى (القدس). | law sa·mah·ti khab·bi·ree·nee 'an·da·maa na·si·lu 'i·laa (al·kuds) f |

Is this seat available?

هل هذا المقعدُ شاغِر؟   hal haa·dhaa al·mak·'ad shaa·ghir

That's my seat.

ذلكَ مقعدي.   dhaa·li·ka mak·'a·dee

I'd like a taxi ...	أريدُ سيارةَ الأجرة ...	'u·ree·du say·yaa·ra·tal 'uj·ra ...
at (9am)	في (الساعةِ التاسعة)	fee (as·saa·'a·ti at·taa·si·'a)
now	الآن	al·'aan
tomorrow	غداً	gha·dan

How much is it to ...?

كم الأجرةِ إلى ...؟   kam al·'uj·ra·ti 'i·laa ...

Please put the meter on.

الأجرة على العداد لو سمحتَ.   al·'uj·ra 'a·laa al·'a·daad law sa·mah·ta

Please take me to (this address).

أوصلني عند (هذا العنوان) لو سمحتَ.   'aw·sal·nee 'ind (haa·dhaa al·'un·waan) law sa·mah·ta

Please ...	لو سمحتَ/ لو سمحتِ ...	law sa·mah·ta/ law sa·mah·ti ... m/f
stop here	قف/قفي هنا	kif/ki·fee hu·naa m/f
wait here	انتظِر/انتظري هنا	'in·ta·dhir/'in·ta·dhi·ree hu·naa m/f

I'd like to hire a …	… أريدُ أن أستأجرَ	'u·ree·du 'an 'as·ta'·ji·ra …
car	سيارةً	say·yaa·ra
4WD	سيارة ذات الدفع الرباعي	say·yaa·ra that ad·daf·'il ru·baa·'ee

| with a driver | مع سائق | ma·'a saa·'ik |
| with air conditioning | ذات مكيف الهواء | that mu·kay·ya·ful ha·waa' |

How much for … hire?	كم الأجرة لـ … ؟	kam al·'uj·ra li …
daily	يومٍ واحد	yaw·min waa·hid
weekly	أسبوع	'us·boo'

I need a mechanic.

أنا بحاجةٍ إلى
ميكانيكي للسيارة.

'a·naa bi haa·ja·tin 'i·laa
mee·kaa·nee·kee as·say·yaa·ra

I've run out of petrol.

نفد الوقود في سيارتي.

na·fa·dul woo·koo·da fee say·yaa·ra·tee

I have a flat tyre.

إطارُ سيارتي
فارغ من الهواء

'i·taa·ru say·yaa·ra·tee
faa·ri·ghun min al·ha·waa'

directions

Where's the …?	أين الـ … ؟	'ay·na al …
bank	بنك	bank
market	سوق	sook
post office	مكتب البريد	mak·ta·bul ba·reed

Is this the road to (the Umayyad Mosque)?

هل هذا الشارعُ إلى
(المسجد الأموي)؟

hal haa·dhaa ash·shaa·ri·'u 'i·laa
(al·mas·ja·dil 'um·ma·wee)

Can you show me (on the map)?

هل يمكنكَ أن توضح لي
(على الخريطة)؟

hal yum·ki·nu·ka 'an tu·wad·da·ha lee
('a·laa al·kha·ree·ta) m

هل يمكنكِ أن توضحي لي
(على الخريطة)؟

hal yum·ki·nu·ki 'an tu·wad·da·hee lee
('a·laa al·kha·ree·ta) f

What's the address?

ما هو العنوان؟ — maa *hu*·wa al-'un·*waan*

How far is it?

كم يبعد المكان من هنا؟ — kam *yab*·u·du al-ma·*kaa*·nu min *hu*·naa

How do I get there?

كيف أصلُ إلى هناك؟ — *kay*·fa 'a·si·lu 'i·laa hu·*naak*

Turn right/left.

اتجه إلى اليمين/اليسار. — 'it·ta·jih 'i·laa al·ya·*meen*/al·ya·*saar* m

اتجهي إلى اليمين/اليسار. — 'it·*ta*·ji·hee 'i·laa al·ya·*meen*/al·ya·*saar* f

It's ...	... هو/هي	hu·wa/hi·ya ... m/f
behind ...	... وراء	wa·*raa*' ...
in front of ...	... أمام	'a·*maam* ...
near to ...	... قريب من	ka·*reeb* min ...
next to ...	... بجانب	bi·*jaa*·ni·bi ...
on the corner	عندَ الزاوية	*'an*·da az·*zaa*·wi·ya
opposite ...	... بمقابل	bi·mu·*kaa*·bil ...
straight ahead	إلى الأمام	'i·laa al·'a·*maam*
there	هناك	hu·*naak*

north	شمال	shi·*maal*
south	جنوب	ja·*noob*
east	شرق	shark
west	غرب	gharb

signs

مدخل	*mad*·khal	Entrance
مخرج	*makh*·raj	Exit
مفتوح	maf·*tooh*	Open
مغلق	*mugh*·lak	Closed
معلومات	ma'·*loo*·maat	Information
الشرطة	ash·*shur*·ta	Police Station
ممنوع	mam·*noo*'	Prohibited
دورات المياه	daw·*raa*·tul mi·*yaah*	Toilets
الرجال	ar·ri·*jaal*	Men
النساء	an·ni·*saa*'	Women
حار	haar	Hot
بارد	*baa*·rid	Cold

accommodation

Where's a ...?	أين أجدُ ...؟	'ay·na 'a·ji·du ...
camping ground	مخيم	mu·khay·yam
guesthouse	بيت للضيوف	bayt li·du·yoof
hotel	فندق	fun·duk
youth hostel	فندق شباب	fun·duk sha·baab

Can you	هل يمكنكَ أن توصيَ	hal yum·ki·nu·ka 'an too·see·ya
recommend	بمكان ...؟	bi·ma·kaan ... m
somewhere ...?	هل يمكنكِ أن توصي	hal yum·ki·nu·ki 'an too·see
	بمكان ...؟	bi·ma·kaan ... f
cheap	رخيص	ra·khees
good	جيّد	jay·yid
nearby	قريب	ka·reeb

I'd like to book a room, please.

أريد أن أحجزَ غرفةً، لو سمحتَ.　　'u·ree·du 'an 'ah·ji·za ghur·fa law sa·mah·ta

I have a reservation.

عندي حجز.　　'in·dee hajz

Do you have	هل عندكم	hal 'in·da·kum
a ... room?	غرفةٌ ...؟	ghur·fa·tun ...
single	بسرير منفردٍ	bi·sa·ree·rin mun·fa·rid
double	بسرير مزدوّج	bi·sa·ree·rin muz·daw·waj
twin	بسريرين منفردين	bi·sa·ree·ray·ni mun·fa·ri·day·ni

How much is	كم ثمنه	kam tha·ma·nu·hu
it per ...?	لـ ...؟	li ...
night	ليلوٍ واحدة	lay·la·tin waa·hid
person	شخصٍ واحدة	shakh·sin waa·hid

I'd like to stay for (three) nights.

أريد الإقامةَ لمدّة　　'u·ree·du al·'i·kaa·ma li·mud·da·ti
(ثلاث) ليالي.　　(tha·laa·thi) lay·yaa·lee

Am I allowed to camp here?

هل من الممكن أن أخيم هنا؟　　hal min al·mum·kin 'an 'u·khay·ya·ma hu·naa

Could I have my key, please?

هل من الممكن أن تعطني/تعطيني　　hal min al·mum·kin 'an tu'·ti·nee/tu'·tee·nee
مفتاحي؟　　mif·taa·hee m/f

Can I get another (blanket)?

هل من الممكن أن تعطني/تعطيني (بطانية) إضافية؟

hal min al-*mum*-kin 'an tu'-ti-nee/tu'-*tee*-nee (ba-*taa*-ni-ya) 'i-*daa*-fee m/f

The (air conditioning) doesn't work.

لا يعملُ (مكيّف الهواء).

la ya'-ma-lu (mu-*kay*-ya-ful ha-*waa*')

This (sheet) isn't clean.

هذا الـ(شرشف) ليس نظيف.

haa-dhi-hi al-(*shar*-shaf) *lay*-sat na-*dhee*-fa

Is there an elevator/a safe?

هل يوجدُ مصعد/خزانة الأمانات؟

hal *yoo*-ja-du *mas*-'ad/kha-*zaa*-na-tul 'a-maa-*naat*

What time is checkout?

في أيِّ ساعةٍ المغادرة؟

fee '*ay*-yee *saa*-'a-tin al-mu-*ghaa*-da-ra

Could I have my ..., please?

هل يمكنني أن أستردَ ...، لو سمحتَ.

hal yum-*ki*-nu-nee 'an 'as-ta-*rid*-da ... law sa-*mah*-ta

deposit	وديعتي	wa-*dee*-'a-tee
passport	جواز سفري	ja-*waa*-zu *sa*-fa-ree
valuables	أشيائي القيمة	'ash-*yaa*-'ee al-*kay*-yi-ma

banking & communications

Where's a/an ...?

أينَ ...؟

'*ay*-na ...

ATM	جهاز الصرافة	ji-*haaz* as-sar-*raa*-fa
foreign exchange office	مكتب صرافة	*mak*-ta-bu sar-*raa*-fa

I'd like to ...

أريدُ أن ...

'u-*ree*-du an ...

arrange a transfer	أقومَ بتحويل مالي	'a-*koo*-ma bi-tah-*wee*-li *maa*-lee
cash a cheque	أصرفَ شيكَ	'as-ru-fa sheek
change a travellers cheque	أحولَ شيكاً سياحيَّ	'u-*haw*-wi-la *shee*-kan see-*yaa*-hee
change money	أحولَ النقود	'u-*haw*-wi-la an-nu-*kood*
withdraw money	أسحبَ نقودَ	'as-*hu*-ba nu-*kood*

What's the ...?

ما ...؟

maa ...

charge for that	العمولة	al-'u-*moo*-la
exchange rate	سعر التحويل	*si*-'ru at-tah-*weel*

Where's the local internet café?

أيَن أقرب مقهى الانترنت؟   'ay·na 'ak·ra·bu mak·ha al·'in·tir·net

How much is it per hour?

ما تكلفة الساعة الواحدة   maa tak·li·fa·tu as·saa·'a·til waa·hi·da

I'd like to ...   ... أريد أن   'u·ree·du an ...

check my email	أفحص البريدَ	'af·hu·sa al·ba·ree·dal
	الالكتروني	'i·lik·troo·nee·ya
get internet	أستخدم	'as·takh·di·ma
access	الانترنت	al·'in·tir·net
use a printer	أستخدمَ آلة	'as·takh·di·ma 'aa·lat
	الطباعة	at·ta·baa·'a
use a scanner	أستخدمَ نسخَ	'as·takh·di·ma nas·kha
	الكتروني	'i·lik·troo·nee

I'd like ...   ... أريد   'u·ree·du ...

to hire a mobile/	أن أستأجرَ	'an 'as·ta'·ji·ra
cell phone	هاتفاً محمولا	haa·ti·fan mah mool
a SIM card for	بطاقة السيم	bi·taa·ka tu seem
your network	لشبكتكم	li·sha·ba·ka·ti·kum

What are the rates?

ما الأسعار؟   maa al·'as·'aar

What's your phone number?

ما رقم هاتفكم؟   maa rak·mu haa·ti·fi·kum

The number is ...

الرقم هو ...   ar·rak·mu hu·wa ...

Where's the nearest public phone?

أيَن أقربُ هاتف عمومي؟   'ay·na 'ak·ra·bu haa·ti·fin 'u·moo·mee

I'd like to buy a phonecard.

أريد أن أشتريَ بطاقة   'u·ree·du an 'ash·ta·ree·ya bi·taa·ka
تلفونية.   ti·li·foo·nee·ya

How much does a (three)-minute call cost?

كم تكلفة الاتصال لمدّة   kam tak·li·fa·til 'it·ti·saa·li li·mud·da·ti
(ثلاث) دقائق؟   (tha·laa·thi) da·kaa·'ik

I want to ...	... أريد أن	'u·*ree*·du an ...
call (Canada)	أتصل بـ(كندا)	'at·*ta*·si·la bi·(*ka*·na·daa)
make a	أقوم باتصال	'a·*koo*·ma bi·'it·ti·*saa*·li
local call	محلي	ma·ha·lee
reverse the	أقومَ باتصال والأجرة	'a·*koo*·ma bi·'it·ti·*saa*·li wal·'*uj*·ra
charges	على الشخص	'a·laa ash·*shakh*·sil
	المتلقّي الاتصال	mut·la·kee al·'it·ti·*saal*

I want to send a ...	... أريد أن أبعَثَ	'u·*ree*·du an '*ab*·'u·tha ...
fax	فاكس	faaks
parcel	طرداً بريدي	tar·dan ba·*ree*·dee

I want to buy ...	... أريد أن أشتريَ	'u·*ree*·du an ash·*ta*·ree·ya ...
an envelope	ظرفٍ	dharf
a stamp	طابع	taa·bi'

Please send it (to	يرجى بعثَهُ	yur·jaa bu'·thu·hu
Australia) by ...	(إلى أستراليا) بـ ...	('i·laa us·traa·li·yaa) bi ...
airmail	البريد الجوّي	al·ba·*ree*·di al·*jaw*·wee
surface mail	البريد العادي	al·ba·*ree*·di al·'*aa*·dee

sightseeing

What time does it open/close?

متى يفتح/يغلق؟   ma·*taa* yaf·tah/yugh·lak

What's the admission charge?

ما ثمن الدخول؟   maa *tha*·ma·nu ad·du·*khool*

Is there a discount for students/children?

هل يوجد خصم للطلاب/للأطفال؟   hal *yoo*·ja·du *kha*·sim lit·tul·*laab*/lil·'at·*faal*

I'd like to see ...

... أريد أن أشاهدَ   'u·*ree*·du an 'u·*shaa*·hi·da ...

What's that?

ما ذلكَ؟   maa *dhaa*·lik

Can I take a photo?

هل من الممكن أن آخذ صورة؟   hal min al·*mum*·kin 'an '*aa*·khu·dha *soo*·ra

I'd like a ...	... أريد	'u·*ree*·du ...
catalogue	فَهْرَس	*fah*·ras
guide	دليل	da·*leel*
local map	خريطة المنطقة	kha·*ree*·ta·tul *man*·ta·ka

24

When's the next ...?	متى الـ...	ma·taa al·...
	القادم؟	al·kaa·dim
day trip	رحلة يومية	rih·la yaw·mee·ya
tour	دورة	daw·ra

Is ... included?	هل يتضمّن على ...؟	hal ya·ta·dam·ma·nu 'a·laa ...
accommodation	سكن	sa·kan
the admission charge	ثمن الدخول	tha·man ad·du·khool
food	الطعام	at·ta·'aam
transport	المواصلات	al·mu·waa·sa·laat

How long is the tour?

كم مدّة الدورة؟   kam mud·da·ti ad·daw·ra

What time should we be back?

في أيّ ساعةٍ يجب   fee 'ay·yee saa·'a·tin ya·ji·bu
أن نرجع إلى هنا؟   'an nar·ja·'a 'i·laa hu·naa

sightseeing

castle	قلعة	kal·'a f
church	كنيسة	ka·nee·sa f
main square	ساحة رئيسية	saa·ha ra·'ee·see·ya f
mosque	مسجد	mas·jad m
old city	مدينة قديمة	ma·dee·na ka·dee·ma f
palace	قصر	kasr m
pyramids	الأهرام	al·'ah·raam f
ruins	آثار	'aa·thaar m

shopping

Where's a ...?	أين ...؟	'ay·na ...
bookshop	مكتبة	mak·ta·ba
camera shop	محل التصوير	ma·hal at·tas·weer
department store	محل المنوعات	ma·hal al·mu·naw·wa·'aat
grocery store	البقالة	al·ba·kaa·la
newsagency	وَكالة أنباء	wa·kaa·la·tu 'an·baa'
souvenir shop	دكان التذكارات	duk·kaan at·tidh·kaa·raat
supermarket	مَتْجَر كبير	mat·jar ka·beer

I'm looking for ...

أبحثُ عن ...

'ab·ha·thu 'an ...

Can I look at it?

هل يمكنني أن أراه؟

hal yum·ki·nu·nee 'an 'a·raa·hu

Do you have any others?

هل عندكم غيره؟

hal 'in·da·kum ghay·ru·hu

Does it have a guarantee?

هل له ضمانة؟

hal la·hu da·maa·na

Can I have it sent overseas?

هل من الممكن أن تبعثه
إلى الخارج؟

hal min al·mum·kin 'an tab·'a·thu·hu 'i·laa al·khaa·rij

Can I have my ... repaired?

هل يمكنك أن تصلّح لي ...؟

hal yum·ki·nu·ka 'an tus·li·ha lee ...

It's faulty.

هذا لا يعمل.

haa·dhaa laa ya'·mal

How much is it?

كم سعره؟

kam si'·ru·hu

Can you write down the price?

هل يمكنك أن تكتب لي السعر؟

hal yum·ki·nu·ka 'an tak·tu·ba lee as·si'r m

هل يمكنك أن تكتبي لي السعر؟

hal yum·ki·nu·ki 'an tak·tu·bee lee as·si'r f

That's too expensive.

هذا غال جدّاً.

haa·dhaa ghaa·lin jid·dan

What's your lowest price?

ما أحسن سعر لديكم؟

maa 'ah·sa·nu si'·ri la·day·kum

I'll give you (50 lira).

سأدفع (خمسين ليرة).

sa·'ad·fa·'u (kham·seen lee·ra)

There's a mistake in the bill.

في خطأ في الحساب.

fee kha·ta' feel hi·saab

Do you accept ...?	هل تقبلون ...؟	hal tak·ba·loo·na ...
credit cards	بطاقات الرصيد	bi·taa·kaat ar·ra·seed
debit cards	بطاقات الاقتراض	bi·taa·kaat al·'ik·ti·raad
travellers cheques	شيكات سياحية	shee·kaat see·yaa·hee·ya

I'd like ..., please.	أريد ... لو سمحتَ.	'u·ree·du ... law sa·mah·ta
a bag	كيسٍ	kees
a refund	استرداد مال	'is·tir·daad maal
to return this	أن أرجع هذا لكم	'an 'ur·ji·'a haa·dhaa la·kum

العربية – shopping

I'd like ..., please.	أريد ... ، لو سمحت	'u·ree·du ... law sa·mah·ta
my change	الباقي	al·baa·kee
a receipt	وصل	wa·sil

I'd like ...	أريد ...	'u·ree·du ...
(100) grams	(مائة) غراماً	(mi·'a) ghraam ...
(four) kilos	(أربع) كيلو	('ar·ba·'a) kee·loo
(three) pieces	(ثلاث) قطع	(tha·laa·tha) ka·ta'

| Less./More. | أقلّ./أكثر. | 'a·kal·lu/'ak·tha·ru |
| Enough. | كفاية. | ki·faa·ya |

photography

Can you ...?	هل يمكنك ...؟	hal yum·ki·nu·ka ... m
	هل يمكنك ...؟	hal yum·ki·nu ki ... f
burn a CD	تجهز قرصا	tu·jah·hi·za kur·san
from my	مدمج من بطاقة	mu·dam·maj min
memory card	الذاكرة	bi·taa·ka·til dhaa·ki·ra
	التي لديّ	al·la·tee la day·yee
develop this	تحمض هذا	tu·ham·mi·da haa·dhaa
film	الفيلم	al·feelm
load my film	يحمّل فيلمي	yu·ham·mi·la feel·mee

I need a ... film	أحتاج إلى فيلما ...	'ah·taa·ju 'i·laa feel·man ...
for this camera.	لهذه الكاميرا!	li·haa·dhi·hil kaa·mee·raa
B&W	أسود وأبيض	'as·wad wa 'ab·yad
colour	ملون	mu·law·wan
slide	شريحة	sha·ree·ha
(200) speed	سريعة (مائتين)	sa·ree·'a (mi·'a·tayn)

| When will it be ready? | متى يكون جاهزاً؟ | ma·taa ya·koo·nu jaa·hiz |

making conversation

Hello.	السلام عليكم.	as·sa·laa·mu 'a·lay·kum
Good night.	تصبح على الخير.	tus·bi·hu 'a·laa al·khayr
Goodbye.	إلى اللقاء.	'i·laa al·li·kaa'

| Mr | سيّد | say·yeed |
| Mrs/Miss | سيدة | say·yee·da |

How are you?	كيف حالكَ/حالكِ؟	kay·fa haa·lu·ka/haa·lu·ki m/f
Fine, thanks. And you?	بخير شكراً. وأنتَ/أنتِ؟	bi·khay·rin shuk·ran wa·'an·ta/wa·'an·ti m/f
What's your name?	ما اسمكَ/اسمكِ؟	maa 'is·mu·ka/'is·mu·ki m/f
My name is ...	اسمي ...	'is·mee ...
I'm pleased to meet you.	أنا سعيد/سعيدة بالتعرّف عليك.	'a·naa sa·'ee·dun/sa·'ee·da·tun bit·ta·'ar·ruf 'a·layk m/f

This is my ...	هذا/هذه ...	haa·dhaa/haa·dhi·hi ... m/f
brother	أخي	'a·khee
daughter	ابنتي	'ib·na·tee
father	أبي	'a·bee
friend	صديقي/صديقتي	sa·dee·kee/sa·dee·ka·tee m/f
husband	زوجي	zaw·jee
mother	أمّي	'um·mee
sister	أختي	'ukh·tee
son	ابني	'ib·nee
wife	زوجتي	zaw·ja·tee

Here's my ...	هذا ...	haa·dhaa ...
(email) address	عنواني (البريد الالكتروني)	'un·waa·nee (al·ba·reed al·'i·lik·troo·nee)
phone number	رقم هاتفي	rak·mu haa·ti·fee

What's your ...?	ما ...؟	maa ...
(email) address	عنوانك/عنوانك (البريدي الالكتروني)	'un·waa·nu·ka/'un·waa·nu·ki (al·ba·ree·deel 'i·lik·troo·nee) m/f
phone number	رقم هاتفِك/ هاتفَك	rak·mu haa·ti·fu·ka/ haa·ti·fu·ki m/f

| Where are you from? | من أين أنتَ/أنتِ؟ | min 'ay·na 'an·ta/'an·ti m/f |

I'm from ...	أنا من ...	'a·naa min ...
Australia	أستراليا	'us·traa·li·yaa
Canada	كندا	ka·na·daa
the UK	بريطانيا	ba·ree·taa·ni·ya
the USA	أمريكا	'am·ree·kaa

What's your occupation?	ما مهنتكَ/مهنتكِ؟	maa *mih*·na·tu·ka/*mih*·na·tu·ki m/f
I'm a/an ...	أنا ...	'a·naa ...
businessperson	رجل أعمال	*ra*·ju·lu 'a'·*maal* m
	سيّدة أعمال	say·*yee*·da·tu 'a'·*maal* f
office worker	موظف	mu·*wadh*·dhaf m
	موظفة	mu·*wadh*·dha·fa f
tradesperson	حِرفيّ/حِرفيّة	hi·ra·*fee*/hi·ra·*fee*·ya m/f
Do you like ...?	هل تحبّ/تحبّينَ ...؟	hal tu·*hib*·bu/tu·hib·*bee*·na ... m/f
I (don't) like ...	أنا (لا) أحبّ ...	'a·naa (laa) 'u·*hib*·bu ...
art	الفنّ	al-*fann*
movies	الأفلام	al·'af·*laam*
music	الموسيقى	al·moo·*see*·kaa
reading	المطالعة	al·mu·*taa*·la·'a
sport	الرياضة	ar·ree·*yaa*·da

eating out

Can you recommend a ...?	هل يمكنكَ أن توصي ...؟	hal yum·*ki*·nu·ka 'an too·*see*·ya ... m
	هل يمكنكِ أن توصي ...؟	hal yum·*ki*·nu·ki 'an too·*see* ... f
bar	بار	baar
café	مقهى	*mak*·han
restaurant	مطعم	mat·'am
I'd like ..., please.	أريدُ ... ، لو سمحتَ.	'u·*ree*·du ... law sa·*mah*·ta
a table for (four)	طاولة لـ(أربعة) أشخاص	taa·*wi*·la·tan li·('ar·ba·'a·ti) 'ash·*khaas*
the (non)smoking section	قسم (غير) المدخنين	*kis*·ma (*ghay*·ri) al·mu·dakh·khi·*neen*
breakfast	فطور	fu·*toor* m
lunch	غداء	gha·*daa*' m
dinner	عشاء	'a·*shaa*' m

What would you recommend?

ماذا توصي/توصينَ؟ *maa*·dhaa *too*·see/too·*see*·na m/f

What's the local speciality?

ما الوجبة الخاصّة maa al·*waj*·ba·tul *khaa*·sa

لهذه المنطقة؟ li·*haa*·dhi·hil *man*·ta·ka

What's that?

ما ذلك؟ maa *dhaa*·lik

I'd like ..., please.	أريد ... , لو سمحتَ.	*'u·ree*·du ... law sa·*mah*·ta
the bill	الحساب	hi·*saab*
the drink list	قائمة المشروبات	kaa·*'i*·ma·tal mash·roo·*baat*
the menu	قائمة الطعام	kaa·*'i*·ma·tu at·ta·*'aam*
that dish	تلك الوجبة	*til*·kal *waj*·ba

drinks

I'll have ...

سآخذُ ... sa·*'aa*·khu·dhu ...

I'll buy you a drink.

أدعوكَ/أدعوكِ إلى مشروب. 'ad·*'oo*·ka/ad·*'oo*·ki mash·*roob* m/f

What would you like?

ماذا تريد؟ *maa*·dhaa tu·*reed*

(cup of) coffee ...	(فنجانُ) قهوة ...	(fin·*jaa*·nu) *kah*·wa ...
(cup of) tea ...	(كأس) شاي ...	(*ka'*·su) *shaa*·ee ...
with milk	بحليب	bi·ha·*leeb*
without sugar	بدون سكّر	bi·*doo*·ni *suk*·kar
boiled water	ماء مغلي	maa' *magh*·lee m
mineral water	مياه معدنية	mi·*yaah* ma'·da·*nee*·ya f
(orange) juice	عصير (برتقال)	'a·*see*·ru (bur·tu·*kaal*) m
soft drink	مشروب بارد	mash·*roob* *baa*·rid m
a bottle/glass of beer	زجاجة/كأسة بيرة	zu·*jaa*·ja·tu/ka'·*sa*·tu *bee*·ra
a shot of whisky	جرعة ويسكي	*jur*·'at *wees*·kee
a bottle/glass	زجاجة/كأسة	zu·*jaa*·ja·tu/ka'·*sa*·tuu
of ... wine	نبيذ ...	na·*bee*·dhin ...
red	أحمر	*'ah*·mar
sparkling	فوّار	faw·*waar*
white	أبيض	*'ab*·yad

special diets & allergies

Is there a vegetarian restaurant near here?

هل يوجدُ مطعماً نباتياً
قريب من هنا؟

hal *yoo*·ja·du mat·'a·man na·baa·*tee*·yan
ka·*ree*·bu min *hu*·naa

Do you have ... food?	هل لديكم طعامٌ ...؟	hal la·*day*·ku·mu ta·'aa·mun ...
halal	حلال	ha·*laal*
kosher	كوشر	*koo*·shir
vegetarian	نباتيّ	na·*baa*·tee

Could you prepare a meal without ...?	هل من الممكن أن تعدّ/تعدّي وجبةً بدون ...؟	hal min al·*mum*·kin 'an tu·'id·da/tu·'id·dee *waj*·ba·tan bi·*doo*·ni ... m/f
butter	زبدة	*zub*·da
eggs	بيض	bayd
meat stock	مرق اللحم	*ma*·rak al·*lah*·mi

I'm allergic to ...	أنا عندي حساسية من ...	'a·naa 'an·dee has·saa·*see*·ya min ...
dairy produce	الألبان	al·'al·*baan*
gluten	الغلوتين	al·ghloo·*teen*
nuts	مكسّرات	mu·kas·si·*raat*
seafood	الطعام البحري	at·ta·*'aa*·mil *ba*·ha·ree

emergencies

Help!	ساعدني!/ساعديني!	saa·'i·du·nee/saa·'i·*dee*·nee m/f
Stop!	قف!/قفي!	kif/*ki*·fee m/f
Go away!	اتركني!/اتركيني!	'it·*ruk*·nee/'it·ru·*kee*·nee m/f
Thief!	سارق!	*saa*·rik
Fire!	نار!	naar
Watch out!	احذر!/احذري!	'ih·dhar/'ih·dha·ree m/f

Call ...!	اتصلْ/اتصلي بـ ...!	'it·ta·sil/'it·*ta*·si·lee bi ... m/f
a doctor	طبيب	ta·*beeb*
an ambulance	سيارة الإسعاف	say·*yaa*·ra·til 'is·*'aaf*
the police	الشرطة	ash·*shur*·ta

Could you help me, please?

هل من الـمـمـكن أن
تـساعدني/تـساعديني؟

hal min al-*mum*-kin 'an
tu-saa-'*i*-du-nee/tu-saa-'*i*-*dee*-na-nee m/f

I have to use the phone.

أحتاج إلى أستخدامَ الهاتف

'ah-*taa*-ju 'i-laa 'is-tikh-*daa*-mal *haa*-tif

I'm lost.

أنا ضائع/ضائعة.

'a-naa *daa*-'i'/*daa*-'i-'a m/f

Where are the toilets?

أينَ دورات المياه؟

'ay-na daw-*raa*-tul mee-*yaah*

Where's the police station?

أينَ الشرطة؟

'ay-na ash-*shur*-ta

I want to report an offence.

أريدُ أن أبلغ عنَ جريمة.

'u-*ree*-du 'an 'u-*bal*-li-gha 'an ja-*ree*-ma

I have insurance.

عندي تأمين.

'*in*-dee al-ta'-*meen*

I want to contact my consulate/embassy.

أريد أن اتّصل
بقنصليتي/بسفارتي.

'u-*ree*-du 'an 'at-*ta*-si-la
bi-kun-su-*li*-ya-tee/bi-sa-*faa*-ra-tee

I've been ...

assaulted — اعتدى عليّ شخص. — *i*'-ta-daa 'a-la-yee shakhs

raped — اغتصبني شخص. — 'igh-ta-*sa*-ba-nee shakhs

robbed — سرقني شخص. — sa-*ra*-ka-nee shakhs

I've lost my ... — ضيعتُ ... — da-*ya*'-tu ...

My ... was/were — ... كان مسروق — ... *kaa*-na mas-*rook* m

stolen. — ... كانت مسروقة — ... *kaa*-nat mas-*roo*-ka f

bag — حقيبتي — ha-*kee*-ba-tee f

credit card — بطاقتي الرصيد — bi-*taa*-ka-tee ar-ra-*seed* f

money — نقودي — nu-*koo*-dee f

passport — جواز سفري — ja-*waa*-zu sa-*fa*-ree m

travellers — شيكاتي — shee-*kaa*-tee

cheques — السياحية — as-see-yaa-*hee*-ya f

wallet — محفظتي — mah-*fa*-dha-tee f

العربية – emergencies

32

health

Where's the nearest ...?	أين أقرب ...؟	'ay·na 'ak·ra·bu ...
dentist	طبيب الأسنان	ta·bee·bul 'as·naan
doctor	طبيب/طبيبة	ta·beeb/ta·bee·ba m/f
hospital	مستشفى	mus·tash·faa
(night) pharmacist	صيدلية (ليلية)	say·da·lee·ya (lay·lee·ya)

I need a doctor (who speaks English).

أحتاج إلى طبيب
(يتكلم الانجليزية).

'ah·taa·ju 'i·laa ta·bee·bin
(ya·ta·kal·la·mu al·'inj·lee·zee·ya)

Could I see a female doctor?

هل من الممكن أن أقابل طبيبة؟

hal min al·mum·kin 'an 'u·kaa·bi·la ta·bee·ba

I've run out of my medication.

لقد نفذتُ جميع أدويتي.

la·kad na·fadh·tu ja·mee·'u 'ad·wi·ya·tee

| I'm sick. | أنا مريض. | 'a·naa ma·reed |
| It hurts here. | عندي ألم هنا. | 'in·dee 'a·lam hu·naa |

I have (a) ...	عندي ...	'in·dee ...
asthma	الربو	ar·rabw
constipation	الإمساك	al·'im·saak
diarrhoea	الإسهال	al·'is·haal
fever	حمى	hum·maa
headache	صداع	su·daa'
heart condition	مشاكل بالقلب	mu·shaa·kil bil·kalb
nausea	غَثَيان	gha·tha·yaan
pain	الم	'a·lam
sore throat	الم في حلقي	'a·la·mu feel hal·kee
toothache	الم في الأسنان	'a·la·mu feel 'as·naan

I'm allergic to ...	عندي حساسيّة من ...	'an·dee has·saa·see·ya min ...
antibiotics	مضاد حيوي	mu·daa·dun hay·ya·wee
anti-inflammatories	مضاد للالتهاب	mu·daa·dun lil·'il·ti·haab
aspirin	الأسبرين	al·'as·pi·reen
bees	نَحَل	nahl
codeine	الكودين	al·koo·deen
penicillin	البنسلين	al·bi·ni·si·leen

english–arabic (msa) dictionary

Words in this dictionary are marked as n (noun), a (adjective), v (verb), sg (singular), pl (plural), ⓜ (masculine) and ⓕ (feminine) where necessary. Verbs are given in the present tense in the third-person singular ('he/she'), in both masculine and feminine forms.

A

A

accident حادث haa-dith ⓜ
accommodation سكن sa-kan
adaptor الموصّل al-mu-was-sil
address n عنوان 'an-waan ⓜ
after بعد ba'-da
air-conditioned مكيّف mu-kay-yaf
airplane طائرة taa-'i-ra ⓕ
airport مطار ma-taar ⓜ
alcohol الكحول al-ku-hool ⓜ
Algeria الجزائر al-ja-zaa-'ir ⓕ
all كلّ kul-lu
allergy حساسية has-sa-si-ya ⓕ
ambulance سيارة الإسعاف say-yaa-ra-tul 'is-'aaf ⓜ
and و wa
ankle كاحل kaa-hil ⓜ
Arabic (language) العربية al-'a-ra-bee-ya ⓕ
arm ذراع dhi-raa' ⓕ
ashtray صحن السجارة sah-nu as-si-jaa-ra ⓜ
ATM جهاز الصرافة ji-haaz as-sar-raa-fa ⓜ

B

baby طفلٌ صغير/طفلة صغيرة tif-lun sa-gheer/tif-la-tun sa-ghee-ra ⓜ/ⓕ
back (body) ظهر dhahr ⓜ
backpack شنطة ظهر shan-ta-tu dhahr ⓕ
bad سيء/سيئة say-yi'/say-yi-'a ⓜ/ⓕ
bag حقيبة ha-kee-ba ⓕ
baggage claim مكان جمع الأمتعة ma-kaa-nun li-jam-'il'am-ti-'a ⓜ
bank بنك bank ⓜ
bar بار baar ⓜ
bathroom غرفة الحمام ghur-fa-tul ham-maam ⓕ
battery بطارية ba-taa-ri-ya ⓕ
beautiful جميل/جميلة ja-meel/ja-mee-la ⓜ/ⓕ
bed سرير sa-reer ⓜ
beer بيرة bee-ra ⓕ
before قبل kab-la
behind وراء 'wa-raa
bicycle دراجة dar-raa-ja ⓕ
big كبير/كبيرة ka-beer/ka-bee-ra ⓜ/ⓕ
bill حساب hi-saab ⓜ
black أسود/سوداء 'as-wad/saw-daa' ⓜ/ⓕ
blanket بطانية ba-taa-ni-ya ⓕ
blood group فئة الدم fi-'a-tu ad-dam ⓜ

blue أزرق/زرقاء 'az-rak/zar-kaa' ⓜ/ⓕ
boat سفينة sa-fee-na ⓕ
book (make a reservation) v يحجز/تحجز yah-ji-zu/tah-ji-zu ⓜ/ⓕ
bottle زجاجة zu-jaa-ja ⓕ
bottle opener فاتح الزجاجات faa-ti-hu az-zu-jaa-jaat ⓜ
boy ولد wa-lad ⓜ
brakes (car) فرامل fa-raa-mil ⓜ
breakfast فطور fu-toor ⓜ
broken (faulty) مكسور/مكسورة mak-soor/mak-soo-ra ⓜ/ⓕ
bus باص baas ⓜ
business عمل 'a-mal ⓜ
buy يشتري/تشتري yash-ta-ree/tash-ta-ree ⓜ/ⓕ

C

café مقهى mak-han ⓜ
camera آلة التصوير 'aa-la-tu at-tas-weer ⓕ
camp site مخيم mu-khay-yam ⓜ
cancel يلغي/تلغي yul-ghee/tul-ghee ⓜ/ⓕ
can opener فاتح التنكة faa-ti-hu at-tan-ka ⓜ
car سيارة say-yaa-ra ⓕ
cash n نقد nukd ⓜ
cash (a cheque) v تصرف/يصرف yas-ru-fu/tas-ru-fu ⓜ/ⓕ
cell phone هاتف محمول haa-ti-fu mah-mool ⓜ
centre مركز mar-kaz ⓜ
change (money) v يصرّف/تصرّف yu-sar-ri-fu/tu-sar-ri-fu ⓜ/ⓕ
cheap رخيص/رخيصة ra-khees/ra-khee-sa ⓜ/ⓕ
check (bill) حساب hi-saab ⓜ
check-in مكتب التسجيل mak-ta-bu at-tas-jeel ⓜ
chest صدر sadr ⓜ
child طفل/طفلة tif-la/tif-la ⓜ/ⓕ
cigarette سجارة si-jaa-ra ⓕ
city مدينة ma-dee-na ⓕ
clean a نظيف/نظيفة na-dheef/na-dhee-fa ⓜ/ⓕ
closed مغلق/مغلقة mugh-lak/mugh-la-ka ⓜ/ⓕ
coffee قهوة kah-wa ⓕ
coins فراطة fu-raa-ta ⓕ
cold a بارد/باردة baa-rid/baa-ri-da ⓜ/ⓕ
collect call
اتصال والأجرة على الشخص المتلقي الاتصال it-ti-saal wal-'uj-ra-'a-laa al-shakh-sil mut-la-kee al-'it-ti-saal ⓜ
come يجيء/تجيء ya-jee-'u/ta-jee-'u ⓜ/ⓕ

computer جهاز الكمبيوتر ji-*haa*-zul kum-bi-*yoo*-ta

condom الواقي al-*waa*-kee ⓜ

contact lenses عدسة لاصقة 'a-da-sa-tun laa-*si*-ka ①

cook v يطبخ جخُ/نطبخ *yat*-bu-khu/*tat*-bu-khu ⓜ/①

cost n تكلفة *tak*-lu-fa ①

credit card بطاقة الرصيد bi-*taa*-ka-tu ar-ra-*seed* ①

cup فنجان fin-*jaan* ⓜ

currency exchange صرافة sa-*raa*-fa ①

customs (immigration) جمارك ja-*maa*-rik ①

D

dangerous خطر/خطرة khatr/*khat*-ra ⓜ/①

date (time) تاريخ taa-*reekh* ⓜ

day يوم yawm ⓜ

delay n تأخير ta'-*kheer* ⓜ

dentist طبيب الأسنان ta-*bee*-bul 'as-*naan*

depart يغادر/تغادر yu-*ghaa*-di-ru/tu-*ghaa*-di-ru ⓜ/①

diaper حفاظة طفل ha-*faa*-dha-tu tifl ①

dictionary قاموس *qaa*-moos

dinner عشاء *a-shaa'*

direct مباشر/مباشرة mu-*baa*-shir/mu-*baa*-shi-ra ⓜ/①

dirty وسخ/وسخة waskh/*was*-kha ⓜ/①

disabled معاق/معاقة mu-*'aak*/mu-*'aa*-ka ⓜ/①

discount n خصم *kha*-sim

doctor طبيب/طبيبة ta-*beeb*/ta-*bee*-ba ⓜ/①

double bed سرير مزدوج sa-*ree*-run muz-*daw*-waj ⓜ

double room غرفة لشخصين *ghur*-fa-tun li-shakh-*sayn*

drink n مشروب mash-*roob* ⓜ

drive v يسوق/تسوق ya-*soo*-ku/ta-*soo*-ku ⓜ/①

drivers licence رخصة القيادة *rukh*-sa-tul kee-*yaa*-da ①

drug (illicit) مخدر mu-*khad*-dir ⓜ

dummy (pacifier) مصاصة mas-*saa*-sa ①

E

ear أذن *u*-dhun ①

east شرق shark ⓜ

eat يأكل/تأكل *ya*-ku-lu/*ta*-ku-lu ⓜ/①

economy class الدرجة العادية ad-*da*-ra-ja-tul *'aa*-diy-ya ①

Egypt مصر misr ⓜ

electricity كهرباء kah-ra-*baa'* ①

elevator مصعد *mas*-'ad ⓜ

email البريد الكتروني al-ba-*ree*-dul 'i-lik-*troo*-nee ⓜ

embassy سفارة sa-*faa*-ra ①

emergency طارئ *taa*-ri' ⓜ

English (language) الإنجليزية al-'inj-lee-*zee*-ya ①

entrance مدخل *mad*-khal ⓜ

evening مساء ma-*saa'* ⓜ

exchange rate سعر التحويل *si*-'ru at-tah-*weel* ⓜ

exit n مخرج *makh*-raj ⓜ

expensive غال/غالية *ghaa*-lin/*ghaa*-lee-ya ⓜ/①

express mail البريد سريع al-ba-*ree*-du as-sa-*ree'* ⓜ

eye عين 'ayn ①

F

far (from) بعيد (عن) ba-*'ee*-du ('an)

fast سريع/سريعة sa-*ree'*/sa-*ree*-'a ⓜ/①

father أب 'ab ⓜ

film (camera) فيلم feelm ⓜ

finger إصبع *is*-ba' ⓜ

first-aid kit صندوق للإسعاف الأولي sun-*doo*-kun lil-'is-*'aa*-fil *'aw*-wa-lee

first class الدرجة الأولى ad-*da*-ra-ja-tul *'oo*-la ①

fish n سمك *sa*-mak

food طعام ta-*'aam* ⓜ

foot قدم *ka*-dam ⓜ

fork شوكة *shaw*-ka ①

free (of charge) مجاناً ma-*jaa*-nan

friend صديق/صديقة sa-*deek*/sa-*dee*-ka ⓜ/①

fruit فاكهة *faa*-ki-ha ①

full شبعان/شبعانة shab *'aan*/shab-*'uu*-na ⓜ/①

funny مضحك/مضحكة *mud*-hik/*mud*-hi-ka ⓜ/①

G

Gaza غزّة *ghaz*-za ①

gift هدية ha-*di*-ya ①

girl بنت bint ①

glass (drinking) كأس ka's ⓜ

glasses (eyesight) نظارات na-*dhaa*-raat ①

go يذهب/تذهب *yadh*-ha-bu/*tadh*-ha-bu ⓜ/①

good جيد/جيدة *jay*-yid/*jay*-yi-da ⓜ/①

green أخضر/خضراء *akh*-dar/khad-*raa'* ⓜ/①

guide n دليل/دليلة da-*leel*/da-*lee*-la ⓜ/①

H

half n نصف nusf ⓜ

hand يد yad ①

handbag محفظة يد mah-*fa*-dha-tu yad ①

happy سعيد/سعيدة sa-*'eed*/sa-*'ee*-da ⓜ/①

have عند 'ind

he هو *hu*-wa

head رأس ra's ⓜ

heart قلب kalb ⓜ

heat n حرارة ha-*raa*-ra ①

heavy ثقيل/ثقيلة tha-*keel*/tha-*kee*-la ⓜ/①

help v يساعد/تساعد yu-*saa*-'i-du/tu-*saa*-'i-du ⓜ/①

here هنا *hu*-naa

high عال/عالية *'aa*-lin/*'aa*-li-ya ⓜ/①

highway طريق عام ta-*ree*-ku *'aam* ⓜ

I

hike v يقيم/نقوم بنزهة طويلة سيراً على القدمين
ya-koo-mu/ta-koo-mu bi-naz-ha-tin ta-wee-la-tin
see-ran ʿa-laal ka-da-mayn ⓜ/ⓕ

holiday إجازة ʾi-jaa-za ⓕ

homosexual a لوطيّ/سحاقيّة
loo-tee/su-haa-kee-ya ⓜ/ⓕ

hospital مستشفى mus-tash-faa ⓜ

hot حارّ/حارة haar/haa-ra ⓜ/ⓕ

hotel فندق fun-duk ⓜ

hungry جائع/جائعة jaaʾiʿ/jaaʾiʿi-ʾa ⓜ/ⓕ

husband زوج zawj ⓜ

I

identification (card) (بطاقة) شخصية
(bi-taa-ka-tu) shakh-see-ya ⓕ

ill مريض/مريضة ma-reed/ma-ree-da ⓜ/ⓕ

important مهمّ/مهمّة mu-him/mu-him-ma ⓜ/ⓕ

included متضمّن/متضمّنة
mu-ta-dam-man/mu-ta-dam-ma-na ⓜ/ⓕ

injury ضرر da-rar ⓜ

insurance تأمين taʾ-meen ⓜ

internet الإنترنت ʾin-tir-net ⓜ

interpreter مترجم فوري/مترجمة فورية
mu-tar-jim faw-ree/mu-tar-ji-ma faw-ree-ya
ⓜ/ⓕ

Iraq العراق al-ʿi-raak ⓕ

Israel إسرائيل ʾis-raa-ʾeel ⓕ

J

jewellery مجوهرات mu-jaw-ha-raat ⓕ

job عمل ʿa-mal ⓜ

Jordan الأردن al-ʾur-dun ⓜ

K

key مفتاح mif-taah ⓜ

kilogram كيلوغرام kee-loo-ghraam ⓜ

kitchen مطبخ mat-bakh ⓜ

knife سكين sik-keen ⓜ

L

laundry (place) مغسل magh-sal ⓜ

lawyer محام/محامية
mu-haa-min/mu-haa-mee-ya ⓜ/ⓕ

Lebanon لبنان lub-naan ⓜ

left (direction) يسار ya-saar ⓜ

left-luggage office مكتب للاحتفاظ بالأمتعة
mak-ta-bun li-li-ʾih-ti-faa-dhi bil-ʾam-ti-ʾa ⓜ

leg رجل rijl ⓜ

lesbian a سحاقيّة su-haa-kee-ya ⓕ

less (من) أقلّ ʾa-kal-lu (min) ⓜ

letter (mail) رسالة ri-saa-la ⓕ

lift (elevator) مصعد mas-ʿad ⓜ

light n ضوء daw ⓜ

like v يحبّ/تحبّ yu-hib-bu/tu-hib-bu ⓜ/ⓕ

lock n قفل kufl ⓜ

long طويل/طويلة ta-weel/ta-wee-la ⓜ/ⓕ

lost ضائع/ضائعة daaʾiʿ/daaʾiʿi-ʾa ⓜ/ⓕ

lost-property office مكتب للأغراض الضائعة
mak-ta-bu lil-ʾagh-raa-di ad-daaʾi-ʾa ⓜ

love v يحبّ/تحبّ yu-hib-bu/tu-hib-bu ⓜ/ⓕ

luggage أمتعة ʾam-ti-ʾa ⓕ

lunch غداء gha-daaʾ ⓜ

M

mail n البريد al-ba-reed ⓜ

man رجل ra-jul ⓜ

map خريطة kha-ree-ta ⓕ

market سوق sook ⓕ

matches كبريت kib-reet ⓜ

meat لحم lahm ⓜ

medicine دواء da-waaʾ ⓜ

menu قائمة الطعام kaaʾi-ma-tu at-ta-ʿaam ⓕ

message رسالة ri-saa-la ⓕ

milk حليب ha-leeb ⓜ

minute دقيقة da-kee-ka ⓕ

mobile phone هاتف محمول
haa-ti-fun mah-mool ⓜ

money نقد nukd ⓜ

month شهر shahr ⓜ

morning صباح sa-baah ⓜ

Morocco المغرب al-magh-rib ⓜ

mother أمّ ʾum ⓕ

motorcycle دراجة نارية dar-raa-ja-tun naa-ree-ya ⓕ

motorway أوتوستراد ʾoo-too-straad ⓜ

mouth فمّ fam ⓜ

music الموسيقى al-moo-see-kaa ⓕ

N

name اسم ʾism ⓜ

napkin محرمة mah-ra-ma ⓕ

nappy حفاظة طفل ha-faa-dha-tu tifl ⓕ

near قريب من ka-ree-bu min

neck رقبة ra-ka-ba ⓕ

new جديد/جديدة ja-deed/ja-dee-da ⓜ/ⓕ

news الأخبار al-ʾakh-baar ⓜ

newspaper جريدة ja-ree-da ⓕ

night ليل layl ⓜ

no لا laa

noisy ضجيج/ضجيجة da-jeej/da-jee-ja ⓜ/ⓕ

nonsmoking غير المدخنين
ghay-ri al-mu-dakh-khi-neen

north شمال sha-maal ⓜ

nose أنف ʾanf ⓜ

now الآن al-ʾaan

number رقم rakm ⓜ

O

OK تمام ta·maam
oil (engine) نفط naft ⑰
old قديم/قديمة ka·deem/ka·dee·ma ⑰/①
Oman عُمان u·maan ⑰
one-way ticket تذكرة ذهاب فقط
tadh·ki·ra·tu dha·haab fa·kat ①
open a مفتوح/مفتوحة maf·tooh/maf·too·ha ⑰/①
outside خارج khaa·rij

P

package طرد tard ⑰
paper ورقة wa·ra·ka ①
park (car) v يوقف/توقف yoo·ki·fu/too·ki·fu ⑰/①
passport جواز سفر ja·waa·zu sa·far ⑰
pay v يدفع/تدفع yad·fa·'u/tad·fa·'u ⑰/①
pen قلم ka·lam ⑰
petrol نفط naft ⑰
pharmacy صيدلية say·da·lee·ya ①
phonecard بطاقة التلفون bi·taa·ka·tu at·ti·li·foon ①
photo صورة soo·ra ①
plate صحن sahn ⑰
police شرطة shur·ta ①
postcard بطاقة المعايدة bi·taa·ka·tul mu·'aa·ya·da ①
post office مكتب البريد mak·ta·bul ba·reed ⑰
pregnant حامل haa·mil
price ثمن tha·man ⑰

Q

quiet هادئ/هادئة haa din/haa dee ya ⑰/①

R

rain n مطر ma·tar ⑰
razor موسى moo·saa ①
receipt n وصول wu·sool ⑰
red أحمر/حمراء 'ah·mar/ham·raa' ⑰/①
refund n إعادة مال 'i·'aa·da·tu maal ①
registered mail بريد مسجّل
ba·ree·dun mu·saj·jal ⑰
rent v يستأجر/تستأجر
yas·ta·'ji·ru/tas·ta·'ji·ru ⑰/①
repair v يُصلح/تُصلح yus·li·hu/tus·li·hu ⑰/①
reservation حجز hajz ⑰
restaurant مطعم mat·'am ⑰
return v يرجع/ترجع yar·ja·'u/tar·ja·'u ⑰/①
return ticket تذكرة ذهاب وإياب
tadh·ki·ra·tu dha·haab·bi wal·'ee·yaab ⑰
right (direction) يمين ya·meen ⑰
road شارع shaa·ri' ⑰
room غرفة ghur·fa ①

S

safe a آمن/آمنة 'aa·min/'aa·mi·na ⑰/①
sanitary napkin منديل نسائي
min·dee·lun ni·saa·'ee ⑰
Saudi Arabia المملكة العربية السعودية
al·mam·la·ka·tul al·'a·ra·bee·ya·tun
as·sa·'u·dee·ya ①
seat مقعد mak·'ad ⑰
send v يبعث/تبعث yab·'a·thu/tab·'a·thu ⑰/①
service station محطة البنزين
mu·hat·ta·tul bin·zeen ①
sex جنس jins ⑰
shampoo الشامبو ash·shaam·boo ⑰
share (a dorm etc) يشارك/تشارك
yu·shaa·ri·ku/tu·shaa·ri·ku ⑰/①
shaving cream محجون الحلاقة
ma·'joo·nul hal·laa·ka ⑰
she هي hi·ya ①
sheet (bed) شرشف shar·shaf ⑰
shirt قميص ka·mees ⑰
shoes حذاء hi·dhaa' ⑰
shop n دكان duk·kaan ⑰
short قصير/قصيرة ka·seer/ka·see·ra ⑰/①
shower n دوش doosh ⑰
single room غرفة لشخص واحد
ghur·fa·tun li·sfakh·sin waa·hid ①
skin جلد jild ⑰
skirt تنّورة tan·noo·ra ①
sleep v ينام/تنام ya·naa·mu/ta·naa·mu ⑰/①
slowly ببطء bi·but
small صغير/صغيرة sa·gheer/sa·ghee·ra ⑰/①
smoke (cigarettes) v يدخّن/تدخّن
yu·dakh·khi·nu/tu·dakh·khi·nu ⑰/①
soap صابون saa·boon ⑰
some بعض ba·'du
soon قريبا ka·ree·ban
south جنوب ja·noob ⑰
souvenir shop دكان التذكارات
duk·kaa·nu at·tidh·kaa·raat ⑰
speak v تتكلّم/يتكلّم
ya·ta·kal·la·mu/ta·ta·kal·la·mu ⑰/①
spoon ملعقة mal·'a·ka ①
stamp طابع taa·bi' ⑰
stand-by ticket تذكرة بديلة
tadh·ki·ra·tun ba·dee·la ①
station (train) محطة mu·hat·ta·tu ①
stomach معدة ma·'i·da ①
stop v يقف/يقف ya·ki·fu/ta·ki·fu ⑰/①
stop (bus) موقف maw·ki·fu ⑰
street شارع shaa·ri' ⑰
student طالب/طالبة taa·lib/taa·li·ba ⑰/①
sun شمس shams ⑰
sunscreen معجون واقي من الشمس
ma·'joo·nun waa·kee min ash·shams ⑰
swim v يسبح/يسبح yas·ba·hu/tas·bu·hu ⑰/①
Syria سوريا soo·ri·ya ①

T

tampons الصمام النسائيّ ⓕ
as·si·*maa*·mu an·ni·*saa*·ee

taxi سيارة الأجرة *say*·yaa·ra·tul *uj*·ra ⓕ

teaspoon ملعقة شاي mal·*a*·ka·tu *shaa*·ee ⓕ

teeth أسنان *as*·naan ⓕ

telephone هاتف *haa*·tif ⓜ

television تلفزيون ti·li·fi·*zi*·yoon ⓜ

temperature (weather) درجة الحرارة
da·ra·ja·tul ha·*raa*·ra ⓕ

tent خيمة *khay*·ma ⓕ

that (one) ذلك/تلك *dhaa*·li·ka/*til*·ka ⓜ/ⓕ

they هم/هنّ hum/*hun*·na ⓜ/ⓕ

thirsty عطشان/عطشانة
at·shaan/*at*·shaa·na ⓜ/ⓕ

this (one) هذا/هذه *haa*·dhaa/*haa*·dhi·hi ⓜ/ⓕ

throat حلق khalk ⓜ

ticket تذكرة *tadh*·ki·ra ⓕ

time وقت wakt ⓜ

tired تعبان/تعبانة ta·*baan*/ta·*baa*·na ⓜ/ⓕ

tissues محارم ma·*haa*·ram ⓕ

today اليوم al·*yawm* ⓜ

toilet دورات المياه daw·*raa*·tul mi·*yaah* ⓕ

tomorrow غدًا *gha*·dan

tonight ليلة اليوم *lay*·la·tul yawm ⓜ

toothbrush فرشاة الأسنان far·*shaa*·tul *as*·naan ⓕ

toothpaste معجون الأسنان *maj*·joo·nul *as*·naan ⓜ

torch (flashlight) مشعل كهربائيّ
mish·a·lun kah·ra·*ba*·ee ⓜ

tour n دورة *daw*·ra ⓕ

tourist office مكتب السياحة
mak·ta·bu as·si·*ya*·ha ⓜ

towel منشفة *man*·sha·fa ⓕ

train قطار ki·*taar* ⓜ

translate نترجم/يترجم
yu·*tar*·ji·mu/tu·*tar*·ji·mu ⓜ/ⓕ

travel agency وكالة سفر wa·*kaa*·la·tu *sa*·far ⓕ

travellers cheque شيك سياحي
shee·kun si·*ya*·hee ⓜ

trousers بنطلون ban·ta·*loon* ⓜ

Tunisia تونس *too*·nis ⓕ

twin beds سريرين منفردين
sa·ree·*ray*·ni mun·fa·ri·*dayn* ⓜ

tyre إطار السيارة *i*·taa·ru as·say·*yaa*·ra ⓜ

U

underwear ملابس داخلية
ma·*laa*·bi·sun daa·khi·*lee*·ya ⓕ

United Arab Emirates الإمارات العربية المتحدة
al·*i*·maa·*raa*·tun al·a·ra·*bee*·ya·tun
al·mut·*ta*·hi·da ⓕ

V

urgent مستعجل/مستعجلة
mus·*ta*·jal/mus·*ta*·ja·la ⓜ/ⓕ

V

vacant شاغر/شاغرة *shaa*·ghir/*shaa*·ghi·ra ⓜ/ⓕ

vacation n إجازة *i*·*jaa*·za ⓕ

vegetable n خضراوات khud·raa·*waat* ⓕ

vegetarian a نباتي/نباتية
na·*baa*·tee/na·baa·*tee*·ya ⓜ/ⓕ

visa تأشيرة ta·*shee*·ra ⓕ

W

waiter نادل/نادلة *naa*·dil/*naa*·di·la ⓜ/ⓕ

walk v يمشي/تمشي yam·*shee*/tam·*shee*

wallet محفظة *mah*·fa·dha ⓕ

warm a دافئ/دافئة *daa*·fi·/*daa*·fi·a ⓜ/ⓕ

wash (something) يغسل/تغسل
yagh·*si*·lu/tagh·*si*·lu ⓜ/ⓕ

watch n ساعة اليد *saa*·a·tul yad ⓕ

water ماء *maa*·a ⓜ

we نحن *nah*·nu

weekend نهاية الأسبوع ni·*haa*·ya·tul *us*·boo· ⓜ

west غرب *gharb* ⓜ

West Bank الضفة الغربية
ad·*daf*·fa·tun al·ghar·*bee*·ya ⓕ

wheelchair كرسي المقعدين
kur·see al·muk·a·*deen* ⓜ

when متى ma·*taa*

where أين *ay*·na

white أبيض/بيضاء *ab*·yad/bay·*daa*· ⓜ/ⓕ

who مَن man

why لماذا li·*maa*·dhaa

wife زوجة *zaw*·ja ⓕ

window شبّاك shub·*baak* ⓜ

wine نبيذ na·*beedh* ⓜ

with مع *ma*·a

without بدون bi·*doo*·ni

woman امرأة *im*·ra·a ⓕ

write يكتب/تكتب *yak*·tu·bu/*tak*·tu·bu ⓜ/ⓕ

Y

yellow أصفر/صفراء *as*·far/saf·*raa*· ⓜ/ⓕ

Yemen اليمن al·*ya*·man ⓕ

yes نعم *na*·am

yesterday أمس *am*·si ⓜ

you sg أنت/أنت *an*·ta/*an*·ti ⓜ/ⓕ

you pl أنتم/أنتنّ *an*·tum/*an*·tun·na ⓜ/ⓕ

Egyptian
Arabic

language difficulties

Do you speak English?

بتتكلم/بتتكلمي إنجليزي؟   bi·tit·*ka*·lim/bi·tit·ka·*lim*·ee in·gi·*lee*·zee m/f

Do you understand?

فاهم/فهمة؟   fa·him/*fah*·ma m/f

I understand.

فاهم/فهمة.   fa·him/*fah*·ma m/f

I don't understand.

مش فاهم/فهمة.   mish fa·him/*fah*·ma m/f

Could you please ...?	ممكن ...؟	*mum*·kin ...
repeat that	تقوله/تقوليه تاني	ti·'ool/ti·'oo·lee ta·nee m/f
speak more slowly	تكلم/تكلمي براحة	ti·*kal*·im/ti·*kal*·im·ee bi *raa*·ḥa m/f
write it down	تكتبه/تكتبيه	tik·ti·*booh*/tik·ti·*beeh* m/f

numbers

0	زيرو	*zee*·ro	20	عشرين	'ish·*reen*
1	واحد	*wa*·hid	30	ثلاثين	ta·la·*teen*
2	إثنين	it·*nayn*	40	عربعين	ar·ba·*'een*
3	ثلاثة	ta·*la*·ta	50	خمسين	kham·*seen*
4	أربعة	ar·*ba*·a	60	ستين	si·*teen*
5	خمسة	*kham*·sa	70	سبعين	sa·ba·*'een*
6	ستة	*si*·ta	80	ثمنين	ta·ma·*neen*
7	سبعة	sa·*ba*·a	90	تسعين	ti·sa·*'een*
8	ثمانية	ta·*man*·ya	100	مئة	*mee*·ya
9	تسعة	ti·*sa*·a	1000	آلف	alf
10	عشرة	*'a*·sha·ra	1,000,000	مليون	mil·*yon*

For Arabic numerals, see the box on page 14.

time & dates

What time is it?	الساعة كم؟	is·sa·'a kam
It's (one) o'clock.	الساعة (واحدة).	is·sa·'a (wa·hi·da)
It's (two) o'clock.	الساعة (إثنين).	is·sa·'a (it·nayn)
Quarter past (two).	الساعة (إثنين) و ربع.	is·sa·'a (it·nayn) wi rub'
Half past (two).	الساعة (إثنين) و نص.	is·sa·'a (it·nayn) wi nus
Quarter to (two).	الساعة (إثنين) إلّا ربع.	is·sa·'a (it·nayn) il·a rub'
At what time ...?	إمتى ...؟	im·ta ...

am	صباحاً	sa·baa·han
pm (afternoon)	بعد الظهر	ba'd i·duhr
pm (evening)	بالليل	bi·layl

Monday	يوم الإثنين	yom il·it·nayn
Tuesday	يوم الثلاث	yom it·ta·lat
Wednesday	يوم الأربع	yom il·ar·ba'
Thursday	يوم الخميس	yom il·kha·mees
Friday	يوم الجمعة	yom il·gu·ma'
Saturday	يوم السبت	yom is·sabt
Sunday	يوم الحد	yom il·had

last ...		
week	الأسبوع اللي فات	il·us·boo' il·i fat
month	الشهر اللي فات	ish·shahr il·i fat
year	السنة اللي فاتت	is·sa·na il·i fat·it

next ...		
week	الأسبوع اللي جاي	il·us·boo' il·i gay
month	الشهر اللي جاي	ish·shahr il·i gay
year	السنة جاية	is·sa·na ga·ya

yesterday ...		
morning	إمبارح الصبح	im·ba·rih subh
afternoon	إمبارح بعد الظهر	im·ba·rih ba'd duhr
evening	إمبارح بالليل	im·ba·rih bi·layl

tomorrow ...		
morning	بكرة الصبح	buk·ra is·subh
afternoon	بكرة بعد الظهر	buk·ra ba'd duhr
evening	بكرة بالليل	buk·ra bi·layl

What date is it today?

النهارده كم؟   i·na·*har*·da kam

It's (15 December).

(خمسة‌عشر ديسمبر.)   (kham·as·*taa*·shir di·*sem*·bir)

border crossing

I'm here ...	... أنا هنا	*a*·na *hi*·na ...
in transit	في ترانسيت	fi tir·an·*seet*
on business	في شغل	fi shughl
on holiday	في أجازة	fi a·*ga*·za

I'm here for ...	... أنا حاقعد	*a*·na ha·'ad ...
(10) days	(عشرة) أيام	('a·sha·rat) ay·am
(three) weeks	(ثلاث) أسابيع	(ta·lat) as·a·*bee*'
(three) months	(ثلاث) أشهر	(ta·lat) ash·hur

I'm going to (Cairo).

أنا رايح/رايحة (القاهرة).   *a*·na raa·yih/ray·ha (il·*kaa*·hi·ra) m/f

I'm staying at the (Marriott).

أنا نزل/نزلة في (المريوت).   *a*·na niz·il/naz·la fil (*mar*·yot) m/f

I have nothing to declare.

مش معيا حاجة أسبتها.   mish ma'·ya ha·ga as·*bit*·ha

I have something to declare.

معيا حاجة أسبتها.   ma'·ya ha·ga as·*bit*·ha

That's (not) mine.

ده (مش) بتاعي.   da (mish) bi·*ta*·'ee

tickets & luggage

Where can I buy a ticket?

أشتري تذكرة منين؟   ash·*ti*·ri taz·*ka*·ra min·*ayn*

Do I need to book a seat?

لازم أحجز؟   *la*·zim *ah*·giz

One ... ticket (to Luxor), please.	تذكرة ... (للقصر) من فضلَك/فضلِك.	taz·ka·rit ... (li·lu'·sor) min fad·lak/fad·lik m/f
one-way	ذهاب	zi·hab
return	عودة	'aw·da

I'd like to ... my ticket, please.	عايز/عايزة ... تذكرتي من فضلَك/فضلِك.	'a·iz/'ai·za ... taz·kar·tee min fad·lak/fad·lik m/f
cancel	ألغى	al·ghee
change	أغير	a·ghay·ar

I'd like a ... seat, please.	عايز/عايزة مكان ... من فضلَك/فضلِك.	'a·iz/'ai·za ma·kan ... min fad·lak/fad·lik m/f
nonsmoking	من غير تدخين	min ghayr tad·kheen
smoking	تدخين	tad·kheen

Is there air conditioning?

فيه تكييف؟   fee tak·yeef

Is there a toilet?

فيه توالیت؟   fee tu·wa·lit

How long does the trip take?

الرحلة هي كم ساعة؟   i·rih·la hee·ya kam sa·'a

Is it a direct route?

الطريق مباشر؟   it·taa·ree' mu·ba·shir

My luggage has been ...	شنطي ...	sho·na·tee ...
damaged	باظت	baa·zit
lost	ضاعت	daa·'it
stolen	إتسرقت	it·sa·ra'·it

transport

Where does flight (007) arrive/depart?

من فين توصل/تمشي رحلة   min fayn too·sal/tim·shee rih·la
نمرة (زيرو زيرو سبعة)؟   nim·ra (zee·ro zee·ro sa·ba·'a)

Is this the ... to (Aswan)?	... الى (أسوان)؟	... i·la (as·waan)
boat	دي المركب	dee il·mar·kib
bus	ده الأوتوبيس	da il·o·to·bees
plane	دي الطيارة	dee i·ta·yaa·ra
train	ده القطر	da il·'atr

What time's	... أتوتوبيس	... o-to-*bees*
the ... bus?	الساعة كم؟	i-*sa*-'a kam
first	الأوّل	il *aw*-il
last	الآخر	il *a*-khir
next	الثاني	i-*ta*-nee

How long will it be delayed?

حايتأخّر كم ساعة؟   ha-yit-*akh*-ir kam *sa*-'a

What station/stop is this?

المحطة دي إسمها/   il-ma-*ha*-ta di is-*ma*-ha/

الموقف ده إسمه إيه؟   il-*maw*-if da ismuh ay

Please tell me when we get to (Minya).

من فضلَك/فضلِك ممكن تقولي/   min *fad*-lak/*fad*-lik *mum*-kin ti-'*ul*-ee/

تقوليلي لمّا نوصل (المنيا)؟   ti-'*ul*-ee-lee *la*-ma *nuw*-sil (il-*min*-ya) m/f

Is this seat available?

الكرسي ده فاضي؟   il-*kur*-si da *faa*-dee

That's my seat.

الكرسي ده بتاعي.   il-*kur*-si da bi-*ta*'-ee

I'd like a taxi ...	... عايز/عايزة تكسي	'*a*-iz/'*ai*-za taks ... m/f
at (9am)	الساعة	i-*sa*-'a
	(تسعة صباحاً)	(*ti*-sa'-a sa-*baa*-han)
now	دلوقتي	dil-*wa*'-tee
tomorrow	بكرة	*buk*-ra

How much is it to ...?

بكم إلى ...؟   bi-*kam* i-la ...

Please take me to (Midan Tahrir).

عايز/عايزة أروح (ميدان التحرير)   '*a*-iz/'*ai*-za a-*ruh* (may-*dan* i-*tah*-reer)

من فضلَك/فضلِك.   min *fad*-lak/*fad*-lik m/f

Please put the meter on.

إفتح العداد من فضلَك/فضلِك.   if-tah il '*ad*-ad min *fad*-lak/*fad*-lik m/f

Please ...	... من فضلَك/فضلِك	min *fad*-lak/*fad*-lik ... m/f
stop here	وقّف هنا	*wa*'-if *hi*-na
wait here	إستنّى هنا	is-*ta*-na *hi*-na

I'd like to hire a ...	... عايز/عايزة	'*a*-iz/'*ai*-za a-*'ag*-ar ... m/f
car	عربية	'*a*-ra-*bee*-ya
4WD	جيب	zheeb

الحركة – transport

with ...		
a driver	مع سوّاق	ma'sa·wa'
air conditioning	بتكييف	bi·tak·yeef

How much for ... hire?	...بكم لإجار ؟	bi·kam li·'ig·aar ...
daily	يومي	yom·ee
weekly	أسبوعي	us·boo'·ee

I need a mechanic.

محتاج/محتاجة ميكانيكي.   mih·tag/mih·ta·ga mi·ka·nee·kee m/f

I've run out of petrol.

البنزين خلص.   il·ben·zeen khi·lis

I have a flat tyre.

الكاوتش نائم.   il·ka·witsh nay·im

directions

Where's the ...?	...فين ؟	fayn ...
bank	البنك	il·bank
market	السوق	is·soo'
post office	البسطة	il·bus·ta

Is this the road to (the Red Sea)?

ده الطريق (للبحر الاحمر)؟   da i·taa·ree' (lil·bahr il·ah·mar)

Can you show me (on the map)?

ممكن تورّيني (على الخريطة)؟   mum·kin ti·wa·ree·nee ('al il·kha·ree·ta)

What's the address?

العنوان أيه؟   il·'un·wan ay

How far is it?

كم كيلو من هنا؟   kam kee·lu min hi·na

How do I get there?

أروح إزّاي؟   a·ruh i·zay

Turn left/right.

حود شمال/يمين.   haw·id shi·mal/yi·meen

It's ...	... هو/هي	hu·wa/hi·ya ... m/f
behind ...	... ورا	wa·ra ...
in front of ...	... قدام	'u·dam ...
near to ...	... قريب من	'u·ray·ib min ...
next to ...	... جمب	gamb ...
on the corner	على الناصية	'a·lal nas·ya
opposite ...	... قصاد	'u·saad ...
straight ahead	على طول	'a·la tool
there	هناك	hi·nak

north	شمال	sha·mal
south	جنوب	ga·noob
east	شرق	shar'
west	غرب	gharb

signs

مدخل	mad·khal	**Entrance**
خروج	kha·roog	**Exit**
مفتوح	maf·tooh	**Open**
مغلق	mugh·lak	**Closed**
إستعلامات	is·ta'·la·mat	**Information**
قسم الشرطة	'ism i·shur·ta	**Police Station**
ممنوع	mam·noo'	**Prohibited**
دورة الميّة	door·it il·mee·ya	**Toilets**
رجال	ri·gal	**Men**
سيّدات	sa·yi·dat	**Women**
سخن	sukhn	**Hot**
بارد	ba·rid	**Cold**

accommodation

Where's a ...?	... فين؟	fayn ...
camping ground	المخيّم	il·mu·khay·am
guesthouse	البنسيون	il·ban·see·yon
hotel	الفندق	il·fun·du'
youth hostel	بيت شباب	bayt sha·bab

Can you recommend	ممكن تقترح/	*mum*·kin tik·*ta*·rah/
somewhere ...?	تقترحي مكان ...؟	tik·*ta*·rah·ee ma·*kan* ... m/f
cheap	رخيص	ra·*khees*
good	كويس	*kway*·is
nearby	قريب من هنا	'u·*rai*·yib min *hi*·na

I'd like to book a room, please.

عايز/عايزة أحجز أوضة من   '*a*·iz/'*ai*·za ah·giz *o*·da min
فضلَك/فضلِك m/f   *fad*·lak/*fad*·lik m/f

I have a reservation.

عندي حجز   '*an*·dee hagz

Do you have	عندَك/عندِك أوضة ...؟	'*an*·dak/'*an*·dik *o*·da ... m/f
a ... room?		
single	لواحد	li·*wa*·hid
double	للإتنين	lil·it·*nayn*
twin	بسريرين	bi·si·ree·*rayn*

How much is it per ...?	بكم ...؟	bi kam ...
night	الليلة	il·*lay*·la
person	الشخص	i shakhs

I'd like to stay for (two nights).

عايز/عايزة أقعد (ليلتين).   '*a*·iz/'*ai*·za '*a*·'ad (layl·*tayn*) m/f

Am I allowed to camp here?

ممكن أخيّم هنا؟   *mum*·kin a·*khay*·im *hi*·na

Could I have my key, please?

عايز/عايزة المفتاح من   '*a*·iz/'*ai*·za il·mif·*tah* min
فضلَك/فضلِك m/f   *fad*·lak/*fad*·lik m/f

Can I get another (blanket)?

عايز/عايزة (بطنية) تنية من   '*a*·iz/'*ai*·za (ba·ta·*nee*·ya) *ta*·nya min
فضلَك/فضلِك m/f   *fad*·lak/*fad*·lik m/f

The (air conditioning) doesn't work.

(التكييف) مش شغال.   (i·tak·*yeef*) mish sha·*ghal*

(This sheet) isn't clean.

(الملاية) دي مش نَظيف.   (il·mi·*lay*·a) di mish na·*deef*

Is there an elevator/a safe?

فيه أسانسير/خزنة؟   fee as·an·*seer*/*khaz*·na

What time is checkout?

لازم نحاسب إمتى؟   *la*·zim ni·*ha*·sib im·ta

Could I have	... عايز/عايزة	*'a·iz/'ai·za* ...
my ..., please?	من فضلك/فضلك؟	min *fad·lak/fad·lik* m/f
deposit	مقدّمي	mu·*'ad·am·*ee
passport	بسبوري	bas·*boor·*ee
valuables	ممتلكاتي	mum·ta·la·*kat·*ee

banking & communications

Where's a/an ...?	... فين؟	fayn ...
ATM	بنك شخصي	bank *shakh·*see
foreign exchange office	صرّاف	sa·*raaf*

I'd like to ...	... عايز/عايزة	*'a·iz/'ai·za* ... m/f
arrange a transfer	أحوّل فلوس	a·*haw·*il fi·*loos*
cash a cheque	أصرف شيك	as·raf sheek
change a travellers cheque	أصرف شيك سياحي	as·raf sheek si·ya·hee
change money	أغيّر فلوس	a·*ghay·*ar fi·*loos*
withdraw money	أسحب فلوس	as·hab fi·*loos*

What's the ...?	... كم؟	... kam
charge for that	العمولات	il·*'u·*moo·*lat*
exchange rate	نسبة التحويل	nis·bit i·*tah·*weel

Where's the local internet café?

فين كفاي إنترنت؟   fayn ka·*fay* in·ter·*net*

How much is it per hour?

الساعة بكم؟   i·sa·'a bi·*kam*

I'd like to ...	... عايز/عايزة	*'a·iz/'ai·za* ... m/f
check my email	أشوف الإيميل رتاعي	a·*shoof* il·ee·*mayl* bi·*ta·*'ee
get internet access	أستعمل الإنترنت	as·*ta·*'mil il·in·ter·*net*
use a printer	أستعمل برنتر	as·*ta·*'mil *brin·*tir
use a scanner	أستعمل سكانر	as·*ta·*'mil *ska·*nir

I'd like a ...	... عايز/عايزة	*'a·iz/'ai·za* ... m/f
mobile/cell phone for hire	أجّر محمول	*'ag·*ar *mah·*mool
SIM card for your network	سيم كارد لشبكة دي	sim kard li *sha·*ba·ka di

What's your phone number?

نمرة تليفونك/تليفونِك كم؟   *nim*·rit ti·li·*fon*·ak/ti·li·*fon*·ik kam **m/f**

Where's the nearest public phone?

فين الاقرب تليفون؟   fayn il a'·rab ti·li·*fon*

I'd like to buy a phonecard.

عايز/عايزة أشتري كرت تليفون.   *'a*·iz/*'ai*·za ash·*ti*·ri kart ti·li·*fon* **m/f**

What are the rates?

الدقيقة بكم؟   il·da·*'ee*·'a bi·*kam*

How much does a (three)-minute call cost?

مكلمة (تلات) دقائق بكم؟   mu·*kal*·ma (*ta*·lat) da·*'ay*·i' bi·*kam*

I want to ...	... عايز/عايزة	*'a*·iz/*'ai*·za ... **m/f**
call (Canada)	أتصل بـ(كندا)	a·*tas*·al bi·(*ka*·na·da)
make a local call	أتصل بنمرة محلية	a·*tas*·al bi·*nim*·ra ma·hal·*ee*·ya
reverse the charges	أحوّل التكليف	a·*hu*·wil i·ta·ka·*leef*

I want to send a ...	... عايز/عايزة أبعت	*'a*·iz/*'al*·za ab·'at ... **m/f**
fax	فاكس	faks
parcel	طرد	tard

I want to buy a/an ...	... عايز/عايزة أشتري	*'a*·iz/*'ai*·za ash·*ti*·ree ... **m/f**
envelope	ظرف	zarf
stamp	طابع	*taa*·bi·'a

Please send it	من فضلَك/فضلِك إبعته	min *fad*·lak/*fad*·lik ib·'at·o
(to Australia) by ...	... بـ (لأستراليا)	(li·us·*traa*·lee·ya) bi ... **m/f**
airmail	بريد جوّي	ba·*reed* gaw·ee
surface mail	بريد عادي	ba·*reed* 'a·dee

sightseeing

What time does it open/close?

بيفتح/بيقفل إمتى؟   bi·*yif*·tah/bi·*yi*'·fil im·ta

What's the admission charge?

رسم الدخول كم؟   rasm i·du·*khool* kam

Is there a discount for students/children?

فيه تخفيض للطلبة/للأطفال؟   fee takh·*feed* lil·*tal*·ba/lil·at·*faal*

I'd like a ...	... عايز/عايزة	'a·iz/'ai·za ... m/f
catalogue	دليل	da·leel
guide	كتاب إرشادي	ki·tab ir·sha·dee
local map	خريطة محلّية	kha·ree·ta ma·ha·lee·ya

When's the next ...?	إمتى الـ ... اللي جاية؟	im·ta il ... il·ee ga·ya
day trip	رحلة	rih·la
tour	جولة	gaw·la

Is ... included?	شامل ...؟	sha·mil ...
accommodation	الإقامة	il·i·kaa·ma
the admission charge	رسم الدخول	rasm i·du·khool
food	الأكل	il·akl
transport	النقل	i·na'l

I'd like to see ...

عايز/عايزة أشوف ...   'a·iz/'ai·za a·shoof ... m/f

What's that?

أيه ده؟   ay da

How long is the tour?

الجولة كم ساعة؟   il·gaw·la kam sa·'a

What time should we be back?

المفروض نرجع إمتى؟   il·maf·rood nir·ga' im·ta

Can I take a photo?

ممكن أصوّر؟   mum·kin a·saw·ar

sightseeing

castle	قلعة	'a·la·'a f
church	كنيسة	ki·nee·sa f
main square	الميدان الرئيسي	il·may·dan i·ra·'ee·see m
mosque	مسجد	mas·gid m
old city	مدينة القديمة	ma·dee·nat il·'a·dee·ma f
palace	قصر	'asr m
pharaonic	فرعوني	fa·ra·'on·ee m
pyramids	أهرامات	ah·ra·maat f
the Pyramids of Giza	الأهرام	il·ah·raam m
ruins	آثار	a·saar m
statue	تمثال	tim·sal m
temple	معبد	ma'·bad m
tomb	مقبرة	ma'·ba·ra f

shopping

Where's a ...?   فين ...؟   fayn ...

bookshop	مكتبة	mak·*ta*·ba
camera shop	محل كاميرات	ma·*hal* ka·mi·*raat*
department store	محل	ma·*hal*
grocery store	بقّال	ba·*'al*
newsagency	بايع جرايد	bay·*aa'* ga·*ray*·id
souvenir shop	محل تذكارات	ma·*hal* i·tiz·ka·*raat*
supermarket	سوبرماركت	soo·bir·*mar*·kit

I'm looking for ...

أنا بدوّر على ...   *a*·na ba·*daw* ar *'a* la ...

Can I look at it?

ممكن أشوفه/أشوفها؟   *mum*·kin a·*shoo*·fuh/a·*shoof*·ha m/f

Do you have any others?

فيه تاني؟   fee *ta*·nee

Does it have a guarantee?

فيه ضمان؟   fee da·*maan*

Can I have it sent overseas?

ممكن أبعته/أبعتها برة؟   *mum*·kin a·*ba'*·tuh/a·*ba't*·ha *ba*·ra m/f

Can I have my ... repaired?

ممكن تصلّح الـ ...؟   *mum*·kin ti·*sal*·ah il ...

It's faulty.

مش شغّال.   mish sha·*ghal*

I'd like ..., please.

عايز/عايزة ... من   *'a*·iz/*'ai*·za ... min
فضلَك/فضلِك.   *fad*·lak/*fad*·lik m/f

a bag	كيس	kees
a refund	أسترداد	is·*tir*·dad
to return this	أرجعّه	a·ra·ga·*'oo*

How much is it?

بكم؟   bi-*kam*

Can you write down the price?

ممكن تكتب/تكتبي الثمن؟   *mum*·kin *tik*·tib/tik·*ti*·bee i·*ta*·man m/f

That's too expensive.

ده غالي قوي.   da *gha*·lee 'aw·ee

What's your lowest price?

الاحسن سعر كم؟   il·*ah*·san si'r kam

I'll give you (20 Egyptian pounds).

أدفع (عشرين جني مصري).   ad·fa' ('ish·*reen* gi·*nay* mas·ree)

There's a mistake in the bill.

فيه غلطة في الحساب.   fee *ghal*·ta fil his·*ab*

Do you accept ...?	بتاخد/بتاخدي ...؟	bi·*ta*·khud/bi·*ta*·khu·dee ... m/f
credit cards	كريدت كارد	*kre*·dit kard
travellers cheques	شيكات سياحي	shee·*kat* see·*ya*·hee

I'd like ..., please.	عايز/عايزة ... من	'*a*·iz/'*ai*·za ... min
	فضلَك/فضلِك	fad·lak/fad·lik m/f
my change	الفكة	il *fa*·ka
a receipt	وصل	wasl

I'd like ...	عايز/عايزة ...	'*a*·iz/'*ai*·za ... m/f
(100) grams	(ميّة) جرام	(meet) graam
(two) kilos	(إثنين) كيلو	(it·*nayn*) *kee*·lo
(three) pieces	(ثلاث) حتة	(ta·*lat*) *hi*·tat
(six) slices	(ستة) ترانش	(*si*·ta) traansh

Less.	أقل.	a·'*al*
Enough.	كفاية.	ki·*fay*·a
More.	أكثر.	*ak*·tar

photography

Can you ...?	ممكن ...؟	*mum*·kin ...
burn a CD from	عامل سي دي	'*a*·mal see·*dee*
my memory card	من الميموري كارد	min il·*me*·mo·ree kard
develop this film	تحمّد الفلم ده	ti·*ha*·mad il·*film* da
load my film	تشحن الكاميرة	*tish*·han il·*ka*·mi·ra
	بالفلم	bil·*film*

I need a/an ... film	أنا محتاج/محتاجة	a·na *mih*·tag/*mih*·ta·ga
for this camera.	فلم ... للكاميرة دي.	film ... lil-*ka*·mi·ra dee m/f
APS	أي بي أس	ay bee es
B&W	أبيض و إسود	*ab*·yad wa *is*·wid
colour	ملوّن	mi·*law*·in
slide	شريحة	sha·*ree*·ha
(200) speed	سرعة (ميتين)	su·ra'·a (mee·*tayn*)

When will it be ready?

حيكون جاهز إمتى؟   hay·*koon* ga·hiz im·ta

making conversation

Hello.	أهلا.	*ah*·lan
Good night.	تصبح على خير.	*tis*·bah '*a*·la khayr
Goodbye.	مع السلامة.	ma' sa·*la*·ma
Mr	سيّد	*say*·id
Mrs	سيّدة	say·*id*·a
Miss	آنسة	*a*·ni·sa

How are you?

إزيّك/إزيّك؟   iz·*ay*·ak/iz·*ay*·ik m/f

Fine, thanks. And you?

/كويّس   *kway*·is/

كويّسة. الحمدللّه؟   *kway*·is·a il·*am*·du·li·lah m/f

What's your name?

إسمَك/إسمِك أيه؟   *is*·mak/*is*·mik ay m/f

My name is ...

إسمي ...   *is*·mee ...

I'm pleased to meet you.

تشرّفنا.   ti·shar·*af*·na

This is my ...	... دي/ده	da/dee ... m/f
brother	أخويا	akh·oo·ya
daughter	بنتي	bin·tee
father	أبويا	ab·oo·ya
friend	صديقي/صديقتي	sa·dee·kee/sa·deek·tee m/f
husband	جوزي	goz·ee
mother	أمي	um·ee
sister	أختي	ukh·tee
son	إبني	ib·nee
wife	مراتي	mi·raa·tee

This is my ...	... دي/ده	da/dee ... m/f
address	عنواني	'un·wa·nee m
email address	عنوان إيميل	'un·wan ee·mayl m
phone number	نمرة تلفوني	nim·ra ti·li·fo·nee f

What's your ...?	... أيه؟	... ay
address	عنوانَك/عنوانِك	'un·wa·nak/'un·wa·nik m/f
email address	عنوان إيميل بتاعَك/بتاعِك	'un·wan ee·mayl bi·ta·ak/bi·ta·ik m/f
phone number	نمرت تلفونَك/تلفونِك	nim·rit ti·li·fo·nak/ti·li·fo·nik m/f

Where are you from?

إنتَ/إنتِ منين؟ in·ta/in·ti min·ayn m/f

I'm from ...	... أنا من	a·na min ...
Australia	أستراليا	us·traal·ya
Canada	كندا	ka·na·da
the UK	بريطانيا	bree·taan·ya
the USA	أمريكا	am·ree·ka

What's your occupation?

إنتَ/إنتِ بتشتغل/بتشتغلي أيه؟ in·ta/in·tee bi·tish·taghl/bi·tish·taghl·ee ay m/f

I'm a ...	... أنا	a·na ...
businessman	راجل أعمال	raa·gil a'·mal m
businesswoman	سيّدة أعمال	say·id·at a'·mal f
labourer	عامل/عاملة	'a·mil/'a·mi·la m/f
lawyer	محامي/محامية	mu·ha·mee/mu·ha·mee·ya m/f
teacher	مدرّس/مدرّسة	mu·da·ris/mu·da·ri·sa m/f

54

Do you like ...?	بتحب/بتحبي ...؟	bit·hib/bit·hib·ee ... m/f
I like/	أنا بحب/	a·na ba·hib/
don't like ...	مابحبش ...	ma·ba·hib·ish ...
art	الفن	il·fan
movies	الأفلام	il·af·lam
music	الموسيقى	il·ma·see·ka
reading	القراءة	il·ki·raa'
sport	الرياضة	i·ree·yaa·da

eating out

Can you recommend	ممكن	mum·kin
a ...?	تفترحلي/	tik·ti·rah·lee/
	تفترحيلي ...؟	tik·ti·ra·hee·lee ... m/f
bar	بار	baar
café	قهوة	'ah·wa
restaurant	مطعم	ma·ta·'am

I'd like a table (for four), please.

عايز/عايزة تربيزة (لأربع)   'a·iz/'ai·za ta·ra·bay·za (li·ar·ba')
من فضلَك/فضلِك.   min fad·lak/fad·lik m/f

What would you recommend?

تقترح أيه؟   tik·tar·ah ey

What's the local speciality?

الأطباق المحلية أيه؟   il at·baa' il ma·ha·lee·ya ay

What's that?

أيه ده؟   ay da

breakfast	فطار	fi·taar m
lunch	غدا	gha·da f
dinner	عشاء	'ash·a' m

I'd like (the) ...,	عايز/عايزة ... من	'a·iz/'ai·za ... min
please.	فضلَك/فضلِك	fad·lak/fad·lik m/f
bill	الحساب	il·hi·sab
drink list	لستة مشروبات	lis·tat mash·roo·bat
menu	المنيو	il·men·yu
that dish	التبق ده	il·ta·ba' da

drinks

| I'll have ... | عايز/عايزة ... | 'a·iz/'ai·za ... m/f |

What would you like to drink?

تشرب أيه؟   tish·rab ay

(cup of) coffee ...	(كبايّة) قهوة ...	(ku·bay·it) 'ah·wa ...
(cup of) tea ...	(كبايّة) شاي ...	(ku·bay·it) shay ...
with milk	مع لبن	ma·'a la·ban
without sugar	بدون سكّر	bi·doon su·kar

| (orange) juice | عصير (برتقان) m | 'as·eer (bur·tu·'aan) m |
| soft drink | حاجة ساقع f | ha·ga sa·'a f |

... water	ميّة ...	ma·ya ... f
boiled	مغلية	magh·lee·ya
mineral	معدنية	ma·'·da·nee·ya

| a bottle/glass of beer | إزازة/كباية بيرة | i·za·zit/ku·bay·it bee·ra |
| a shot of whisky | وسكي | wis·kee |

a bottle/glass	إزازة/كاس	i·za·zit/kas
of ... wine	نبيد ...	ni·beet ...
red	أحمر	ah·mar
sparkling	شمبانيا	sham·ban·ya
white	أبيض	ab·yad

special diets & allergies

Is there a vegetarian restaurant near here?

فيه مطعم نباتي قرّيب   fee *ma·ta·am na·ba·*tee *'ur·ay·*ib
من هنا؟   min *hi·*na

Do you have ... food?	عندّك/عندِك أكل ... ؟	*'an·*dak/*'an·*dik akl ... m/f
halal	هلال	ha·*lal*
vegetarian	نباتي	na·*ba·*tee

Could you prepare	ممكن تعمل أكل	*mum·*kin ta·*'mil* akl
a meal without ...?	من غير ... ؟	min ghayr ...
butter	زبدة	*zib·*da
eggs	بيض	bayd
meat stock	شربة لحمة	*shor·*bit *lah·*ma

I'm allergic to ...	عندي حساسية لـ ...	*'an·*dee ha·sa·*see·*ya li ...
dairy produce	الألبان	al·*ban*
nuts	مكسّرات	mi·ka·sa·*raat*
seafood	أسماك البحر	*as·*mak il·*bahr*

emergencies

Help!	الحقني!	il·*ha·*'nee
Stop!	أقف!	u·*'af*
Go away!	إمشي!	im·*shee*
Thief!	حرامي!	ha·*raa·*mee
Fire!	حريق!	ha·*ree'*
Watch out!	خالي بالَك/بالِك!	*kha·*lee ba·*lak/*ba·*lik* m/f

Call ...!	إتصل ب ... !	i·*tas·*al bi ...
a doctor	دكتور/دكتورة	duk·*toor/*duk·*too·*ra m/f
an ambulance	الإسعاف	il·is·*'af*
the police	البوليس	il·bu·*lees*

Could you help me, please?

ممكن تساعدني من   *mum·*kin ti·sa·*'id·*nee min
فضلَك/فضلِك؟   *fad·*lak/*fad·*lik m/f

I have to use the phone.

لازم أتكلم في التليفون. *la*·zim at·*kal*·im fi ti·li·*fon*

I'm lost.

أنا تايه/تهت. *a*·na *tay*·ih/tuht m/f

Where are the toilets?

فين التواليت؟ fayn i·tu·wa·*leet*

Where's the police station?

فين قسم الشرطة؟ fayn ism i·*shur*·ta

I want to report an offence.

عايز/عايزة أبلغ البوليس. *'a*·iz/*ai*·za a·*bal*·agh il·bu·*lees* m/f

I have insurance.

عندي تأمين. *'an*·dee ta·*'meen*

I want to contact my embassy.

عايز/عايزة أتصل بالسفارة. *'a*·iz/*ai*·za a·*ta*·sal bil·si·*faa*·ra m/f

I've been ...	... أنا	*a*·na ...
assaulted	مغتصبة	mugh·*ta*·sa·ba
raped	مغتصبة	mugh·*ta*·sa·ba
robbed	إتسرقت	it·*sar*·'at

I've lost my ...	ضاعت الـ ... بتاعي.	*daa*·'it il ... bi·*ta*·'ee
My ... was/were	الـ ... بتاعي	il ... bi·*ta*·'ee
stolen.	إتسرقت.	it·*sa*·ra·'it
bag	شنطة	*shan*·ta
credit card	كريدت كارد	*kre*·dit kard
money	فلوس	fi·*loos*
passport	بسبور	bas·*boor*
travellers cheques	شيكات سياحية	shee·*kat* si·ya·*hee*·ya

health

Where's the nearest ...?	فين الاقرب ...	fayn il·*'a*·rab ...
dentist	دكتور/دكتورة السنان	duk·*toor*/duk·*too*·ra i·si·*nan* m/f
doctor	دكتور/دكتورة	duk·*toor*/duk·*too*·ra m/f
hospital	مستشفى	mus·*tash*·fa
pharmacist	صيدلية	say·da·*lee*·ya

I need a doctor (who speaks English).

عايز/عايزة دكتور
(بيكلّمة إنجليزي).

'a·iz/'ai·za duk·*toor*
(biy·*ka*·lim in·gi·*lee*·zee) m/f

Could I see a female doctor?

ممكن أشوف دكتورة؟

mum·kin a·*shoof* duk·*too*·ra

I've run out of my medication.

الدواء بتاعي خلص.

i·*da*·wa bi·*ta*'·ee *khi*·lis

I'm sick.

أنا عيّان/عيّانة.

a·na ay·*an*/ay·*an*·a m/f

It hurts here.

بيوجعني هنا.

bi·yiw·*ga*'·nee *hi*·na

I have nausea.

عايز/عايزة أرجع.

'a·iz/*'ai*·za a·*ra*·ga' m/f

I have (a) ...	... عندي	*'an*·dee ...
asthma	أزمة ريو	*az*·mit *ra*·boo
constipation	إمساك	im·*sak*
diarrhoea	إسهال	is·*hal*
fever	همّة	*hu*·ma
headache	سداع	su·*daa*'
heart condition	حاجة في القلب	*ha*·ga fil 'alb
pain	وجع	*wa*·ga'
sore throat	إلتهاب في الزور	il·ti·*hab* fil zor
toothache	وجع في الضرس	*wa*·ga' fi *dirs*

I'm allergic to ...	عندي حساسية	*'an*·dee ha·sa·*see*·ya
	... من	min ...
antibiotics	مضاد حيوي	mu·*daad* ha·ya·wee
anti-inflammatories	حاجة للألم	*ha*·ga lil·*a*·lam
aspirin	أسبرين	as·bi·*reen*
bees	نحل	nahl
codeine	كدايين	ko·da·*yeen*
penicillin	بنسلين	be·ni·si·*leen*

english–egyptian arabic dictionary

Words in this dictionary are marked as n (noun), a (adjective), v (verb), sg (singular), pl (plural),
ⓜ (masculine) and ⓕ (feminine) where necessary. Verbs are given in the present tense in the third-
person singular ('he/she'), in both masculine and feminine forms.

A

accident حدثه *had-sa* ⓕ
accommodation إقامة i-*kaa-ma* ⓕ
adaptor ادابتار a-*dab-taar* ⓜ
address n عنوان *'un-wan* ⓜ
after بعد *ba-'d*
air-conditioned مكيف/مكيفة
mu-*kay-if*/mu-*kay-i-fa* ⓜ/ⓕ
airplane طيارة ta-*yaa-ra* ⓕ
airport مطار *ma-taar* ⓜ
alcohol خمرة *kham-ra* ⓕ
all كل *kul*
allergy حساسية ha-sa-*see-ya* ⓕ
ambulance إسعاف is-*'af* ⓜ
and و *wa*
ankle كعب *ka'b* ⓜ
arm دراع di-*raa'* ⓜ
ashtray طفاية ta-*faa-ya* ⓕ
ATM بنك شخصي bank *shakh-see* ⓜ

B

baby بايبي *bay-bee* ⓕ
back (body) ظهر *dahr* ⓜ
backpack شنطة ظهر *shan-tit dahr* ⓕ
bad وحش/وحشة *wi-hish*/*wih-sha* ⓜ/ⓕ
bag شنطة *shan-ta* ⓕ
baggage claim الأخد الهقائب
il-*akh*-ad il-ha-*kaa-ib* ⓜ
bank بنك *bank* ⓜ
bar بار *baar* ⓜ
bathroom حمام *ham-am* ⓜ
battery بطارية ba-*ta-ree-ya* ⓕ
beautiful جميل/جميلة ga-*meel*/ga-*mee-la* ⓜ/ⓕ
bed سرير *sir-eer* ⓜ
beer بيرة *bee-ra* ⓕ
before قبل *'abl*
behind وراء *wa-ra*
bicycle عجلة *a-ga-la* ⓕ
big كبير/كبيرة ki-*beer*/ki-*bee-ra* ⓜ/ⓕ
bill حساب hi-*sab* ⓜ
black إسود/سوداء *is-wid*/*so-da* ⓜ/ⓕ
blanket بطانية ba-*taa-nee-ya* ⓕ

blood group صنف الدم sanf i-*dam* ⓜ
blue أزرق/زرقاء *az-ra*/*zar-a* ⓜ/ⓕ
boat مركب *mar-kib* ⓜ
book (make a reservation) v يحجز/تحجز
yih-*giz*/tih-*giz* ⓜ/ⓕ
bottle قزازة i-*zo-za* ⓕ
bottle opener فتاحة fa-*ta-ha* ⓕ
boy ولد *wa-lad* ⓜ
brakes (car) فرملة far-*ma-la* ⓕ
breakfast فطار fi-*taar* ⓜ
broken (faulty) بايظ/بايظة *baa-yiz*/*bay-za* ⓜ/ⓕ
bus أوتوبيس o-to-*bees* ⓜ
business شغل *shughl* ⓜ
buy يشتري/تشتري yish-*ti-ri*/tish-*ti-ri* ⓜ/ⓕ

C

café قهوة *'ah-wa* ⓕ
camera كاميرة *ka-mi-ra* ⓕ
camp site مخيم mu-*khay-am* ⓜ
cancel يلغي/تلغي *yil-ghee*/*til-ghee* ⓜ/ⓕ
can opener فتاحة fa-*ta-ha* ⓕ
car عربية a-ra-*bee-ya* ⓕ
cash n كاش *kash* ⓜ
cash (a cheque) v يصرف شيك/تصرف شيك
yis-rif *sheek*/tis-rif *sheek* ⓜ/ⓕ
cell phone محمول mah-*mool* ⓜ
centre n مركز *mar-kaz* ⓜ
change (money) v يغير/تغير
yi-*ghay-ar*/ti-*ghay-ar* ⓜ/ⓕ
cheap رخيص/رخيصة ra-*khees*/ra-*khee-sa* ⓜ/ⓕ
check (bill) حساب hi-*sab* ⓜ
check-in تسجيل ودخول tas-*geel* wi da-*khool*
chest صدر sidr ⓜ
child طفل/طفلة tifl/*tif-la* ⓜ/ⓕ
cigarette سجارة si-*gaa-ra* ⓕ
city مدينة ma-*dee-na* ⓕ
clean a نظيف/نظيفة na-*deef*/na-*dee-fa* ⓜ/ⓕ
closed مقفول/مقفولة *ma'-fool*/*ma'-fo-la* ⓜ/ⓕ
coffee قهوة *'ah-wa* ⓕ
coins فكة *fa-ka* ⓕ
cold (feel) بردان/بردانة bar-*dan*/bar-*da-na* ⓜ/ⓕ
cold (weather) a برد *bard* ⓜ
come يجيء/تجيء *yee-gi*/*tee-gi* ⓜ/ⓕ

computer كمبيوتر kom-bi-yoo-tar ⓜ
condom كبوت ka-boot ⓜ
contact lenses عدسة لاصقة 'ad-a-sat las-'a ①
cook v يطبخ/تطبخ yut bukh/tut bukh ⓜ/①
cost n تكلفة tak-li-fa ①
credit card كريدت كارد kre-dit kard ⓜ
cup فنجان fin-gan ⓜ
currency exchange صراف sa-raaf ⓜ
customs (immigration) جمرك gom-ruk ⓜ

D

dangerous خطير/خطيرة kha-teer/kha-tee-ra ⓜ/①
date (time) تاريخ ta-reekh ⓜ
day يوم yom ⓜ
delay n تأخيرة ta'-khee-ra ①
dentist دكتور/دكتورة أسنان duk-toor/duk-too-ra as-nan ⓜ/①
depart يمشي/تمشي yim-shee/tim-shee ⓜ/①
diaper بامبرز bam-bers ⓜ
dictionary قاموس kaa-moos ⓜ
dinner عشاء a-sha ⓜ
direct مباشر/مباشرة mu-ba-shir/mu-ba-shi-ra ⓜ/①
dirty وسخ/وسخة wi-sikh/wis-kha ⓜ/①
disabled معاق/معاوقة mu-'aw-ak/mu-'a-wa-ka ⓜ/①
discount n تخفيض takh-feed ⓜ
doctor دكتور/دكتورة duk-toor/duk-too-ra ⓜ/①
double bed سرير مزدوج si-reer muz-da-wag ⓜ
double room أوضة للاثنين o-da lil-it-nayn ①
drink n مشروب mash-roob ⓜ
drive v يسوق/تسوق yi-soo'/ti-soo' ⓜ/①
drivers licence رخصة سواقة rukh-sat si-wa'-a ①
drug (illicit) مخدرات mu-kha-daa-raat ①
dummy (pacifier) تتينة ti-tee-na ①

E

ear ودن widn ⓜ
east شرق shar' ⓜ
eat يأكل/تأكل ya-kul/ta-kul ⓜ/①
economy class (plane only) درجة ثانية da-ra-ga tan-ya ①
electricity كهرباء kah-ra-ba ①
elevator أسانسير as-an-seer ⓜ
email إميل ee-mayl ⓜ
embassy سفارة si-faa-ra ①
emergency طواريء ta-waa-ri' ⓜ
English (language) إنجليزي in-glee-zee ⓜ
entrance مدخل mad-khal ⓜ

evening مساء mi-sa ⓜ
exchange rate نسبة التحويل nis-bit i-tah-weel ①
exit n مخروج makh-roog ⓜ
expensive غالي/غالية gha-lee/ghal-ya ⓜ/①
express mail بريد مستعجل ba-reed mis-ta'-gil ⓜ
eye عين 'ayn ⓜ

F

far بعيد/بعيدة ba-'eed/ba-'ee-da ⓜ/①
fast سريع/سريعة sa-ree'/sa-ree-'a ⓜ/①
father أب ab ⓜ
film (camera) فيلم film ⓜ
finger صباع su-baa' ⓜ
first-aid kit شنطة إسعاف أولّي shan-tit is-'af aw-wa-lee ①
first class درجة أولى da-ra-ga oo-la ①
fish n سمك sam-ak ⓜ
food أكل 'akl ⓜ
foot رجل rigl ⓜ
fork شوكة sho-ka ①
free (of charge) بلاش bi-ba-lash
friend صاحب/صاحبة sa-hib/sah-ba ⓜ/①
fruit فكهة fak-ha ①
full مليان/مليانة mal-yan/mal-ya-na ⓜ/①
funny مضحك/مضحكة mud-hik/mud-hi-ka ⓜ/①

G

gift هديّة hi-di-ya ①
girl بنت bint ①
glass (drinking) كبايّة ku-bay-a ①
glasses (eyesight) نظارة na-daa-ra ①
go يروح/تروح yi-rooh/ti-rooh ⓜ/①
good كويّس/كويّسة kway-is/kway-sa ⓜ/①
green أخضر/خضرا akh-dar/khad-ra ⓜ/①
guide n مرشد/مرشدة mur-shid/mur-shi-da ⓜ/①

H

half نص nus ⓜ
hand يد eed ⓜ
handbag شنطة shan-ta ①
happy مبسوط/مبسوطة mab-soot/mab-soo-ta ⓜ/①
he هو hu-wa
head راس ras ⓜ
heart قلب 'alb ⓜ
heat n حرارة ha-raa-ra ①
heavy ثقيل/ثقيلة ti-'eel/ti-'ee-la ⓜ/①

help v يساعد/تساعد yi·sa·'id/ti·sa·'id ⓜ/ⓕ
here هنا hi·na
high عالية/عالي 'a·lee/'al·ya ⓜ/ⓕ
highway الطريق السريع it·taa·ree'·is·sa·ree·'a ⓕ
hike v يمشي/تمشي yim·shee/tim·shee ⓜ/ⓕ
holiday إجازة a·ga·za ⓕ
holiday (religious) عيد 'eed ⓜ
homosexual n لوطي/سحاقية
loo·tee/su·haa·kee·ya ⓜ/ⓕ
hospital مستشفى mus·tash·fa ⓜ
hot (to be) حرّان/حرّانة har·aan/ha·raa·na ⓜ/ⓕ
hot (weather) حار har
hotel فندق fun·du' ⓜ
hungry جعان/جعانة ga·'an/ga·'a·na ⓜ/ⓕ
husband جوز goz ⓜ

I

I أنا a·na
identification (card) كرنيه kar·nay ⓜ
ill عيّان/عيّانة 'a·yan/'a·ya·na ⓜ/ⓕ
important مهم/مهمة mu·him/mu·hi·ma ⓜ/ⓕ
included شامل/شاملة sha·mil/sham·la ⓜ/ⓕ
injury جرح garh ⓜ
insurance تأمين ta'·meen
internet إنترنت in·ter·net ⓜ
interpreter مترجم/مترجمة
mu·tar·gim/mu·tar·gi·ma ⓜ/ⓕ

J

jewellery مجوهرات mu·gaw·ha·raat ⓕ
job شغلة shugh·la ⓕ

K

key مفتاح mif·tah ⓜ
kilogram كيلو kee·lo ⓜ
kitchen مطبخ mat·bakh ⓜ
knife سكينة si·kee·na ⓕ

L

laundry (place) تنتورلي tan·tor·lee ⓜ
lawyer محامي/محامية
mu·ha·mee/mu·ha·mee·ya ⓜ/ⓕ
left (direction) شمال shi·mal
left-luggage office أمانات a·ma·nat ⓕ
leg رجل rigl ⓜ
lesbian n سحاقية su·haa·kee·ya ⓕ
less أقل a·'al

letter (mail) جواب ga·wab ⓜ
lift (elevator) أسانسير as·an·seer ⓜ
light n نور noor ⓜ
like v يحب/تحب yi·hib/ti·hib ⓜ/ⓕ
lock n قفل 'ifl ⓜ
long طويل/طويلة ta·weel/ta·wee·la ⓜ/ⓕ
lost ضايع/ضايعة daa·yi'/daa·yi·'a ⓜ/ⓕ
lost-property office مكتب مفقودات
mak·tab maf·koo·dat ⓜ
love v يحب/تحب yi·hib/ti·hib ⓜ/ⓕ
luggage شنط sho·nat ⓕ
lunch غدا gha·da ⓕ

M

mail n بوسطة bus·ta ⓕ
man راجل raa·gil ⓜ
map خريطة kha·ree·ta ⓕ
market سوق soo' ⓜ
matches كبريت kab·reet ⓜ
meat لحمة lah·ma ⓕ
medicine دوا da·wa ⓜ
menu منيو men·yu ⓜ
message رسالة ri·sa·la ⓕ
milk لبن la·ban ⓜ
minute دقيقة di·'ee·'a ⓕ
mobile phone محمول mah·mool ⓜ
money فلوس fi·loos ⓕ
month شهر shahr ⓜ
morning صبح subh ⓜ
mother أم um ⓕ
motorcycle موتوسيكل mo·to·sikl ⓜ
motorway الطريق السريع it·taa·ree'·is·sa·ree·'a ⓜ
mouth بوق bo' ⓜ
music مزيقة ma·zee·ka ⓕ

N

name إسم ism ⓜ
napkin فوطة foo·ta ⓕ
nappy بمبرس bam·bers ⓜ
near قريب/قريبة u·ray·ib/u·ray·ib·a ⓜ/ⓕ
neck رقبة ra·'a·ba ⓕ
new جديد/جديدة ga·deed/ga·dee·da ⓜ/ⓕ
news خبر kha·bar ⓜ
newspaper جورنال gur·naal ⓜ
night ليل lay·la ⓕ
no لا x 'la
noisy ده دوشة قوي da daw·sha 'aw·ee
nonsmoking غير تدخين ghayr tad·kheen
north شمال sha·mal
nose مناخير ma·na·kheer ⓜ

now دلوقتي dil-wa'-tee
number (numeral) نمرة num-ra ①
number (quantity) عدد 'a-dad ⓜ

O

oil (engine) زيت zayt ⓜ
old (person) عجوز/عجوزة 'a-gooz/'a-goo-za ⓜ/①
old (thing) قديم/قديمة 'a-deem/'a-dee-ma ⓜ/①
one-way ticket تذكرة ذهاب taz-kar-rit zi-hab ①
open a مفتوح/مفتوحة maf-tooh/maf-too-ha ⓜ/①
outside برّة ba-ra

P

package لفّة la-fa ①
paper ورق wa-ra' ⓜ
park (car) v تركن/تركن yir-kin/tir-kin ⓜ/①
passport بسبور bas-boor ⓜ
pay v يدفع/تدفع yid-fa/tid-fa ⓜ/①
pen قلم 'al-am ⓜ
petrol بنزين ben-zeen ⓜ
pharmacy صيدليّة say-da lee ya ①
phonecard كرت تليفون kart ti-li-fon ①
photo صورة soo-ra ①
plate طبق ta-ba' ⓜ
police شرطة shur-ta ①
postcard كرت بوستال kart bus-tal ⓜ
post office مكتب بستي mak-tab bus-ta ⓜ
pregnant حامل ha-mil
price سعر si'r ⓜ

Q

quiet هادي/هادية ha-dee/ha-dya ⓜ/①

R

rain n مطار mo-tar ⓜ
razor موس moos v
receipt فتورة fa-too-ra ①
red احمر/حمرا ah-mar/ham-ra ⓜ/①
refund n استرداد is-tir-dad v
registered mail جواب مسجّل ga-wab mu-sa-gil ⓜ
rent v يأجر/تأجر yi-'ag-ar/ti-'ag-ar ⓜ/①
repair v يصلح/تصلح yi-sa-lah/ti-sa-lah ⓜ/①
reservation حجز hagz ⓜ
restaurant مطعم mat-am ⓜ
return v يرجع/ترجع yir-ga/tir-ga ⓜ/①
return ticket تذكرة عودة taz-kar-rit 'aw-da ①
right (direction) يمين yi-meen

road طريق ta-ree ⓜ
room أوضة o-da ①

S

safe a أمان/أمانة a-man/a-ma-na ⓜ/①
sanitary napkin فوطة صحيّة foo-ta si-hi-ya ①
seat كرسي kur-see ⓜ
send v يبعت/تبعت yib-'at/tib-'at ⓜ/①
service station محطة بنزين ma-ha-tit i-ben-zeen ⓜ
sex جنس gins ⓜ
shampoo شامبو sham-boo ⓜ
share (a dorm etc) v تشارك/تشارك yi-sha-rik/ti-sha-rik ⓜ/①
shaving cream كريم حلاقة kreem hi-la-'a ⓜ
she هيّ hee-ya
sheet (bed) ملاية mi-lay-a ①
shirt قميص 'a-mees ⓜ
shoes جزمة gaz-ma ①
shop n محل ma-hal ⓜ
short قصير/قصيرة 'u-ay-ar/us-ay-ar-a ⓜ/①
shower n دوش doosh ⓜ
single room غرفة لواحد ghur-fa li-wa-hid ⓜ
skin جلد qild ⓜ
skirt جيبة zhee-ba ①
sleep v ينام/تنام yi-nam/ti-nam ⓜ/①
slowly بشويش bi-shweesh
small صغير/صغيرة su-ghay-ar/su-ghay-ar-a ⓜ/①
smoke (cigarettes) v يدخّن/تدخّن yi-dakh-an/ti-dakh-an ⓜ/①
soap صابون sa-boon ⓜ
some بعض ba'd
soon قرّيب 'u-ay-ib
south جنوب ga-noob ⓜ
souvenir shop محل التذكرات ma-hal it-tiz-kar-at ⓜ
speak v يكلّم/تكلّم yi-kal-lm/ti-kal-lm ⓜ/①
spoon معلقة ma'-la-'a ①
stamp طابع taa-bi' ⓜ
stand-by ticket تذكرة في قائمة الإنتظار taz-kar-it kee-mat li-in-ti-zaar ①
station (train) محطة قطار ma-ha-tit 'atr ⓜ
stomach معدة mi'-da ①
stop (do) v يقف/تقف yu-'af/tu-'af ⓜ/①
stop (bus) n موقف maw-'if ⓜ
street شارع sha-ri-a ⓜ
student طالب/طالبة taa-lib/taa-li-ba ⓜ/①
sun شمس shams ⓜ
sunscreen كريم ضد الشمس kreem did ish-shams ⓜ
swim v يسبح/تسبح yis-bah/tis-bah ⓜ/①

T

tampons تامبونات tam-bo-*nat* ①

taxi تكسي taks ⓜ

teaspoon معلقة شاي ma'-*la*-'it shai

teeth سنان si-*nan*

telephone n تليفون ti-li-*fon* ⓜ

television تلفزيون ti-li-viz-*yoon*

temperature (weather) حرارة ha-*raa*-ra ①

tent خيمة *khay*-ma ①

that (one) ده/دي (واحد) da/dee (wa-hid) ⓜ/①

they هما hu-*ma* ⓜ&①

thirsty عطشان/عطشانة
'at-*shaan*/at-*shaa*-na ⓜ/①

this (one) ده/دي (واحد) da/dee (wa-hid) ⓜ/①

throat زور zor ⓜ

ticket تذكرة taz-*ka*-ra ①

time وقت wa't ⓜ

tired تعبان/تعبانة ta'-*ban*/ta'-*ba*-na ⓜ/①

tissues منديل man-*deel* ⓜ

today النهارده i-na-*har*-da

toilet تواليت tu-wa-*lit* ⓜ

tomorrow بكرة *buk*-ra

tonight الليلة دي il-*lay*-la di

toothbrush فرشة سنان for-shit si-*nan* ①

toothpaste معجون سنان ma'-*goon* si-*nan*

torch (flashlight) بطاريّة ba-taa-*ree*-ya ①

tour n رحلة *rih*-la ①

tourist office مكتب السياحة
mak-tab i-si-*ya*-ha ⓜ

towel فوطة *foo*-taa ①

train قطر 'atr ⓜ

translate يترجم/تترجم
yi-*tar*-gim/ti-*tar*-gim ⓜ/①

travel agency مكتب سياحة *mak*-tab si-*ya*-ha ①

travellers cheque شيك سياحي
sheek si-ya-*hee*

trousers بانطلون ban-ta-*lon* ⓜ

twin beds سريرين sir-*eer*-ayn ①

tyre كاوتش kaw-*itsh* ⓜ

U

underwear كلوت ki-*lot* ⓜ

urgent مستعجل/مستعجلة
mis-ta'-gil/mis-ta'-*gi*-la ⓜ/①

V

vacant فاضي/فاضية faa-dee/faa-*dya* ⓜ/①

vacation إجازة a-*ga*-za ①

vegetable n خضار khu-*daar*

vegetarian a نباتي na-ba-*tee*/na-ba-*tee*-ya ⓜ/①

visa تأشيرة ta'-*shee*-ra ①

W

waiter جارسون gar-*son* ⓜ

walk v يمشي/تمشي *yim*-shee/*tim*-shee ⓜ/①

wallet محفظة mah-*fa*-za ①

warm (to feel) a دافيانة/دافيانة
daf-*yaan*/daf-*yaa*-na ⓜ/①

warm (weather) a دافية/دافي
da-fee/daf-*ya* ⓜ/①

wash (something) يغسل/تغسل
yigh-sil/*tigh*-sil ⓜ/①

watch n ساعة *sa*-'a ①

water ميّة *mai*-ya ①

we إحنا ih-*na*

weekend نهاية الأسبوع ni-*ha*-yit il-us-*boo*' ①

west غرب gharb

wheelchair كرسي متحرك *kur*-si mu-ta-har-ik ⓜ

when إمتى im-ta

where فين fayn

white أبيض/بيضاء *ab*-yad/*bay*-da ⓜ/①

who مين meen

why ليه lay

wife زوجة *zo*-ga ①

window شباك shu-*bak* ⓜ

wine نبيذ ni-*beet* ⓜ

with مع ma'-a

without من غير min ghayr

woman ستّ sit ①

write كتب *ka*-ta-b/*yik*-tib ⓜ/①

Y

yellow أسفر/سفراء *as*-far/*saf*-ra ⓜ/①

yes أيوة *ai*-wa

yesterday إمبارح im-*ba*-rih

you sg إنت/إنتِ in-ta/in-tee ⓜ/①

you pl إنتو *in*-to ⓜ&①

Gulf
Arabic

language difficulties

Do you speak English?

تتكلم انجليزية؟   tit·*kal*·am in·glee·*zee*·ya m

تتكلمي انجليزية؟   tit·*ka*·la·mee in·glee·*zee*·ya f

Do you understand?

فاهم/فهما؟   *faa*·him/*faa*·hi·ma m/f

I understand.

فاهم.   *faa*·him

I don't understand.

مو فاهم.   moo *faa*·him

Could you please ...?   لو سمحت...؟   law sa·*maht* ...

     repeat that   تعيد/تعيدي   ta·*'eed*/ta·*'ee*·dee m/f

     speak more slowly   اتكلم/اتكلمي بشوية   it·*kal*·am/it·*ka*·la·mee bi·*sway*·a m/f

     write it down   اكتبه/اكتبيه لي   ik·ti·*boo*/ik·ti·*bee* lee m/f

numbers

0	صفر	*si*·fir		20	عشرين	'ash·*reen*
1	واحد	*waa*·hid		30	ثلاثين	tha·la·*theen*
2	اثنين	ith·*nayn*		40	اربعين	ar·ba·*'een*
3	ثلاثة	tha·*laa*·tha		50	خمسين	kham·*seen*
4	اربع	*ar*·ba'		60	ستين	sit·*een*
5	خمسة	*kham*·sa		70	سبعين	sa·ba·*'een*
6	ستة	*si*·ta		80	ثمانين	tha·ma·*neen*
7	سبعة	*sa*·ba'		90	تسعين	ti·sa·*'een*
8	ثمانية	tha·*maan*·ya		100	مية	*mee*·ya
9	تسعة	*tis*·a'		1000	الف	alf
10	عشرة	'ash·*ar*·a		1,000,000	مليون	mel·*yoon*

For Arabic numerals, see the box on page 14.

time & dates

What time is it?	الساعة كم؟	i-*saa*-a' kam
It's one o'clock.	الساعة واحدة.	i-*saa*-a' *waa*-hi-da
It's (two) o'clock.	الساعة (ثنتين).	i-*saa*-a' (thin-*tayn*)
Quarter past (two).	الساعة (ثنتين) و ربع.	i-*saa*-a' (thin-*tayn*) wa *ru*-ba'
Half past (two).	الساعة (ثنتين) و نس.	i-*saa*-a' (thin-*tayn*) wa nus
Quarter to (three).	الساعة (ثلاثة) الا ربع.	i-*saa*-a' (tha-*laa*-tha) *il*-a *ru*-ba'
At what time ...?	الساعة كم ...؟	i-*saa*-a' kam ...
At ...	الساعة ...	i-*saa*-a'...

am	الصبح	sa-*baah*
pm	بعد الظهر	ba'd a-*thuhr*

Monday	يوم الاثنين	yawm al-ith-*nayn*
Tuesday	يوم الثلاثة	yawm a-tha-*laa*-tha
Wednesday	يوم الاربعة	yawm al-*ar*-ba'
Thursday	يوم الخميس	yawm al-kha-*mees*
Friday	يوم الجمعة	yawm al-*jum*-a'
Saturday	يوم السبت	yawm a-*sibt*
Sunday	يوم الاحد	yawm al-*aa*-had

last ...	ماضي ...	*maa*-dee ...
next ...	قادم ...	*yuu*-dlim ...
night	ليلة	*lay*-la
week	اسبوع	us-*boo*-a'
month	شهر	*sha*-har
year	سنة	*sa*-na

yesterday ...	البارح ...	il-*baa*-rih ...
tomorrow ...	باكر ...	*baa*-chir ...
morning	صباح	sa-*baah*
afternoon	بعد الظهر	ba'd a-*thuhr*
evening	مساء	mi-*saa*

What date is it today?

اش اليوم؟   aysh al-*yawm*

It's (15 December).

اليوم (خمسطاش ديسامبر).   al-*yawm* (kha-mas-*taash* dee-*sam*-bur)

border crossing

I'm here ...	... انا هنا	a·na hi·na ...
in transit	في ترانسيت	fee tran·sit
on business	في العمل	fil·'am·al
on holiday	في الاجازة	fil·ee·jaa·za

I'm here for ...	... انا هنا مدة	a·na hi·na mud·at ...
(10) days	(عشرة) ايام	('ash·a·rat) ai·yaam
(three) weeks	(ثلاثة) اسابيع	(tha·laa·tha) a·saa·bee·a'
(five) months	(خمسة) شهور	(kham·sa) shu·hoor

I'm going to (Dubai).

اروح الى (دبي).   a·roh i·la (du·bai)

I'm staying at the (Burj al-Arab Hotel).

انا قائد في (برج العرب).   a·na gaa·id fee (borj al·'ar·ab)

I have nothing to declare.

ما معيا هاجة.   maa ma'·ya haa·ja

I have something to declare.

انا معيا هاجة.   a·na ma'·ya haa·ja

That's (not) mine.

هاذاك (مو) مالي.   haa·dhaa·ka (moo) maa·lee

tickets & luggage

Where can I buy a ticket?

وين اقدر اشري تذكرة؟   wayn ag·dar ash·ree tadh·ka·ra

Do I need to book a seat?

لازم احجز كرسي؟   laa·zim ah·jiz kur·see

One ... ticket	تذكرة ... (الدوحة)	tadh·ka·ra ... (a·do·ha)
(to Doha), please.	من فضلك.	min fad·lak
one-way	ذهاب بص	dhee·haab bas
return	ذهاب و اياب	dhee·haab wa ai·yaab

I'd like to ... my	اريد ... تذكرتي	a·reed ... tadh·ki·ra·tee
ticket, please.	من فضلك.	min fad·lak
cancel	الغا	al·ghaa
change	احاول	a·haa·wil
collect	استلم	as·ta·lam

I'd like a ... seat,	اريد مقعد ...	a·reed mag·'ad ...
please.		
nonsmoking	ممنوع تدخين	mam·noo·a' tad·kheen
smoking	مسموح تدخين	mas·mooh tad·kheen

Is there air conditioning?

فيه كنديشان؟ fee kan·day·shan

Is there a toilet?

فيه مرحاض؟ fee mir·haad

How long does the trip take?

كم الرحلة تستغرق؟ kam i·rah·la tis·tagh·rik

Is it a direct route?

الرحلة متواصلة؟ i·rah·la moo·ta·wau·si·la

My luggage	جنتي ...	ju·na·tee ...
has been ...		
damaged	مكسورة	mak·soo·ra
lost	مفقودة	maf·koo·da
stolen	مسروقة	mas·roo·ka

transport

Where does flight (654) arrive/depart?

من وين توصل/تطلع min wayn too·sil/tat·la'
طيارة رقم (٦٥٤)؟ tay·aa·ra ra·kam (si·ta kham·sa ar·ba')

Is this the ...	هاذا ال ... يروح	haa·dha al ... yi·roh
(to Riyadh)?	(الرياض)؟	(li·ree·yaad)
boat	سفينة	sa·fee·na
bus	باص	baas
plane	طيارة	tay·aa·ra
train	قطار	gi·taar

What time's	الساعة كم	a·saa·a' kam
the ... bus?	الباص ...؟	il·baas ...
first	الاول	il·aw·al
last	الاخر	il·aa·khir
next	القادم	il·gaa·dim

How long will it be delayed?

| كم دقيقة يتاخر؟ | kam da·gee·ga yit·aa·khir |

What station/stop is this?

| ما هي المحطة هاذي؟ | maa hee·ya il·ma·ha·ta haa·dhee |

Please tell me when we get to (Al Ain).

| لو سمحت خبرني/خبريني | law sa·maht kha·bir·nee/kha·bir·ee·nee |
| وقت ما نوصل الي (العين). | wokt ma noo·sil i·la (al·'ain) m/f |

Is this seat available?

| مقعد هاذا فارغ؟ | ma·ga'd haa·dhee faa·righ |

That's my seat.

| هاذاك مقعدي. | haa·dhaak ma·ga·d·ee |

I'd like a taxi ...	اريد تكسي ...	a·reed tak·see ...
at (9am)	الساعة (تسعة)	a·saa·a' (tis·a')
now	الحين	il·heen
tomorrow	باكر	baa·chir

How much is it to (Sharjah)?

| بكم الى (شارقة)؟ | bi·kam i·la (shaa·ri·ka) |

Please put the meter on.

| من فضلك شكل عدات. | min fad·lak sha·kal 'ad·aat |

Please take me to (this address).

| من فضلك خذني | min fad·lak khudh·nee |
| (علعنوان هاذا). | ('al·'un·waan haa·dha) |

Please stop here.

| لو سمحت وقف هنا. | law sa·maht wa·gif hi·na |

Please wait here.

| لو سمحت استنا هنا. | law sa·maht is·ta·na hi·na |

I'd like to hire a ...	اريد استأجر ...	a·reed ist·'aj·ir ...
car	سيارة	say·aa·ra
4WD	سيارة فيها دبل	say·aa·ra fee·ha du·bal

with ...	مع ...	ma' ...
a driver	دريول	dray·wil
air conditioning	كنديشان	kan·day·shan

How much for ... hire?	كم الإيجار ...؟	kam il·ee·jaar ...
daily	كل يوم	kul yawm
weekly	كل اسبوع	kul us·boo·a'

I need a mechanic.

احتاج ميكانيك   ah·taaj mee·kaa·neek

I've run out of petrol.

ينضب البنزين   yan·dab al·ban·zeen

I have a flat tyre.

عندي بنشار   'und·ee ban·shar

directions

Where's the ...?	من وين ...؟	min wayn ...
bank	البنك	il·bank
market	السوق	i·soog
post office	مكتب البريد	mak·tab il·ba·reed

Is this the road to (Abu Dhabi)?

هاذا الطريق الى (ابو ظبي)؟   haa·dha i·ta·reeg i·la (a·boo da·bee)

Can you show me (on the map)?

لو سمحت وريني (علخريطة)؟   law sa·maht wa·ree·nee ('al·kha·ree·ta)

What's the address?

ما العنوان؟   ma il·'un·waan

How far is it?

كم بعيد؟   kam ba·'eed

How do I get there?

كيف ممكن اوصل هناكا؟   kayf mum·kin aw·sil hoo·naak

Turn (left/right).

لف/لفي (يسار/يمين).   lif/li·fee (yee·saar/yee·meen) m/f

It's ...	... هو/هي	hoo·wa/hee·ya ... m/f
behind ...	... ورا	wa·raa ...
in front of ...	... قدام	gu·daam ...
near to ...	... قريب من	ga·reeb min ...
next to ...	... جنب	janb ...
on the corner	علزاوية	'a·zaa·wee·ya
opposite ...	... مقابل	moo·gaa·bil ...
straight ahead	سيدا	see·da
there	هناك	hoo·naak

north	شمال	sha·maal
south	جنوب	ja·noob
east	شرق	sharg
west	غرب	gharb

signs

مدخل	mad·khal	Entrance
خروج	kha·rooj	Exit
مفتوح	maf·tooh	Open
مقفول	mag·fool	Closed
معلومات	ma·'·loom·aat	Information
مركز الشرطة	mar·kaz a·shur·ta	Police Station
ممنوع	mam·noo·a'	Prohibited
المرحاض	al·mir·haad	Toilets
رجال	ri·jaal	Men
نساء	ni·saa	Women

accommodation

Where's a ...?	... وين؟	wayn ...
camping ground	مخيم	moo·khay·am
hotel	فندق	fun·dug
Can you recommend somewhere ...?	ممكن تقترح/تقترحي مكان...؟	mum·kin tig·ta·rah/tig·ta·rah·ee ma·kaan ... m/f
cheap	رخيص	ra·khees
good	جيد	jay·id
nearby	قريب	ga·reeb

Am I allowed to camp here?

ممكن اخيم هنا؟   *mum·kin a·khay·am hi·na*

I'd like to book a room, please.

اريد احجز غرفة من فضلك.   *a·reed ah·jiz ghur·fa min fad·lak*

I have a reservation.

عندي حجز.   *'and·ee hu·jiz*

Do you have	عندك/عندك	*'and·ak/'and·ik*
a ... room?	غرفة ...؟	*ghur·fa ... m/f*
single	لشخص واحد	li·*shakhs waa·hid*
double	لشخصين	li·*shakh·sayn*
twin	مع سريرين	ma' sa·ree·*rayn*

How much is it per ...?	بكم كل ...؟	bi·*kam kul ...*
night	ليلة	*lay·la*
person	شخص	*shakhs*

I'd like to stay for (three) nights.

اريد اقعد (ثلاثة) ليالي.   *a·reed og·'od (tha·laa·tha) lay·aa·lee*

Could I have my key, please?

مفتاحي من فضلك؟   *mif·taa·hee min fad·lak*

Can I get another (blanket)?

احتاج الى (برنوس)   *ah·taaj i·la (bar·noos)*

الثاني من فضلك؟   *i·thaa·nee min fad·lak*

The (air conditioning) doesn't work.

(الكنديشان) ما يشتغل.   *(il·kan·day·shan) ma yish·ta·ghil*

This (sheet) isn't clean.

هاذا (الشرشف) مو نظيف.   *haa·dha (i·shar·shaf) moo na·dheef*

Is there an elevator/a safe?

فيه مصعد/صندوق؟   *fee mis·'ad/sun·doog*

What time is checkout?

كم ساعة شك اوت؟   *kam saa·a' shak awt*

Could I have my ..., please?	ممكن تعطني/تعطيني ... مالي من فضلك؟	mum·kin ta'·ta·nee/ta'·tee·nee ... maa·lee min fad·lak m/f
deposit	العملة	il·'um·la
passport	جواز السفر	jaw·aaz i·saf·ar
valuables	الغالي	il·ghaa·lee

banking & communications

Where's a/an ...?	من وين ...؟	min wayn ...
ATM	مكينة صرف	ma·kee·nat sarf
foreign exchange office	صراف	si·raaf

I'd like to ...	اريد ...	a·reed ...
arrange a transfer	تحويل مالي	tah·weel maa·lee
cash a cheque	اصرف شك	as·raf shek
change a travellers cheque	اصرف شك سياحي	as·raf shek see·yaa·hee
change money	اصرف فلوس	as·raf floos
withdraw money	اسحب فلوس	as·hab floos

What's the ...?	ما هو ...؟	maa hoo·wa ...
charge for that	السعر	i·sa'r
exchange rate	السعر	i·sa'r

Where's the local internet café?

من وين انترنيت كفي؟   min in·ter·net ka·fay

How much is it per hour?

بكم كل ساعة؟   bi·kam kul saa·a'

I'd like to ...	اريد ...	a·reed ...
check my email	اشوف يميل	a·shoof ee·mayl
get internet access	اشوف انترنيت	a·shoof in·ter·net
use a printer	استخدم برينتر	as·takh·dam prin·ter
use a scanner	استخدم سكنر	as·takh·dam skan·er

I'd like a ...	... اريد	a-reed ...
mobile/cell phone	موبيل	moo-bail
for hire	للكراء	lil-ki-raa
SIM card for your	سم كرت	sim kart
network	لشبكة مالكم	li-shab-ka maal-kum

What's your phone number?

ما الرقم تلفون
مالَك/مالِك؟

maa i-rag-am til-foon
maal-ak/maal-ik m/f

The number is ...

الرقم هو ...

i-rag-am hoo-wa ...

Where's the nearest public phone?

وين اقرب تلفون عمومي؟

wayn ak-rab til-foon 'u-moo-mee

I'd like to buy a phonecard.

اريد اشري كرت لتلفون.

a-reed ish-ree kart li-til-foon

How much does a (three)-minute call cost?

بكم مكلمة (ثلاثة)
دقائق؟

bi-kam moo-ka-li-ma (tha-laa-tha)
da-yuu-iy

What are the rates?

بكم دقيقة؟

bi-kam da-gee-ga

I want to ...	... اريد	a-reed ...
call (Canada)	اكلم (كندا)	a-ka-lim (ka-na-da)
make a local call	مكلمة محلية	moo-ka-li-ma ma-ha-lee-ya

I want to send a ...	... اريد ارسل	a-reed ar-sil ...
fax	فكس	faks
parcel	طرد	tard

I want to buy a/an ...	... اريد اشري	a-reed ish-ree ...
envelope	ظرف	tharf
stamp	طابع	taa-bi'

Please send it	ارسله/ارسليه	ir-sil-oo/ir-sil-ee
(to Australia) by ...	(لاستراليا)	(li-os-traa-lee-ya)
	بـ... من فضلك	bil ... min fad-lak m/f
airmail	بريد جوي	ba-reed jaw-ee
surface mail	بريد عادي	ba-reed 'aa-dee

sightseeing

What time does it open/close?
الساعة كم مفتوح/مغفول؟ i·saa·a' kam maf·tooh/magh·fool

What's the admission charge?
بكم الدخول؟ bi·kam i·du·khool

Is there a discount for students/children?
فيه تخفيذ لطلاب/جاحل؟ fee takh·feedh li·tu·laab/li·jaa·hil

I'd like to see ...
اريد اشوف ... a·reed a·shoof ...

I'd like a ...	... اريد	a·reed ...
catalogue	كتالوغ	ka·ta·loog
guide	دليل	da·leel
local map	خريطة محلية	kha·ree·ta ma·ha·lee·ya

When's the	الساعة كم ...	i·saa·a' kam ...
next ...?	القادمة؟	il·gaa·di·ma
day trip	الرحلة	i·rah·la
tour	الجولة	i·jaw·la

Is ... included?	... شامل؟	... shaa·mil
accommodation	السكن	i·su·kun
the admission charge	الدخول	i·du·khool
food	الاكل	il·ak·il
transport	الوصلات	il·wa·sa·laat

How long is the tour?
كم ساعة الرحلة؟ kam saa·a' i·rah·la

What time should we be back?
كم ساعة نرجع؟ kam saa·a' nar·ja'

What's that?
اش هاذا؟ aash haa·dha

Can I take a photo?
ممكن اتصور؟ mum·kin at·saw·ar

castle	قصر	ka·sar m
church	كنيسة	ki·nee·sa f
main square	الساحة	i·saa·ha f
mosque	المسجد	il·mas·jid m
old city	المدينة القديمة	il·ma·dee·na il·ga·dee·ma f
palace	قصر	ka·sar m
ruins	الاثار	a·la·thaar f

shopping

Where's a ...?	... من وين	min wayn ...
bookshop	مكتبة	mak·ta·ba
camera shop	مصور	moo saw·ir
department store	محل ضخم	ma·hal dukh·um
grocery store	محل ابقالية	ma·hal ih·gaa·lee·ya
newsagency	محل يبيع جرائد	ma·hal yi·bee·a' ja·raa·id
souvenir shop	محل سياحي	ma·hal say·aa·hee
supermarket	سوبرمركت	soo·ber·mar·ket

I'm looking for ...

مدور/مدورة على ...   moo·daw·ir/moo·daw·i·ra 'a·la ... m/f

Can I look at it?

ممكن اشوف؟   mum·kin a·shoof

Do you have any others?

عندَك/عنوك اخرين؟   'and·ak/'and·ik ukh·reen m/f

Does it have a guarantee?

عنده ضمان؟   'and·oo da·maan

Can I have it sent overseas?

ممكن ترسله/ترسليه   mum·kin tur·sil·oo/tur·sil·ee
في الخارج؟   fil khaa·rij m/f

Can I have my ... repaired?

ممكن تصلي ... مالي؟   mum·kin it·sal·ee ... mau·lee

It's faulty.

فيه خلل.   fee kha·lal

How much is it?

بكم؟   bi·*kam*

Can you write down the price?

ممكن تكتبلي/تكتبيلي السعر؟   *mum*·kin tik·*tib*·lee/tik·*tib*·ee·lee i·*si'r* **m/f**

That's too expensive.

غالي جدا.   *ghaa*·lee *jid*·an

What's your lowest price?

اش السعر الاخر؟   aash i·*si'r* il·*aa*·khir

I'll give you (nine dirhams).

اعطيك/اعطيكي (تسعة دراهم).   *'a·teek*/*'a·tee*·kee (*tis*·a' *draa*·him) **m/f**

There's a mistake in the bill.

فيه غلط في الفطورة.   fee *gha*·lat fil fa·*too*·ra

Do you accept ...?	تقبلي/تقبلي ...؟	*tag*·bil/*tag*·bil·ee ... **m/f**
credit/debit cards	كارت	kart
travellers cheques	شيكات سياحية	shee·*kaat* say·aa·*hee*·ya

I'd like ..., please.	اريد ... من فضلك.	a·*reed* ... min *fad*·lak
a bag	شنطة	*jan*·ta
my change	كمالة فلوسي	ka·*maa*·lit *floo*·see
a receipt	ايصال	ee·*saal*
a refund	مبلغ مردود	*mab*·lagh mar·*dood*
to return this	ارجع هاذا	ar·*ja'* *haa*·dha

I'd like ...	اريد ...	a·*reed* ...
(100) grams	(مية) غرام	(*mee*·yat) gram
(two) kilos	(اثنين) كيلوات	(ith·*nayn*) kee·loo·*waat*
(three) pieces	(ثلاثة) قطعات	(tha·*laa*·tha) gi·taa·*'aat*
(six) slices	(ستة) شرائح	(*si*·ta) sha·*raa*·ih

Less.	اقل.	a·*gul*
Enough.	كافية.	*kaa*·fee·ya
More.	زيادة.	zee·*yaa*·da

الخليجية – shopping

photography

Can you ...?	... تقدر/تقدري ...؟	tig-dir/tig-dir-ee ... m/f
burn a CD from my memory card	تنسخ/تنسخي سي دي من مموري كارت	tan-sakh/tan-sa-khee see dee min me-moo-ree kart m/f
develop this film	تحمض/تحمضي الفلم هاذا	tah-mid/tah-mid-ee il-film haa-dha m/f
load my film	تركب/تركبي الفلم في كميرة	tir-kib/tir-ki-bee il-film fee ka-mee-ra m/f

I need a/an ... film for this camera.	احتاج فلم ... للكميرة هاذي.	ah-taaj film ... lil-ka-mee-ra haa-dhee
APS	اي بي اس	ay pee es
B&W	اسود و ابيض	as-wad wa ab-yad
colour	ملون	moo-law-an
slide	الشفافة	i-sha-faa-fa
200 speed	ميتين	mee-ya-teen

| When will it be ready? | منى تكون جاحز؟ | ma-ta ta-koon haa-jlz |

making conversation

Hello.	اهلا و سهلا.	ah-lan was ah-lan
Good night.	تصبح/تصبحي على خير.	tis-bah/tis-bah-ee 'a-la khayr m/f
Goodbye.	مع السلامة.	ma' sa-laa-ma

Mr	السيد	a-say-id
Mrs	السيدة	a-say-id-a
Miss	الانسة	al-aa-ni-sa

How are you?

كيف حالَك/حالِك؟   kayf haa-lak/haa-lik m/f

Fine, thanks. And you?

بخير الحمد الله. و انتَ/انتِ؟   bi-khayr il-ham-du-li-laa win-ta/win-ti m/f

What's your name?

اش اسمَك/اسمِك؟   aash is-mak/is-mik m/f

My name is ...

اسمي ...   is·mee ...

I'm pleased to meet you.

تشرفنا.   nit·sha·raf·na

This is my ...	هاذا/هاذي ...	haa·dha/haa·dhee ... m/f
brother	اخي	akh·ee
daughter	بنتي	bin·tee
father	ابي	ab·ee
friend	صديقي	sa·dee·gee m
	صديقتي	sa·dee·ga·tee f
husband	زوجي	zaw·jee
mother	امي	um·ee
sister	اختي	ukh·tee
son	ولدي	wa·la·dee
wife	زوجتي	zaw·ja·tee

Here's my ...	اعطيك/اعطيكي ...؟	'a·teek/'a·tee·kee ... m/f
What's your ...?	اش العنوان ...؟	aash il·'un·waan ...
address	مالك	maa·lak
email address	إيميل	ee·mayl
phone number	رقم تلفون	ra·gam til·foon

Where are you from?   انتَ/انتِ من وين؟   in·ta/in·ti min wayn m/f

I'm from ...	انا من ...	a·na min ...
Australia	استراليا	os·traa·lee·ya
Canada	كندا	ka·na·da
New Zealand	نيوزيلاندا	noo zee·land
the UK	المملكة المتحدة	al·mam·la·ka al·moo·ta·hi·da
the USA	الولايات المتحدة	il·wu·lay·aat al·moo·ta·hi·da

What's your occupation?	اش تشتغل/تشتغلي؟	aash tish·ta·ghil/tish·ta·ghi·lee m/f

I'm a/an ...	اشتغل ...	ash·ta·ghil ...
businessperson	راجل عمال	raa·jil 'u·maal
office worker	موظف/موظفة	moo·wadh·af/moo·wadh·fa m/f
tradesperson	صناعي/صناعية	sa·naa·'ee/sa·naa·'ee·ya m/f

Do you like ...?	تحب/تحبي ...؟	ti-*heb*/ti-*he*-bee ... **m/f**
I (don't) like ...	(ما) احب ...	(maa) a-*heb* ...
art	فن	fan
movies	سينيما	see-nee-*ma*
music	موسيقى	moo-*see*-ka
reading	قراءة	ki-*raa*
sport	رياضة	ree-*yaa*-da

eating out

Can you recommend a ...?	ممكن تنصح/ تنصحي ...؟	*mum*-kin *tan*-sah/ *tan*-sa-hee ... **m/f**
bar	بار	baar
café	قهوة	*gah*-wa
restaurant	مطعم	*ma*-ta'm
I'd like ..., please.	اريد ... من فضلك	a-*reed* ... min fad-lak
a table for (four)	طاولة (اربعة)	*taa*-wi-lat (ar-ba')
	اشخاص	ash-*khaas*
the (non)smoking section	المكان ممنوع تدخين	il-ma-*kaan* mam-*noo*-a' tad-*kheen*

breakfast	فطر	*fa*-tar **m**
lunch	غداء	*gha*-da **m**
dinner	عشاء	'*ash*-aa **m**

What would you recommend?

اش تنصح/تنصحي؟   aash *tan*-sah/*tan*-sa-hee **m/f**

What's the local speciality?

اش الطبق المحلي؟   aash i-*ta*-bak il-*ma*-ha-lee

What's that?

اش هاذا؟!   aash *haa*-dhee

I'd like (the) ..., please.	عطني/عطيني الـ ... من فضلك	'a·ti·nee/'a·tee·nee il ... min fad·lak m/f
bill	قائمة	kaa·'i·ma
drink list	قائمة المشروبات	kaa·'i·mat il·mash·roo·baat
menu	قائمة الطعام	kaa·'i·mat i·ta·'aam
that dish	الطبق هاذاك	i·tab·ak haa·dhaa·ka

drinks

I'll have ...
اخذ ...   aa·kudh ...

I'll buy you a drink.
اشري تَك/لِك مشروبة.   ash·ree lak/lik mash·roo·ba m/f

What would you like?
اش تحب تشرب؟   aash ti·hib tish·rub m
اش تحبي تشربي؟   aash ti·hib·ee tish·rub·ee f

(cup of) coffee ...	نقهوة ...	kah·wa ...
(cup of) tea ...	شاي ...	shay ...
with milk	بالحليب	bil·ha·leeb
without sugar	بدون شكر	bi·doon shi·ker

| (orange) juice | عصير (برتقال) | 'a·seer (bor·too·gaal) m |
| soft drink | مشروبة باردة | mash·roo·ba baa·ri·da f |

... water	ماي ...	may ...
boiled	مغلي	mugh·lee
mineral	معدني	ma'a·da·nee

| a bottle/glass of beer | بوتل/قلاس بيرة | boo·til/glaas bee·ra m |
| a shot of (whisky) | ويسكي | wee·skee m |

a bottle/glass of ... wine	بوتل/قلاس ... خمر	boo·til/glaas ... kha·mar
red	احمر	ah·mer
sparkling	فوار	fa·waar
white	ابيض	ab·yad

special diets & allergies

Do you have ... food?	عندك طعم ... ؟	'an·dak ta·'am ...
halal	حلال	ha·laal
vegetarian	نباتي	na·baa·tee
Could you prepare a meal without ...?	ممكن تطبخها/ تطبخيها بدون ... ؟	mum·kin tat·bakh·ha/ tat·bakh·ee·ha bi·doon ... m/f
butter	زبدة	zib·da
eggs	بيض	bayd
meat stock	مرق لهم	ma·rak la·ham
I'm allergic to ...	عندي حساسية لـ ...	'an·dee ha·saa·see·ya li ...
dairy produce	الألبان	il·al·baan
gluten	قمح	ka·mah
nuts	كرزات	ka·ra·zaat
seafood	السمك و المحارات	i·sa·mak wa al·ma·haa·raat

emergencies

Help!	مساعد!/مساعدة!	moo·saa·'id/moo·saa·'id·a m/f
Stop!	وقف!/وقفي!	oo·gif/oo·gif·ee m/f
Go away!	ابعد!/ابعدي!	ib·'ad/ib·'ad·ee m/f
Thief!	حرامي!/حراميه!	ha·raa·mee/ha·raa·mee·ye m/f
Fire!	حريقة!	ha·ree·ga
Watch out!	انتبه!/انتبهي!	in·ta·bee/in·tab·hee m/f
Call ...!	تصل/تصلي على ...!	ti·sil/ti·si·lee 'a·la ... m/f
a doctor	طبيب	ta·beeb
an ambulance	سيارة الاسعف	say·aa·rat al·as·'af
the police	الشرطة	i·shur·ta

Could you help me, please?

ممكن تساعدني/ تساعديني من فضلك؟	mum·kin ta·saa·'ad·nee/ ta·saa·'a·dee·nee min fad·lak m/f

I have to use the phone.

احتاج اتكلم في تلفون. ah-*taaj* at-*ka*-lam fee til-*foon*

I'm lost.

انا ضعت. *a*-na duht

Where are the toilets?

وين المرحاض؟ wayn il-mir-*haad*

Where's the police station?

وين مركز الشرطة؟ wayn *mar*-kaz i-*shur*-ta

I want to report an offence.

اريد ابلغ على جرم. a-*reed* ab-lagh *'a*-la jurm

I have insurance.

عندي تامين. *'an*-dee taa-*meen*

I want to contact my embassy.

اريد اتصل بسفارتي. a-*reed* a-ta-sal bi-si-*faa*-ra-tee

I've been ...	... حد	had ...
assaulted	اعتدائني	*'it*-ee-*daa*-nee
raped	اغتصبني	igh-ta-*sab*-nee
robbed	سرقني	sa-*rag*-nee

I've lost my ...	... افقد	af-*gad* ...
My ... was/were stolen.	... سرقوني	sar-*goo*-nee ...
bag	جنطتي	*jan*-ta-tee
credit card	كارتي	*kaar*-tee
money	فلوسي	*floo*-see
passport	جواز السفر	jaw-*aaz* i-*sa*-far
travellers cheques	شيكات سياحية	shee-*kaat* say-aa-*hee*-ya

health

Where's the nearest ...?	وين الاقرب ...؟	wayn al-*ak*-rab ...
dentist	طبيب/طبيبة الاسنان m/f	ta-*beeb*/ta-*bee*-ba al-is-*naan* m/f
doctor	طبيب/طبيبة m/f	ta-*beeb*/ta-*bee*-ba m/f
hospital	مستشفى	mus-*tash*-fa
(night) pharmacist	صيدلية مفتوح في ليل	say-da-*lee*-ya maf-*too*-ha fee layl

I need a doctor (who speaks English).

احتاج طبيب اللي
(يتكلم بالانجليزية).

ah·*taaj* ta·*beeb* il·ee
(yit·*kal*·am in·glee·*zee*·ya)

Could I see a female doctor?

اريد اشوف طبيبة؟

a·*reed* a·*shoof* ta·*bee*·ba

I've run out of my medication.

خلص الدوا.

kha·*las* i·*da*·waa

I'm sick.

انا مريض/مريضة.

a·na ma·*reed*/ma·*ree*·da m/f

It hurts here.

يوجعني هنا.

yoo·*ja'*·nee *hi*·na

I have (a) ...	انا مريض ب ...	a·na ma·*reed* bi ...
asthma	الربو	i·*rab*·oo
constipation	الامساك	al·im·*saak*
diarrhoea	الاسهال	al·is·*haal*
fever	حمى	*ha*·mee
headache	وجيع في راسي	oo·jee·a' fee *raas*·ee
heart condition	قلب	kalb
nausea	غشيان	gha·shee·*yaan*
pain	وجيع	oo·jee·*a'*
sore throat	حلق	halk
toothache	الاسنان	al·is·*naan*

I'm allergic to ...	عندي حساسية لـ ...	'and·ee ha·saa·*see*·ya li ...
antibiotics	مضاد حيوي	moo·*daad* hay·a·wee
anti-inflammatories	مضاد الورم	moo·*daad* il·*wa*·ram
aspirin	اسبيرين	as·bi·*reen*
bees	نحل	*na*·hal
codeine	كودين	*koo*·deen
penicillin	البنسلين	ben·ee·*si*·lin

english–gulf arabic dictionary

Words in this dictionary are marked as n (noun), a (adjective), v (verb), sg (singular), pl (plural), ⓜ (masculine) and ⓕ (feminine) where necessary. Verbs are given in the present tense in the third-person singular ('he/she'), in both masculine and feminine forms.

A

accident حادثة *haad-tha* ⓕ
accommodation سكن *sa-kan* ⓜ
adaptor وصلة مهايئة *was-la mu-haa-ya* ⓕ
address n عنوان *'un-waan* ⓜ
after بعد *ba'd*
air-conditioned كنديشاني/كنديشانية
kan-*day*-shan-ee/kan-day-shan-ee-ya ⓜ/ⓕ
airplane طيارة *tay-yaa-ra* ⓕ
airport مطار ma-*taar* ⓜ
alcohol خمر *kha-mar* ⓜ
all كل *kul*
allergy حساسية *ha-saa-see-ya* ⓕ
ambulance سيارة اسعاف *say-yaa-rat is-'aaf* ⓕ
and و *wa*
ankle مفصل قدم *maf-sal kad-am* ⓜ
arm ذراع *dhraa'* ⓜ
ashtray طفاية *ta-fai-ya* ⓕ
ATM مكينة صرف ma-*keen-at sarf*

B

baby جاهل *jaa-hil* ⓜ & ⓕ
back (body) ظهر *dha-har* ⓜ
backpack جنطة *jan-ta* ⓕ
bad شين *shayn/shay-na* ⓜ/ⓕ
bag جنطة *jan-ta* ⓕ
baggage claim حقائب و امتعة
hak-*aa*-'ib wa am-*ti*-'a ⓕ
bank بنك bank ⓜ
bar بار baar ⓜ
bathroom حمام ham-*maam* ⓜ
battery بيتري *bay-tree* ⓜ
beautiful جميلة/جميل ja-*meel*/ja-*mee*-la ⓜ/ⓕ
bed سرير sar-*eer* ⓜ
beer بيرة *bee-ra* ⓕ
before قابل *gaa-bil*
behind ورا *wa-ra*
bicycle سيكل *sai-kal* ⓜ
big كبيرة/كبير ka-*beer*/ka-*bee*-ra ⓜ/ⓕ
bill قائمة *kaa-'im-a* ⓕ
black اسودة/اسود *as-wad*/*soo-da* ⓜ/ⓕ
blanket برنوس bar-*noos* ⓜ

blood group نوع دم *noo-wa' dam* ⓜ
blue زرقة/ازرق *az-rag*/*zar-ga* ⓜ/ⓕ
boat سفينة sa-*fee-na* ⓕ
book (make a reservation) v يحجز/تحجز
yih-*jiz*/tih-*jiz* ⓜ/ⓕ
bottle بوتل *boo-til* ⓜ
bottle opener مفتاح للبوتل mif-*taah lil-boo-til* ⓜ
boy ولد *wa-lad* ⓜ
brakes (car) بريك bi-*rayk* ⓜ
breakfast فطر *fa-tar* ⓜ
broken (faulty) خريانة/خريان
khar-*baan*/khar-*baa-na* ⓜ/ⓕ
bus باص baas ⓜ
business عمل *'am-al* ⓜ
buy يشتري/تشتري yish-*tar-ee*/tish-*tar-ee* ⓜ/ⓕ

C

café مقهى *mag-ha* ⓕ
camera كميرة *kaa-mee-ra* ⓕ
camp site مخيم *moo-khay-am* ⓜ
cancel يلغي/تلغي *yul-ghee*/*tul-ghee* ⓜ/ⓕ
can opener فتاحة علب fa-*taa-hat 'al-ab* ⓕ
car سيارة say-*yaa-ra* ⓕ
cash n فلوس fi-*loos* ⓜ
cash (a cheque) v يصرف/تصرف
yis-*raf*/tis-*raf* ⓜ/ⓕ
cell phone جواز jaw-*aaz* ⓜ
centre n مركز *mar-kaz* ⓜ
change (money) v يصرف/تصرف
yis-*raf*/tis-*raf* ⓜ/ⓕ
cheap رخيصة/رخيص ra-*khees*/ra-*khee-sa* ⓜ/ⓕ
check (bill) قائمة *kaa-'im-a* ⓕ
check-in n شك ان chek in ⓜ
chest صدر *sad-ir* ⓜ
child جاهل *jaa-hil* ⓜ & ⓕ
cigarette جيقارة jee-*gaa-ra* ⓕ
city مدينة mad-*ee-na* ⓕ
clean a نظيفة/نظيف na-*dheef*/na-*dhee-fa* ⓜ/ⓕ
closed مقفولة/مقفول mag-*fool*/mag-*foo-la* ⓜ/ⓕ
coffee قهوة *gah-wah* ⓕ
coins عملات *'um-laat* ⓕ
cold a باردة/بارد baa-*rid*/baa-*ri-da* ⓜ/ⓕ
come v يجي/تجي *yee-jee*/*tee-jee* ⓜ/ⓕ

computer كمبيوتر kom-bew-ter ⓜ
condom كابوت ka-boot ⓜ
contact lenses عدسات ʿad-as-aat ⓕ
cook v يطبخ/تطبخ ylt-bukh/tlt-bukh ⓜ/ⓕ
cost v سعر si-ʿir ⓜ
credit card كارت kart ⓜ
cup كوب koob ⓜ
currency exchange صرف se-raf ⓜ
customs (immigration) جمرك gum-ruk ⓜ

D

dangerous خطير/خطيرة
kha-teer/kha-tee-ra ⓜ/ⓕ
date (time) تاريخ taa-reekh ⓜ
day يوم yawm ⓜ
delay n تاخير taʾ-kheer ⓜ
dentist طبيب/طبيبة الاسنان
ta-beeb/ta-bee-bat al-is-naan ⓜ/ⓕ
depart يخرج/تخرج على
yukh-rij/tukh-rij ʿa-la ⓜ/ⓕ
diaper حفاظ الطفل haf-aadh at-tu-ful ⓜ
dictionary قاموس kaa-moos ⓜ
dinner عشاء ʿash-aa ⓜ
direct مباشر/مباشرة
moo-baa-sher/moo-baa-she-ra ⓜ/ⓕ
dirty وسخ/وسخة wa-sikh/wa-si-kha ⓜ/ⓕ
disabled عاجز/عاجزة ʿa-jiz/ʿa-ji-za ⓜ/ⓕ
discount n تخفيض takh-feedh ⓜ
doctor طبيب/طبيبة ta-beeb/ta-bee-ba ⓜ/ⓕ
double bed سرير لشخصين
sa-reer li-shakh-sayn ⓜ
double room غرفة لشخصين
ghur-fa li-shakh-sayn ⓕ
drink n مشروبة mash-roo-ba ⓕ
drive v يسوق/تسوق yi-soog/ti-soog ⓜ/ⓕ
drivers licence ليسان مال سواقة
lay-san maal si-waa-ga ⓜ
drug (illicit) مخدر moo-kha-der ⓜ
dummy (pacifier) مصاصة ma-saa-a ⓕ

E

ear اذن idh-in ⓜ
east شرق sharg ⓜ
eat ياكل/تاكل yak-il/tak-il ⓜ/ⓕ
economy class دارجة سياحية
daa-ra-ja say-a-hee-ya ⓕ
electricity كهرباء kah-ra-ba ⓕ
elevator مصعد mis-ʿad ⓜ
email بريد الاكترونى ba-reed el-ek-tro-nee ⓜ
embassy سفارة si-faa-ra ⓕ

emergency طارى taa-ree-ʾa ⓜ
English (language) انغليزي in-glee-zee ⓜ
entrance دخول du-khool ⓜ
evening مساء mi-saa ⓜ
exchange rate سعر العملة si-ʿir il-ʿum-la ⓜ
exit n خروج kha-rooj ⓜ
expensive غالي/غالية ghaa-lee/ghaa-lee-ya ⓜ/ⓕ
express mail بريد مستعجل ba-reed must-ʿa-jil ⓜ
eye عين ʿayn ⓜ

F

far بعيد/بعيدة ba-ʿeed/ba-ʿee-da ⓜ/ⓕ
fast سريع/سريعة sa-reeʿ/sa-ree-ʾa ⓜ/ⓕ
father اب ab ⓜ
film (camera) فلم film ⓜ
finger صبيع sbee-yaʿ ⓜ
first-aid kit اسعافات اولية
is-ʿaa-faat aw-aa-lee-ya ⓕ
first class درجة اولة da-ra-ja oo-la ⓕ
fish n سمك sam-ak ⓜ
food اكل ak-il ⓜ
foot رجل rr-jil ⓜ
fork كنفال chin-gaal ⓜ
free (of charge) بلاش ba-laash
friend صديق/صديقة sd-deey/sa-dee-ga ⓜ/ⓕ
fruit ميوة may-wa ⓕ
full متروس/متروسة mat-roos/mat-roo-sa ⓜ/ⓕ
funny مضحك/مضحكة
mudh-hik/mudh-hi-ka ⓜ/ⓕ

G

gift هدية had-ee-ya ⓕ
girl بنت bint ⓕ
glass (drinking) قلاس gi-laas ⓜ
glasses (eyesight) نظارة nadh-aa-ra ⓕ
go يروح/تروح yi-rooh/ti-rooh ⓜ/ⓕ
good جيد/جيدة jay-yid/jay-da ⓜ/ⓕ
green اخضر/خضرة akh-dhar/kha-dhra ⓜ/ⓕ
guide n دليل da-leel ⓜ

H

half n نص nus ⓜ
hand يد eed ⓜ
handbag جنطة jan-ta ⓕ
happy فرحان/فرحانة fur-haan/fur-haa-na ⓜ/ⓕ
have عند ʿind
he هووا hoo-wa
head راس raas ⓜ
heart قلب galb ⓜ

heat n حر har ⓜ

heavy ثقيل/ثقيلة tha-*geel*/tha-*gee*-la ⓜ/ⓕ

help v يساعد/تساعد yi-*saa*-*id*/ti-*saa*-*id* ⓜ/ⓕ

here هنا *hi*-na

high عالي/عالية *aa*-lee/*aa*-lee-ya ⓜ/ⓕ

highway طريق ta-*reeg* ⓜ

hike v يمشي/تمشي yim-*shee*/tim-*shee* ⓜ/ⓕ

holiday عطلة *ut*-la ⓕ

homosexual لوطي *loo*-tee ⓜ

hospital مستشفى mus-*tash*-fa ⓕ

hot حار/حارة haar/*haa*-ra ⓜ/ⓕ

hotel فندق *fun*-dug ⓜ

hungry جوعان/جوعانة joo-*aan*/joo-*aa*-na ⓜ/ⓕ

husband زوج zooj ⓜ

I

I انا *a*-na

identification (card) بطاقة شخصية boo-*taa*-ga shakh-*see*-ya ⓕ

ill مريض/مريضة ma-*reedh*/ma-*ree*-dha ⓜ/ⓕ

important مهم/مهمة ma-*him*/ma-*hi*-ma ⓜ/ⓕ

included بضمن bi-*dhimn*

injury جرح *jar*-ih

insurance تامين ta*'*-meen

internet انترنت in-ter-*net*

interpreter مترجم/مترجمة moo-*taar*-jim/moo-*taar*-ji-ma ⓜ/ⓕ

J

jewellery مجوهرات moo-*jaw*-har-aat ⓕ

job شغل *shu*-ghul ⓜ

K

key مفتاح mif-*taah* ⓜ

kilogram كيلو *kay*-law ⓜ

kitchen مطبخ *mat*-bakh ⓜ

knife سكين se-*cheen* ⓜ

L

laundry (place) مكوي *mak*-wee ⓜ

lawyer محامي/محامية moo-*haa*-mee/moo-*haa*-mee-ya ⓜ/ⓕ

left (direction) يسار yi-*saar*

leg ريل reel ⓜ

lesbian ساحاقية sa-haa-*kee*-ya ⓕ

less اقل a-*gal*

letter (mail) رسالة ri-*saa*-la ⓕ

lift (elevator) مصعد *mis*-*'ad* ⓜ

light n ليت lait ⓜ

like v يحب/تحب yi-*hib*/ti-*hib* ⓜ/ⓕ

lock n قفل *gu*-ful ⓜ

long طويل/طويلة ta-*weel*/ta-*wee*-la ⓜ/ⓕ

lost مفقود/مفقودة naf-*good*/naf-*goo*-da ⓜ/ⓕ

lost-property office امتعة مفقودة am-ti-*'a* maf-*goo*-da ⓕ

love v يحب/تحب yi-*hib*/ti-*hib* ⓜ/ⓕ

luggage جنط jun-*at* ⓕ

lunch غداء *gha*-da ⓜ

M

mail بريد ba-*reed* ⓜ

man ريال ray-*yaal* ⓜ

map خريطة kha-*ree*-ta ⓕ

market سوق soog ⓜ

matches كبريت chi-*breet* ⓜ

meat لحم *la*-ham ⓜ

medicine دواء *da*-wa ⓜ

menu قائمة الاكل kaa-*'im*-at ak-*il* ⓕ

message خبر *kha*-bar ⓜ

milk حليب ha-*leeb* ⓜ

minute دقيقة da-*gee*-ga ⓕ

mobile phone جوال jaw-*aaz* ⓜ

money فلوس fi-*loos* ⓜ

month شهر *sha*-har ⓜ

morning صباح sa-*baah* ⓜ

mother ام um ⓕ

motorcycle موطورسيكل maa-*toor*-si-kil ⓜ

motorway طريق ta-*reeg* ⓜ

mouth فم fum ⓜ

music موسيقة moo-*see*-ga ⓕ

N

name اسم *is*-im ⓜ

napkin كافية cha-*fee*-ya ⓕ

nappy حفاظ الطفل *haf*-aadh at-*tu*-ful ⓜ

near قريب من ga-*reeb* min

neck رقبة *rug*-ba ⓕ

new جديد/جديدة ja-*deed*/ja-*dee*-da ⓜ/ⓕ

news اخبار akh-*baar* ⓜ

newspaper جريدة ja-*ree*-da ⓕ

night ليلة *lay*-la ⓕ

no لا la

noisy مزعج/مزعجة moo-*za*-ij/moo-*za*-i-ja ⓜ/ⓕ

nonsmoking ممنوع تدخين mam-*noo*-*a'* tad-*kheen*

north شمال sha-*maal* ⓜ

nose خشم *kha*-shim ⓜ

now الحين il-*heen* ⓕ

number رقم ra-*gam* ⓜ

O

oil (engine) نفط naft ⓜ
old قديم/قديمة ga-*deem*/ga-*dee*-ma ⓜ/ⓕ
one-way ticket تذكرة ذهاب
tadh-ka-rat dhi-*haab* ⓕ
open a مفتوح/مفتوحة
maf-*tooh*/maf-*too*-ha ⓜ/ⓕ
outside خارج *khaa*-rij

P

package طرد tard ⓜ
paper ورقة wa-ra-ga ⓕ
park (car) v يوقف/توقف
yi-*wag*-gaf/ti-*waq*-qaf ⓜ/ⓕ
passport جواز السفر jà-*waaz* as-*saf*-ar
pay v يدفع/تدفعي yid-*fa*'/tid-*fa*' ⓜ/ⓕ
pen قلم *gal*-am ⓜ
petrol بنزين ban-*zeen* ⓜ
pharmacy صيدلية say-da-*lee*-ya ⓕ
phonecard كرت تليفون kart ti-lee-*foon* ⓜ
photo صورة *soo*-ra ⓕ
plate صحن *sa*-han ⓕ
police شرطة *shur*-ta ⓕ
postcard بطاقة boo-*taa* ga ⓕ
post office مكتب البريد *mak*-tab al-bar-*eed* ⓜ
pregnant حامل *haa*-mil ⓕ
price سعر *si*-'ir ⓜ

Q

quiet هادي/هادية *haa*-dee/*haa*-dee-ya ⓜ/ⓕ

R

rain n مطر *ma*-tar ⓜ
razor موس moos ⓜ
receipt n وصل *wa*-sil ⓜ
red احمر/حمرة *ah*-mer/*ham*-ra ⓜ/ⓕ
refund n ارجاع ir-*jaa*' ⓜ
registered mail بريد مسجل bar-*eed* moo-*saj*-jal ⓜ
rent v يستاجر/تستاجر
yist-*aa*-jar/tist-*aa*-jar ⓜ/ⓕ
repair v يصلح/تصلح yi-*sal*-ih/ti-*sal*-ih ⓜ/ⓕ
reservation حجز *haj*-iz ⓜ
restaurant مطعم mat-*'am* ⓜ
return v يرجع/ترجع yir-*ja*'/tir-ja' ⓜ/ⓕ
return ticket تذكرة ذهاب و اياب
tadh-kar-at dhi-*haab* wi ee-*yaab* ⓕ
right (direction) يمين ya *meen*

S

road طريق ta-*reeg* ⓜ
room غرفة *ghur*-fa ⓕ

S

safe a امن/امنة aa-*min*/aa-*mi*-na ⓜ/ⓕ
sanitary napkin فوطة صحية *foo*-ta se-*hee*-ya ⓕ
seat مقعد *mag*-'ad ⓜ
send يطرش/تطرش yi-*tar*-ish/ti-*tar*-ish ⓜ/ⓕ
service station محطة بنزين
ma-ha-tat ban-*zeen* ⓕ
sex جنس *ji*-nis ⓜ
shampoo شمبو *sham*-boo ⓜ
share (a dorm etc) يتشارك/تتشارك
yit-*shaa*-rak/tit-*shaa*-rak ⓜ/ⓕ
shaving cream كريم حلق kreem *ha*-lak ⓜ
she هي *hee*-ya
sheet (bed) شرشف *shar*-shaf ⓜ
shirt قميص ga-*mees* ⓜ
shoes جوتي *joo*-tee ⓜ
shop n محل *ma*-hal ⓜ
short قصير/قصيرة ga-*seer*/ga-*see*-ra ⓜ/ⓕ
shower n دوش doosh ⓜ
single room غرفة لشخص واحد
ghur-fa li-*shakhs* waa-*hid* ⓕ
skin جلد jild ⓜ
skirt تنورة ta-*noo*-ra ⓕ
sleep v ينام/تنام yi-*naam*/ti-*naam* ⓜ/ⓕ
slowly بشوية bi-*shway*-ya
small صغير/صغيرة sa-*gheer*/sa-*ghee*-ra ⓜ/ⓕ
smoke (cigarettes) v يدخن/تدخن
yi-*dakh*-an/ti-*dakh*-an ⓜ/ⓕ
soap صبون sa-*boon* ⓜ
some بعض *ba*'dh
soon قريب ga-*reeb*-an
south جنوب ja-*noob* ⓜ
souvenir shop محل سياحية
ma-*hal* say-aa-*hee*-ya ⓜ
speak يتكلم/تتكلم yit-*kal*-am/tit-*kal*-am ⓜ/ⓕ
spoon قفشة *gaf*-shah ⓕ
stamp طابع *taa*-bi' ⓜ
stand-by ticket تذكرة انتظار
tadh-ka-ra in-tee-*dhaar* ⓕ
station (train) محطة ma-*ha*-ta ⓕ
stomach بطن *baa*-tin ⓜ
stop v يقف/تقف *yoo*-gaf/*too*-gaf ⓜ/ⓕ
stop (bus) n محطة الباص ma-*ha*-tat al-*baas* ⓕ
street شارع *shaa*-ri' ⓜ
student طالب/طالبة *taa*-lib/*taa*-li-ba ⓜ/ⓕ
sun شمس shams ⓜ
sunscreen كريم شمس kreem shams ⓜ
swim v يسبح/تسبح yis-*bah*/tis-*bah* ⓜ/ⓕ

T

tampons تميكس *tam*-paks ⓜ
taxi تكسي *tik*-see ⓜ
teaspoon قفشة شي *gaf*-shat chay ⓕ
teeth اسنان as-*naan* ⓜ
telephone n تلفون til-*foon* ⓜ
television تلفزيون ti-lee-*fiz*-yoon ⓜ
temperature (weather) درجة الحرارة
    da-ra-jat al-ha-*raa*-ra ⓕ
tent خيمة *khay*-ma ⓕ
that (one) هاذاك/هاذيك
    haa-*dhaak*/haa-*dheek* ⓜ/ⓕ
they هم *hum*-a ⓜ&ⓕ
thirsty عطشان/عطشانة
    'at-*shaan*/'at-*shaa*-na ⓜ/ⓕ
this (one) هاذا/هاذي haa-*dha*/haa-*dhee* ⓜ/ⓕ
throat زردوم zar-*doom* ⓜ
ticket تذكرة *tadh*-ka-ra ⓕ
time وقت *wa*-git ⓜ
tired طعبان/طعبانة ta'-*baan*/ta'-*baa*-na ⓜ/ⓕ
tissues كفافي che-*faa*-fee ⓕ
today اليوم al-*yoom* ⓜ
toilet مرحاض mir-*haadh* ⓜ
tomorrow باكر *baa*-cher ⓜ
tonight الليلة al-*lay*-la ⓕ
toothbrush فرشة الاسنان *fur*-chat al-as-*naan* ⓕ
toothpaste معجون الاسنان ma'-*joon* al-as-*naan* ⓜ
torch (flashlight) تورش *too*-rich ⓜ
tour n جولة *jaw*-la ⓕ
tourist office مكتب السياحي
    mak-tab as-see-*yaa*-ha ⓜ
towel فوطة *foo*-ta ⓕ
train قطار gi-*taar* ⓜ
translate يترجم/تترجم yi-*tar*-jim/ti-*tar*-jim ⓜ/ⓕ
travel agency وكالة السفريات
    wa-*kaa*-lat as-sa-*far*-ee-yaat ⓕ
travellers cheque شيك سياحي
    chayk see-*yaa*-hee ⓜ
trousers بنتلون *bant*-a-loon ⓜ
twin beds سريرين sa-ree-*rayn* ⓜ
tyre تير tayr ⓜ

U

underwear هدوم جوانية he-*doom* jaw-aa-*nee*-ya ⓕ
urgent مستاجل/مستاجلة
    must-*'a*-jil/must-*'a*-ji-la ⓜ/ⓕ

V

vacant فارغ/فارغة *faa*-righ/*faa*-ri-gha ⓜ/ⓕ
vacation عطلة *ut*-la ⓕ
vegetable n خضار khe-*dhaar* ⓜ
vegetarian a نباتي/نباتية
    na-baa-*tee*/na-baa-*tee*-ya ⓜ/ⓕ
visa فيزة *fee*-za ⓕ

W

waiter قرصون gar-*soon* ⓜ
walk v يمشي/تمشي yim-*shee*/tim-*shee* ⓜ/ⓕ
wallet محفظة mih-*fa*-dha ⓕ
warm a ساخن/ساخنة *saa*-khin/*saa*-khi-na ⓜ/ⓕ
wash (something) يغسل/تغسل
    yigh-*sil*/tigh-*sil* ⓜ/ⓕ
watch n ساعة *saa*-'a ⓕ
water ماي may ⓜ
we نحن *nih*-na
weekend عطلة اسبوع *ut*-lat is-*boo*-a' ⓕ
west غرب gharb ⓜ
wheelchair كرسي مقعد *kur*-see *mag*-'ad ⓜ
when متى *ma*-ta
where وين wayn
white ابيض/بيضة *ab*-yadh/*bay*-dha ⓜ/ⓕ
who من man
why لاش laysh
wife زوجة *zoo*-ja ⓕ
window دريشة da-*ree*-sha ⓜ
wine خمر *kha*-mar ⓜ
with مع ma'a
without بدون bi-*doon*
woman حرمة *her*-ma ⓕ
write يكتب/تكتب yik-*tib*/tik-*tib* ⓜ/ⓕ

Y

yellow اصفر/صفرة *as*-far/*saf*-ra ⓜ/ⓕ
yes نعم na'am
yesterday البارح il-*baar*-ha
you sg انت *in*-ta/*in*-tee ⓜ/ⓕ
you pl انتو *in*-too ⓜ&ⓕ

Levantine
Arabic

language difficulties

Do you speak English?

بتحكي إنكليزي؟   *btah·kee 'inj·lee·zee*

Do you understand?

بتفهم؟/بتفهمي؟   *btaf·ham/btaf·ha·mee* **m/f**

I understand.

فهمت.   *fa·he·met*

I don't understand.

ما فهمت.   *maa fa·he·met*

Could you please ...?

اذا بتريد/   *'i·za bit·reed/*
بتريدي ...؟   *bit·ree·dee ...* **m/f**

   repeat that   عيد/عيدي ذالك   *'eed/'ee·dee zaa·lik* **m/f**

   speak more   احكي شوي، شوي   *'ih·kee shway shway*
   slowly

   write it down   اكتبه/اكتبيه   *'ik·tu·bu/'ik·tu·beeh* **m/f**

numbers

0	صفر	*sifr*	20	عشرين	*'ish·reen*
1	واحد	*waa·hed*	30	تلاتين	*ta·laa·teen*
2	اتنين	*'it·nayn*	40	اربعين	*'ar·be·'een*
3	تلاته	*ta·laa·te*	50	خمسين	*kham·seen*
4	اربع	*'ar·ba*	60	ستين	*sit·teen*
5	خمسه	*kham·se*	70	سبعين	*sab·'een*
6	سته	*sit·te*	80	تمانين	*ta·maa·neen*
7	سبعه	*sab·'a*	90	تسعين	*tis·'een*
8	تمانه	*ta·maa·ne*	100	مائة	*mi·'a*
9	تسعة	*tis·'a*	1000	الف	*'elf*
10	عشرة	*'ash·re*	1,000,000	مليون	*mal·yoon*

For Arabic numerals, see the box on page 14.

time & dates

What time is it?	كم الساعة؟	kam 'is·sae·'e
It's one o'clock.	الساعة وحدة.	'is·sae·'e wah·de
It's (two) o'clock.	هي (تنتين).	hi·ye (tin·tayn)
Quarter past (two).	(تنتين) وربع.	(tin·tayn) oo rub'
Half past (two).	(تنتين) ونص.	(tin·tayn) oo nus
Quarter to (two).	(تنتين) إلّا ربع.	(tin·tayn) 'il·la rub'
At what time ...?	امتى ...؟	'em·ta ...
At ...	في ...	fee ...

| am | صبح | su·beh |
| pm | مساء | ma·sae' |

Monday	يوم الأثنين	yawm il·'it·nayn
Tuesday	يوم التلات	yawm il·ta·laat
Wednesday	يوم الاربعة	yawm il·'ar·ba·'a
Thursday	يوم الخميس	yawm il·kha·mees
Friday	يوم الجمع	yawm il·jum·'a
Saturday	يوم السبت	yawm is·sabt
Sunday	يوم الاحد	yawm il·'a·had

last...	يللي راح ...	yil·lee raah ...
next ...	جاي ...	'ij·jae·'ee ...
night	ليله	lay·le
week	أسبوع	us·boo'
month	شهر	shahr
year	سنة	sa·ne

yesterday ...	مبارح ...	mbae·reh ...
tomorrow ...	بكرة ...	buk·ra ...
morning	صبح	su·beh
afternoon	بعد ظهر	ba'd zuhr
evening	مسا	ma·sae

What date is it today?

شو التاريخ؟   shoo 'it·tae·reekh

It's (15 December).

هو (خمستعش ديسمبر).   hu·we (khams·ta·'ash dee·sem·ber)

border crossing

I'm here ...	سبب زيارتي هون ...	sa·bab zee·yae·re·tee hoon ...
in transit to	الترانسيت	it·traan·seet
(Jordan)	لـ(الأردن)	lil·('ur·dun)
on business	التجارة	it·ti·jae·re
on holiday	الإجازة	il·'ee·jae·ze

I'm here for ...	أنا هون لـ...	'a·na hoon li·...
(10) days	(عشرة) أيام	('ash·re) 'ay·yaem
(three) weeks	(تلاته) أسابيع	(ta·lae·te) 'e·sae·bee'
(three) months	(تلات) شهور	(ta·lae·tu) shu·hoor

I'm going to (Homs).

أنا مسافر/
مسافرة لـ(حمص).

'a·na mu·sae·fer/
mu·sae·fa·re la·(homs) **m/f**

I'm staying at the (Hotel Rabee').

أنا مقيم/مقيمة
بـ(فندق الربيع).

'a·na mu·'ee·yem/mu·'ee·ye·me
bil·(fun·du' ar·ra·bee') **m/f**

I have nothing to declare.

ما معي ما لازمه الإقرار.

ma ma·'ee ma lae·zi·mu il·i·'raar

I have something to declare.

معي ما لازمه الإقرار.

ma·'ee ma lae·zi·mu il·'i·raar

That's (not) mine.

هيدا (مش) لإلي.

hay·da (mish) la·'i·lee

tickets & luggage

Where can I buy a ticket?		
من وين اشتري تذكرة؟		min wayn 'ish·ta·ree taz·ki·re
Do I need to book a seat?		
لازم احجز مقعد؟		lae·zim 'ah·jiz ma·'·ad

One ... ticket	تذكرة ...	taz·ki·re
(to Beirut),	(لبيروت)	(la·bay·root)
please.	اذا بتريد.	'iza bit·reed
one-way	ذهاب	za·haeb
return	ذهاب واياب	za·haeb oo 'ee·yaeb

I'd like to ... my ticket, please.	... بدي تذكرتي, اذا بتريد.	bid·dee ... taz·ki·re·tee 'i·za bit·reed
cancel	الغي	'al·ghee
change	اغير	ghay·yir
collect	اخذ	'aa·khud
I'd like a ... seat, please.	.... بدي مقعد اذا بتريد.	bid·dee ma'·'ad ... 'i·za bit·reed
nonsmoking	بقسم غير المدخنين	bi·'ism ghayr il·mu·dakh·khi·neen
smoking	بقسم المدخنين	bi·'ism il·mu·dakh·khi·neen

Is there air conditioning?

في مكيف؟ — fee mu·kay·yef

Is there a toilet?

في حمامات؟ — fee ham·mae·maet

How long does the trip take?

الرحلة, كم ساعة بتاخذ؟ — ar·rih·le kam sae·'a bi·tae·khud

Is it a direct route?

الطريق مباشر؟ — it·ta·ree' mu bac·shir

My luggage has been ...	... شنطايتي	shan·tae·ye·tee ...
damaged	متضررة	mit·dar·ri·re
lost	ضائعة	dae·ya·'e
stolen	مسروقة	mas·roo·'e

transport

Where does flight (687) arrive/depart?

وين بتوصل/بتروح رحلة — wayn bi·too·sal/bit·rooh rih·le
(ستة, ثمانة, سبعة)؟ — (sit·te ta·mae·ne sab·'a)

Is this the ... to (Petra)?	... هيدا الـ لـ(بيترا)؟	hay·dae il· ... la·(bee·tra)
boat	سفينة	sfee·ne
bus	باص	baas
plane	طائرة	tae·'i·re
train	قطار	'i·taar

What time's	أمتى	'em·ta
the ... bus?	الباص...؟	il-baas il-...
first	اول	'aw·wel
last	اخر	'ae·khir
next	قادم	'ae·dim

How long will it be delayed?

| | قديش بيتأخر؟ | 'ad·deesh bya·ta·'akh·khir |

What station/stop is this?

| | شو هيدا المحطة/الموقف؟ | shoo hay·dae il·mhat·te/il·maw·if |

Please tell me when we get to (Martyrs' Square).

| | اولي/اوليلي لما منوصل | 'oo·lee/'oo·lee·lee lam·ma mnoo·sal |
| | عند (الميدان الشهداء). | 'ind (may·daen ish·shu·ha·daa') m/f |

Is this seat available?

| | هيدا الكرسي فاضي؟ | hay·dae il·kur·see fae·dee |

That's my seat.

| | ذالك الكرسي الي. | zae·lik il·kur·see 'i·lee |

I'd like a taxi ...	بدي تكسي ...	bid·dee tak·see ...
at (9am)	في (الساعة	fee (sae·'e tis·'e
	تسعة صبح)	su·beh)
now	هلق	hal·la'
tomorrow	بكرة	buk·ra

How much is it to ...?

| | قديش الاجرة لـ ...؟ | 'ad·deesh il·'uj·re la ... |

Please take me to (this address).

| | اوصلني عند (هيدا العنوان). | 'oo·sal·nee 'ind (hay·dae il·'un·waen) |

Please put the meter on.

| | شغل العداد اذا بتريد. | shughl il·'a·daed 'i·za bit·reed |

Please ...	اذا بتريد ...	'i·za bit·reed ...
stop here	قف هون	'if hoon
wait here	استنا هون	stan·naa hoon

I'd like to hire a ...	بدي استأجر ...	bid·dee 'is·ta'·jir ...
car	سيارة	say·yae·re
4WD	سيارة ذات	say·yae·re zaat
	الدفع الرباعي	id·daf'·er·ru·bae·'ee

اللبنانية – transport

| with a driver | ومعها سائق | oo ma-'aa sae-'i' |
| with air conditioning | بالمكيف | bil-mu-kay-yef |

How much for	قديش	'ad-deesh
... hire?	الاجرة لـ...؟	il-'uj-re la...
daily	يوم	yawm
weekly	أسبوع	'us-boo'

I need a mechanic.

لازمني ميكانيكي.   lae-zim-nee mee-kaa-nee-kee

I've run out of petrol.

خلص البنزين بسيارتي.   kha-las il-bi-trool bi-say-yae-re-tee

I have a flat tyre.

اطار السيارة ما فيه هواء.   'i-taer is-say-yae-re ma fee-hu ha-wae

directions

Where's the ...?	وين الـ...؟	wayn il-...
bank	بنك	bank
market	سوق	soo'
post office	مكتب البريد	mak-tab il-ba-reed

Is this the road to (Tyre)?

هيدا الطريق لـ(صور)؟   hay-dae it-ta-ree' la-(soor)

Can you show me (on the map)?

بتورجني (عالخريطة)؟   btwar-ji-nee ('al-kha-ree-te)

What's the address?

شو العنوان؟   shoo il-'un-waen

How far is it?

قديش هو بعيد من هون؟   'ad-deesh hu-wa ba-'eed min hoon

How do I get there?

كيف بوصل لهناك؟   kayf boo-sal la-hu-naek

Turn (left/right).	اتجه /اتجهي (ليسار/الشمال).	'it·ta·jih/'it·taj·hee (li·ya·saer/li·shi·mael) m/f
It's ...	... هو/هي	hu·we/hi·ye ... m/f
behind ...	... خلف	khalf ...
in front of ...	... قدام	'ad·daem ...
near to ...	... قريب من	'a·reeb min ...
next to ...	... جنب	jinb ...
on the corner	عند الزاوية	'ind az·zae·wi·ye
opposite ...	... مواجه	mu·wae·jeh ...
straight ahead	للقدام	lil·'ad·daem
there	هناك	hu·naek
north	شمال	she·mael
south	جنوب	'ij·noob
east	شرق	shar'
west	غرب	gharb

signs

مدخل	mad·khal	Entrance
مخرج	makh·raj	Exit
مفتوح	maf·tooh	Open
مغلق	mugh·lak	Closed
معلومات	ma'·loo·maat	Information
الشرطة	ash·shur·ta	Police Station
ممنوع	mam·noo'	Prohibited
دورات المياه	daw·raa·tul mi·yaah	Toilets
الرجال	ar·ri·jaal	Men
النساء	an·ni·saa'	Women
حار	haar	Hot
بارد	baa·rid	Cold

accommodation

Where's a ...?	؟... وين	wayn ...
camping ground	مخيّم	mu·khay·yam
guesthouse	بيت الضيوف	bayt id·du·yoof
hotel	فندق	fun·du'
youth hostel	فندق شباب	fun·du' sha·baeb

Can you recommend	بتورجني	bit·war·ji·nee
somewhere ...?	على مكان ...؟	'a·la ma·kaen ...
cheap	رخيص	'ir·khees
good	منيح	mneeh
nearby	قريب	'a·reeb

Do you have	في عندكن	fee 'ind·kun
a ... room?	غرفة ...؟	ghur·fe ...
single	بتخت منفرد	bi·takht mun·fa·rid
double	بتخت مزدوّج	bi·takht muz·daw·wej
twin	بتختين	bi·takh·tayn

How much is	قديش	'ad·deesh
it per ...?	لـ ...؟	li...
night	ليلة	lay·le
person	شخص	shakhs

I'd like to book a room, please.

بدي احجز غرفة، | bid·dee 'ah·jcz ghur·fe
لو سمحت. | law sa·maht

I have a reservation.

عندي حجز. | 'in·dee hajz

I'd like to stay for (three) nights.

أنا مقيم/مقيمة | 'a·na mu·'eem/mu·'ee·me
(تلات) ليالي. | (ta·laet) lay·yae·lee **m/f**

Am I allowed to camp here?

فيني بخيم هون؟ | fee·nee bi·khay·yem hoon

Could I have my key, please?

اعطني/اعطيني | 'a·ti·nee/'a·tee·nec
مفتاحي، اذا بتريد. | mif·tae·hee 'i·za bit·reed **m/f**

Can I get another (blanket)?

اعطني/اعطيني | 'a·ti·nee/'a·tee·nee
(بطانية) تاني. | (ba·taa·nee·ye) tae·nee **m/f**

The (air conditioning) doesn't work.

(المكيف) مانه شغال. | (il·mu·kay·yef) mae·nu sha·ghael

This (sheet) isn't clean.

هيدا (الشرشف) | hay·dae (il·shar·shef)
مش نظيف. | mish na·zeef

Is there an elevator/a safe?

في مصعد/خزانة | fee mas·'ad/kha·zae·nit
الإمانات؟ | il·'i·mae·naet

What time is checkout?

أي ساعة المغادرة؟ | 'a·yee sae·'a il·mu·ghae·de·re

Could I have my ..., please? | اعطني/اعطيني | 'a·ti·nee/'a·tee·nee
| ... اذا بتريد **m/f** | ... 'i·za bit·reed **m/f**
deposit | وديعتي | wa·dee·'e·tee
passport | جواز سفري | ja·waez sa·fe·ree
valuables | اشيائي القيمة | 'esh·yae·ee il·'ee·me

banking & communications

Where's a/an ...? | وين ...؟ | wayn ...
ATM | جهاز الصرافة | je·haez is·sa·rae·fe
foreign exchange office | مكتب صرافة | mak·teb sa·rae·fe

I'd like to ... | بدي ... | bid·dee ...
arrange a transfer | سوي تحويل مالي | saw·wee tah·weel mae·lee
cash a cheque | اصرف شيك | 'es·ref sheek
change a travellers cheque | احول شيك سياحي | 'u·haw·wel sheek see·yae·hee
change money | احول مساري | 'u·haw·wel msae·re
withdraw money | اسحب مساري | 'es·hab msae·re

What's the ...? | شو...؟ | shoo ...
charge for that | العمولة | il·'u·moo·le
exchange rate | سعر التحويل | si'r it·tah·weel

Where's the local internet café?

وين أقرب مقهى الانترنت؟ | wayn 'a·'reb ma·ha il·'in·ter·net

How much is it per hour?

قديش بتكلف لساعة وحدة؟ | 'ad·deesh bit·kal·lef la·sae·'a wah·de

I'd like to ...	بدي ...	*bid·dee* ...
check my email	اشوف بريدي الالكتروني	shoof ba·*ree*·dee il·'i·*lik*·*troo*·nee
get internet access	ادخل عالانترنت	*'ad*·khal 'al·'*in*·*ter*·net
use a printer	استخدم آلة الطباعة	'is·*takh*·dem *'ae*·let it·ta·*bae*·'a
use a scanner	استخدم نسخ الكتروني	'is·*takh*·dem *nas*·ekh 'i·lik·*troo*·nee

I'd like ...	بدي ...	*bid*·dee ...
to hire a mobile/ cell phone	استأجر موبيل	'is·*ta*·'jer moo·*beel*
a SIM card for your network	بطاقة سيم لشبكتكن	hi·*tae*·'et seem li·she·be·*ket*·kun

What's your phone number?

شو رقم تلفونكن؟   shoo ra'm te·li·*foon*·kun

The number is ...

الرقم ...   ir·*ra'm* ...

Where's the nearest public phone?

وين أقرب تلفون عمومي؟   wayn 'a·'reb te·li·*foon* 'u·*moo*·mee

I'd like to buy a phonecard.

بدي اشتري بطاقة تلفون.   *bid*·dee *'ish*·ta·ree bi·*tae*·'e te·li·*foon*

What are the rates?

شو الأسعار؟   shoo il·'as·*'aer*

How much does a (three)-minute call cost?

قديش بتكلف اتصال (تلات) دقائق؟   'ad·*deesh* bit·*kal*·lif 'it·ti·*sael* (ta·*laet*) da·*'ae*·'e'

I want to ...	بدي ...	*bid*·dee ...
call (Canada)	اتصل بـ(كندا)	'it·*ta*·sel bi·(*ka*·na·da)
make a local call	سوي اتصال محلي	saw wee 'it·ti·*sael* *ma*·ha·lee
reverse the charges	سوي اتصال بيرد والأجرة عالذي	saw·wee 'it·ti·*sael* ool·*'uj*·re 'al·*la*·zee biy·*rid*

I want to send a ...	بدي ابعت ...	*bid*·dee '*ib*·'at ...
fax	فكس	faks
parcel	طرد	tard

I want to buy a/an ...	... بدي اشتري	bid·dee 'ish·ta·ree ...
envelope	ظرف	zarf
stamp	طابع	tae·bi'

Please send it	ابعته / ابعتيه	'ib·'a·tu/'ib·'a·tee·hu
(to Australia) by ...	(لاستراليا) بـ...	(li·'us·trae·li·yae) bi·... m/f
airmail	البريد الجوي	il·ba·reed il·jaw·wee
surface mail	البريد العادي	il·ba·reed il·'ae·dee

sightseeing

What time does it open/close?
امتى بيفتح /بيسكر؟   'em·ta byaf·teh/bysak·ker

What's the admission charge?
قديش تمن الدخول؟   'ad·deesh ta·men id·du·khool

Is there a discount for students/children?
في خصم للطلاب /للأطفال؟   fee khasm lit·tu·laeb/lil·'at·fael

I'd like a ...	... بدي	bid·dee ...
catalogue	فهرس	fah·res
guide	دليل	da·leel
local map	خريطة المنطقة	kha·ree·tet il·min·te·'a

When's the next ...?	امتى ... الجائي؟	'em·ta ... ij·jae·'ee
day trip	الرحلة اليومية	ir·rih·le il·yaw·mee·ye
tour	الدورة	id·daw·re

Is ... included?	... بيحتوي على ...؟	byah·ta·wee 'a·la ...
accommodation	السكن	is·se·ken
the admission charge	تمن الدخول	ta·men id·du·khool
food	الطعام	it·ta·'aem
transport	المواصلات	il·mu·wae·se·laet

I'd like to see ...
... بدي شوف   bid·dee shoof ...

What's that?
شو هيدا؟   shoo hay·dae

Can I take a photo?
بتسمحني اخذ صورة؟   btsa·mah·nee 'aa·khud soo·re

How long is the tour?

كم ساعة بتاخذ الرحلة؟   kam sae·'e btae·khud ir·rih·le

What time should we be back?

امتى لازم منرجع؟   'em·ta lae·zim mnar·ja'

sightseeing		
castle	قلعة	kal·'a **f**
church	كنيسة	ka·nee·se **f**
main square	ساحة رئيسية	sae·ha ra·'ee·see·ye **f**
mosque	مسجد	mas·jad **m**
old city	مدينة قديمة	ma·dee·ne 'a·dee·me **f**
palace	قصر	'asr **m**
pyramids	الأهرام	al·'ah·raem **f**
ruins	آثار	'ae·thaar **m**

shopping

Where's a ...?	وين ...؟	wayn ...
bookshop	مكتبة	mak·ta·be
camera shop	محل الكاميرات	ma·hal il·kaa·mee·raet
department store	محل المنوعات	ma·hal il·mu·naw·wa·'aet
grocery store	بقالة	ba·'ae·le
newsagency	وكالة الأنباء	wi·kae·let il·'en·baa'
souvenir shop	محل التذكارات	ma·hal it·tiz·kae·raet
supermarket	سبر مركت	su·ber markt

I'm looking for ...

بدور عن ...   bi·daw·wer 'an ...

Can I look at it?

ورجني/ورجيني ياه؟   war·ji·nee/war·jee·nee yaah **m/f**

Do you have any others?

في عندكن غيره؟   fee 'ind·kun ghay·ru

Does it have a guarantee?

عنده ضمانة؟   'ind·hu da·mae·ne

Can I have it sent overseas?

بتبعته/بتبعتيه لبرى؟   btab·'a·tu/btab·'a·tee·hee la·bar·ra **m/f**

Can I have my ... repaired?

بتصلح لي ...ي؟   btsa·lah·lee ...·ee

It's faulty.

هو خربان.   hu·we khar·baen

How much is it?

قديش هقه؟   'ad·deesh ha'·'u

Can you write down the price?

اكتب/اكتبي الهق.   'ik·tub/'ik·tu·bee il·ha' **m/f**

That's too expensive.

هيدا غالي اكتير.   hay·dae ghae·lee 'ik·teer

What's your lowest price?

شو احسن سعر طبعكن؟   shoo 'ih·sen si'r ta·ba'·kun

I'll give you (50 lira).

بعطيكن (خمسين ليرة).   bu'·tee·kun (kham·seen lee·ra)

There's a mistake in the bill.

في خطأ بالحساب.   fee kha·ta' bil·hi·saeb

Do you accept ...?	بتقبل ...؟	bta·'·bal ...
credit cards	بطاقات رصيد	bi·tae·'aet ra·seed
debit cards	بطاقات اقتراض	bi·tae·'aet 'i'·ti·raed
travellers cheques	شيكات سياحية	shee·kaet see·yae·hee·ye

I'd like ...,	بدي ...،	bid·dee ...
please.	لو سمحت.	law sa·maht
a bag	كيس	kees
my change	الباقي	il·bae·'ee
a receipt	وصل	wa·sil
a refund	استرداد مال	'is·tir·daed mael
to return this	ارجع هيدا	'ir·ja' hay·dae

I'd like ...	... بدي	bid·dee ...
(100) grams	(مائة) غرام	(mi·'e) ghraem
(three) kilos	(تلات) كيلوات	(ta·laet) kee·loo·ael
(three) pieces	(تلات) قطع	(ta·laet) 'i·ta'
(six) slices	(ست) شرائح	(sit) she·rae·'ih

Less.	اقل.	'a·'al
Enough.	كفاية.	ki·fae·ye
More.	اكتر.	'ik·tar

photography

Can you ...?	بتقدر/بتقدري ...؟	bta'·der/bta'·de·ree ... **m/f**
burn a CD from	تجهّز/تجهزي	tu·jah·hez/tu·jah·he·zee
my memory	قرص مدمج من	'irs mu·dam·mej min
card	بطاقتي الذاكرة	bi·tae·'a·tee iz·zae·ki·re **m/f**
develop this	تحمض/تحمضي	tu·ham·mid/tu·ham·mi·dee
film	هيدا الفيلم	hay·dae il·feelm **m/f**
load my film	تحمّل/تحملي	tu·ham·mil/tu·ham·mi·lee
	فيلمي	feel·mee **m/f**

I need a/an ... film	لازمني فيلم ...	lae·zim·nee feelm ...
for this camera.	لهيدا الكميرا.	li·hay·dae il·kaa·mee·raa
B&W	اسود وابيض	'is·wäd oo 'ib·yad
colour	ملون	mlaw·wen
slide	شريحة	sha·ree·he
(200) speed	سريعة (مائتين)	sa·ree·e (mi·'e·tayn)

When will it be ready?	امتى بيكون جاهز؟	'em·ta bee·koon jae·hiz

making conversation

Hello.	مرحبا.	mer·ha·ba
Good night.	تصبح على الخير.	tus·bih 'a·la il·khayr **m**
	تصبحي على الخير.	tus·bi·hee 'a·la il·khayr **f**
Goodbye.	خاطرَك.	khae·trak **m**
	خاطرِك.	khae·trik **f**

| Mr | سيد | *say*·yid |
| Mrs/Miss | سيدة | say·*yi*·de |

How are you?

| | كيفك/كيفك؟ | *kay*·fak/*kay*·fik **m/f** |

Fine, thanks. And you?

| | منيح/منيحة. | mneeh/*mnee*·ha **m/f** |
| | وأنت/أنتي؟ | oo 'ent/'*en*·tee **m/f** |

What's your name?

| | شو اسمَك/اسمك؟ | shoo 'es·mak/'es·mik **m/f** |

My name is ...

| | اسمي ... | 'es·mee ... |

I'm pleased to meet you.

| | تشرفنا. | tash·ar·*raf*·nae |

This is my ...	هيدا/هيدي ...	*hay*·dae/*hay*·dee ... **m/f**
brother	اخي	*'a*·khee
daughter	بنتي	*bin*·tee
father	بيي	*bay*·ee
friend	رفيقي/رفيقتي	ra·*fee*·'ee/ra·*fee*·'tee **m/f**
husband	جوزي	*jaw*·zee
mother	امي	*'im*·mee
sister	اختي	*'ekh*·tee
son	ابني	*'ib*·nee
wife	زوجتي	*zawj*·tee

Here's my ...	هيدا هو ...	*hay*·dae *hu*·we ...
address	عنواني	*'un*·*wae*·nee
email address	عنواني البريد	*'un*·*wae*·nee il-ba·*reed*
	الالكتروني	il·'i·lik·*troo*·nee
phone number	رقم تلفوني	ra'·mu te·li·*foo*·nee

What's your ...?	شو ...؟	shoo ...
address	عنوانك	*'un*·*wae*·nak
email address	عنوانك البريد	*'un*·*wae*·nak il-ba·*reed*
	الالكتروني	il·'il·lik·*troo*·nee
phone number	رقم تلفونك	ra'm te·li·*foo*·nak

Where are you from?	انت/انتي من وين؟	'en·te/'en·tee min wayn **m/f**
I'm from ...	أنا من ...	'a·na min ...
Australia	استراليا	'us·trae·li·ya
Canada	كندا	ka·na·da
New Zealand	نيو زيلندا	nee·yoo zee·lan·da
the UK	بريطانيا	ba·ree·tae·nee·ya
the USA	أمريكا	'am·ree·ka
What's your occupation?	شو بتشتغل/ بتشتغلي؟	shoo btash·taghl/ btash·tagh·lee **m/f**
I'm a/an ...	أنا ...	'a·na ...
businessperson	رجل أعمال	ra·jul 'a·*mael* **m**
	سيدة أعمال	say·yi·det 'a'·mael **f**
office worker	موظف	mu·waz·zef **m**
	موظفة	mu·waz·zi·fe **f**
tradesperson	حرفي	hi·ra·fee **m**
	حرفية	hi·ra·fee·ye **f**
Do you like ...?	يتحب/بحبتي ...؟	bit·hib/bit·hi·bee ... **m/f**
I (don't) like ...	أنا (ما) بحب ...	'a·na (ma) bi·hib ...
art	الفن	il·fenn
movies	الافلام	il·'af·laem
music	الموسيقى	il·moo·see·'a
reading	القراءة	il·'i·rae·'a
sport	الرياضة	ir·ree·yae·da

eating out

Can you recommend a ...?	بتوصي بـ...؟	btoo·see bi·...
bar	بار	baar
café	مقهى	ma'·ha
restaurant	مطعم	mat·'em
I'd like ..., please.	بدي ...، لو سمحت.	bid·dee ... law sa·maht
a table for (four)	طاولة لـ(أربع أشخاص)	tae·wi·le li·('ar·ba·'at 'esh·khaes)
the (non)smoking section	قسم (غير) المدخنين	'ism (ghayr) il·mu·dakh·khi·neen

breakfast	فطور	ftoor m
lunch	غداء	gha·dae m
dinner	عشاء	'a·shae m

I'd like (the) ...,	بدي ...،	bid·dee ...
please.	لو سمحت.	law sa·maht
bill	الحساب	il-hi·saeb
drink list	قائمة	'ae·'i·met
	المشروبات	il-mash·roo·baet
menu	قائمة الطعام	'ae·'i·met it·ta·'aem
that dish	ذالك الوجبة	zae·lik il-waj·be

What would you recommend?

بشو بتوصي؟ | bi-shoo btoo·see

What's the local speciality?

شو الوجبة الخاصة؟ | shoo il-waj·be il-khae·se

What's that?

شو هيدا؟ | shoo hay·dae

drinks

I'll have ...

بدي ... | bid·dee ...

I'll buy you a drink.

بدعوك/بدعوكي | bid·'ook/bid·'oo·kee
الى مشروب. | 'i·la mash·roob m/f

What would you like?

شو بتحب/ بتحبي؟ | shoo bit·hib/bit·hi·bee m/f

(cup of) coffee ...	(فنجان) قهوى ...	(fin·jaen) 'ah·way ...
(cup of) tea ...	(كاسة) شاي ...	(kae·set) shaay ...
with milk	بالحليب	bil-ha·leeb
without sugar	بدون سكر	bi·doon suk·ker

boiled water	ماء مغلي	maay magh·lee m
mineral water	مياه معدنية	mee·yaah ma'·da·nee·ye f
(orange) juice	عصير (برتقال)	'a·seer (bur·te·'ael) m
soft drink	شراب بارد	shi·raeb bae·rid m

| a bottle/glass of beer | زجاجة/كاسة بيرا | zu·jae·je/kae·set bee·ra |
| a shot of (whisky) | جرعة (ويسكي) | jar·'et (wees·kee) |

a bottle/glass	زجاجة/كاسة	zu·jae·jet/kae·set
of ... wine	نبيذ ...	nbeez ...
red	احمر	'ah·mer
sparkling	فوار	faw·waer
white	ابيض	'ib·yad

special diets & allergies

Is there a vegetarian restaurant near here?

في مطعم نباتي قريب؟   fee mat·'em na·bae·tee 'a·reeb

Do you have	في عندكن	fee 'ind·kun
... food?	طعام ...؟	ta·'aem ...
halal	حلال	ha·lael
kosher	كوشر	koo·sher
vegetarian	نباتي	na·bae·tce

Could you prepare	بتقدروا تحضروا	bta·de·roo tu·had·de·roo
a meal without ...?	وجبه بدون ...؟	waj·be bi·doon ...
butter	زبدة	zeb·de
eggs	بيض	bayd
meat stock	مرق لحم	mir' lahm

I'm allergic	أنا عندي حساسية	'a·na 'in·dee ha·sae·see·ye
to ...	من ...	min ...
dairy produce	الألبان	il·'al·baen
gluten	الغلوتين	il·ghloo·teen
nuts	المكسرات	il·mu·kas·si·raet
seafood	الطعام البحري	it·ta·'aem bah·ree

emergencies

Help!	ساعد!/ساعدي!	sae·'id/sae·'i·dee **m/f**
Stop!	قف!/قفي!	'if/'i·fee **m/f**
Go away!	روح!/روحي!	rooh/roo·hee **m/f**
Thief!	سارق!/سارقة!	sae·ri'/sae·ri·'e **m/f**
Fire!	نار!	naar
Watch out!	انتبه!/انتبهي!	'in·ta·bih/'in·tab·hee **m/f**

Call ...!	اتصل بـ...!	'it·ta·sil bi·...
a doctor	دكتور	duk·toor
an ambulance	سيارة الاسعاف	say·yae·ret il·'is·'aef
the police	الشرطة	ish·shur·ta

Could you help me, please?

ساعدني/ساعديني، — sae·'id·nee/sae·'i·dee·nee
لو سمحت. — law sa·maht **m/f**

I have to use the phone.

لازمني استخدم التلفون. — lae·zim·nee 'is·takh·dem it·te·li·foon

I'm lost.

أنا ضائع/ضائعة. — 'a·na dae·'i'/dae·'i·'e **m/f**

Where are the toilets?

وين الحمامات؟ — wayn il·ham·mae·maet

Where's the police station?

وين الشرطة؟ — wayn ish·shur·ta

I want to report an offence.

بدي ابلغ عن جريمة. — bid·dee 'u·bel·legh 'an je·ree·me

I have insurance.

عندي تأمين. — 'in·dee ta'·meen

I want to contact my embassy.

بدي اتصل بسفارتي. — bid·dee 'it·ta·sil bis·fae·ra·tee

I've been ...	... حدا	ha·da ...
assaulted	اعتدى على	'i·ta·da 'a·lay
raped	اغتصبني	'igh·ta·seb·nee
robbed	سرقني	sar·ra·'·nee

I've lost my ...	ضيعت ...ي.	da·ya·'et ...ee
My ... was/were	...ي مسروق/	...ee mas·roo'/
stolen.	مسروقة.	mas·roo·'e **m/f**
bag	حقيبة	ha·'ee·bat **f**
credit card	بطاقة رصيد	bi·tae·'et ra·seed **f**
money	مساري	msae·ree **m**
passport	جواز سفر	ja·waez sa·far **m**
travellers cheques	شيكات سياحية	shee·kaet see·yae·hee·ye **f**

health

Where's the nearest ...?	وين أقرب ... ؟	wayn 'a'·reb ...
dentist	طبيب الأسنان	ta·beeb il·'as·naen
doctor	دكتور	duk·toor
hospital	مستشفى	mus·tash·fae
(night) pharmacist	صيدلية (ليالية)	say·da·lee·ye (lee·yae·lee)

I need a doctor (who speaks English).

لازمني دكتور(بيحكي إنجليزي). lae·zim·nee duk·toor (byah·kee 'inj·lee·zee)

Could I see a female doctor?

بقدر اشوف طبيبة؟ bi'·dir 'a·shoof ta·bee·be

I've run out of my medication.

خلص كل دوائي. kha·las kil da·wae·'ee

I'm sick.

أنا مريض/مريضة. 'a·na ma·reed/ma·ree·de **m/f**

It hurts here.

في ألم هون. fee 'alm hoon

I have (a) ...	عندي ...	'in·dee ...
asthma	الربو	ir·rabw
constipation	الإمساك	il·'im·saek
diarrhoea	الإسهال	il·'is·hael
fever	حمى	hum·ma
headache	صداع	su·dae'
heart condition	مشاكل بالقلب	mu·shae·kil bil·'elb
nausea	غثيان	gha·tha·yaen
pain	ألم	'alm
sore throat	ألم بحلقي	'alm bi·hal·'ee
toothache	ألم في الأسنان	'alm fee il·'as·naen

I'm allergic to ...	أنا حساسي/ حساسية من ...	'a·na ha·sae·see/ ha·sae·see·ye min ... **m/f**
antibiotics	مضاد حيوي	mu·daed ha·ya·wee
anti-inflammatories	مضاد للالتهاب	mu·daed lil·'il·ti·haeb
aspirin	الأسبرين	il·'as·breen
bees	نحل	nahl
codeine	الكودين	il·koo·deen
penicillin	البنسلين	il·bi·ni·si·leen

english–levantine arabic dictionary

Words in this dictionary are marked as n (noun), a (adjective), v (verb), sg (singular), pl (plural), m (masculine) and f (feminine) where necessary. Verbs are given in the present tense in the third-person singular ('he/she'), in both masculine and feminine forms.

A

accident حادث hae-dith m
accommodation سكن se-ke-ne m
adaptor موصّل mu-was-sel
address n عنوان 'un-waen m
after بعد ba'd
air-conditioned عنده مكيف 'in-du mu-kay-yef
airplane طائرة tae-'i-re f
airport مطار ma-taer m
alcohol الكحول il-ku-hool m
all كل kil
allergy حساسية has-sae-see-ye f
ambulance سيارة الإسعاف say-yae-ret il-'is-aef f
and وو oo
ankle كاحل kae-hil m
arm ذراع zi-rae' f
ashtray صحن سيجارة sahn see-jae-re m
ATM جهاز الصرافة ji-haez is-sar-rae-fe m

B

baby طفل صغير/ طفلة صغيرة
    tifl 'iz-gheer/tif-le 'iz-ghee-re f
back (body) ظهر zahr
backpack شنطة ظهر shan-tet zahr f
bad سيء/سيئة say-yi'/say-yi'-e
bag شنطة shan-te f
baggage claim مكان لجمع الشنطيات
    ma-kaen li-ja-mi' ish-shan-tae-yaet m
bank بنك bank m
bar بار baar m
bathroom غرفة الحمام ghur-fet il-ham-maem m
battery بطارية ba-tae-ree-ye f
beautiful جميل/جميلة ja-meel/ja-mee-le m/f
bed تخت takht m
beer بيرا bee-ra m
before قبل 'abl
behind خلف khalf
bicycle بيسكليت bee-see-kleet f
big كبير/كبيرة ka-beer/ka-bee-re m/f
bill حساب hi-saeb m
black اسود/سودا 'is-wad/saw-dae m/f
blanket بطانية ba-tae-nee-ye f

blood group فئة الدم fi-'et id-dam m
blue ازرق/زرقاء 'iz-ra'/zar-'ae m/f
boat سفينة sfee-ne f
book (make a reservation) v يحجز/تحجز
    byah-jiz/btah-jiz m/f
bottle زجاجة zu-jae-je f
bottle opener فاخ الزجاجات
    fae-tih iz-zu-jae-jaet f
boy ولد wa-led m
brakes (car) فرامل fa-rae-mil f
breakfast فطور ftoor m
broken (faulty) خربان/خربانة
    khar-baen/khar-bae-ne m/f
bus باص baas m
business شغل shaghl m
buy بيشتري /بتشتري
    byash-ta-ree/btash-ta-ree m/f

C

café مقهى ma'-hae m
camera كاميرا kae-mee-ra m
camp site مخيم mu-khay-yem m
cancel بيلغي /بتلغي byal-ghee/btal-ghee m/f
can opener فاخ التنكة fae-tih it-tan-ke f
car سيارة say-yae-re f
cash n مصاري msae-re m
cash (a cheque) v بيصرف/بتصرف
    byas-ref/btas-ref m/f
cell phone موبيل moo-beel m
centre n وسط wast m
change (money) v بيصرف/بتصرف
    bya-sar-rif/bit-sar-rif m/f
cheap رخيص/رخيصة ra-khees/re-khee-se m/f
check (bill) حساب hi-saeb m
check-in مكتب التسجيل mak-teb it-tas-jeel m
chest صدر sadr m
child طفل/طفلة tifl/tif-le m/f
cigarette سيجارة see-jae-re f
city مدينة ma-dee-ne f
clean a نظيف/نظيفة na-zeef/na-zee-fe m/f
closed مسكر/مسكرة msak-ker/msak-ki-re m/f
coffee قهوى 'ah-way m
coins فراطة fi-rae-ta f

cold a بارد/باردة bae-rid/bae-ri-de ⓜ/①
collect call اتصال والأجرة عالذي يبرد it-ti-sael ool-'uj-re 'ael-la-zee bya-rid
come v يجي/بتجي byi-jee/bti-jee
computer كمبيوتر kom-byoo-ter
condom الواقي il-waa-'ee
contact lenses عدسة لاصقة 'a-da-set lae-si-'e ①
cook v يطبخ/بتطبخ byat-bukh/btat-bukh ⓜ/①
cost n تكلفة tek-li-fe ①
credit card بطاقة رصيد bi-tae-'et ra-seed ①
cup فنجان fin-jaen ⓜ
currency exchange صرافة sa-rae-fe ①
customs (immigration) جمارك ja-mae-rak ①

D

dangerous a خاطر/خاطرة khae-tir/khae-ti-re ⓜ/①
date (time) تاريخ tae-reekh ⓜ
day يوم yawm ⓜ
delay n تأخير ta-'kheer ⓜ
dentist طبيب الأسنان ta-beeb il-'as-naen ⓜ
depart يغادر/بتفادر byu-ghae-dir/bit-ghae-dir ⓜ/①
diaper حفاظة طفل ha-fae-zat tifl ①
dictionary قاموس 'ae-moos ⓜ
dinner عشاء 'a-shae ⓜ
direct مباشر/مباشرة mu-bae-shir/mu-bae-shi-re ⓜ/①
dirty وسخ/وسخة waskh/was-khe ⓜ/①
disabled معاق/معاقة mu-'ae'/mu-'ae-'e ⓜ/①
discount n خصم khasm ⓜ
doctor دكتور/دكتورة duk-toor/duk-tuu-re ⓜ/①
double bed تخت مزدوج takht muz-daw-wej ⓜ
double room غرفة لشخصين ghur-fe li-shakh-sayn ①
drink n مشروب mash-roob ⓜ
drive v بيسوق/بتسوق bye-sool/bit-soo' ⓜ/①
drivers licence رخصة القيادة rukh-set il-'ee-yae-de ①
drug (illicit) مخدر mu-khad-dir ⓜ
dummy (pacifier) مصاصة mas-sae-se ①

E

ear أذن 'u-zun ①
east شرق shar' ⓜ
eat بياكل/بتاكل byae-kul/btae-kul ⓜ/①
economy class الدرجة العادية id da ra-je il-'ae-dee-ye ①
electricity كهرباء kah-ra-bae' ⓜ
elevator مصعد mas-'ad ⓜ
email بريد الكتروني ba-reed 'i-lik-troo-nee ⓜ

embassy سفارة sa-fae-re ①
emergency طارىء tae-ri' ⓜ
English (language) الإنجليزي il-'inj-lee-zee ⓜ
entrance مدخل mad-khel ⓜ
evening مساء ma-sae ⓜ
exchange rate سعر التحويل si'r it-tah-weel ⓜ
exit n مخرج makh-raj ⓜ
expensive غالي/غالية ghae-lee/ghae-lee-ye ⓜ/①
express mail بريد سريع ba-reed sa-ree' ⓜ
eye عين 'ayn ①

F

far بعيد/بعيدة ba-'eed/ba-'ee-de ⓜ/①
fast سريع/سريعة sa-ree'/sa-ree-'e ⓜ/①
father بي bay
film (camera) فيلم feelm ⓜ
finger إصبع 'is-ba' ⓜ
first-aid kit صندوق للإسعاف الأول sun-doo'lil-'is-'aef il-'ew-wel ⓜ
first class الدرجة الأولى id-da-ra-je il-'oo-le ①
fish n سمك se-mek ⓜ
food طعام ta-'aem ⓜ
foot قدم 'adm ①
fork شوكة shaw-ke ①
free (of charge) مجانا ma-jae-nan
friend رفيق/رفيقة ra-fee'/ra-fee-'e ⓜ/①
fruit فواكه fa-wae-keh ①
full شبعان/شبعانة shab-'aen/shab-'ae-ne ⓜ/①
funny مضحك/مضحكة mud-hik/mud-hi-ke ⓜ/①

G

gift هدية ha-dee-ye ①
girl بنت bint ①
glass (drinking) كاسة kae-se ①
glasses (eye) نظارات na-zaa-raet ①
go بيروح/بتروح bya-rooh/bit-rooh ⓜ/①
good منيح/منيحة mneeh/mnee-ha ⓜ/①
green أخضر/خضرا 'akh-dar/khad-rae ⓜ/①
guide n دليل/دليلة da-leel/da-lee-le ⓜ/①

H

half n نص nuss ⓜ
hand يد yad ①
handbag محفظة يد mah-fa-zet yad ①
happy مبسوط/مبسوطة mab-soot/mab-soo-ta ⓜ/①
have عند 'ind
he هو hu-we ⓜ

113

head راس raas ⓜ
heart قلب 'elb ⓜ
heat n حرارة ha-rae-ra ⒡
heavy ثقيل/ثقيلة ta-'eel/ta-'ee-le ⓜ/⒡
help v يساعد/تساعد
bya-sae-'id/bit-sae-'id ⓜ/⒡
here هون hoon
high عالي/عالية 'ae-lee/'ae-lee-ye ⓜ/⒡
highway طريق عام ta-ree' 'aem
hike v بيتمشى/بتتمشي بطريق طويل في الريف
bya-ta-ma-shae/bta-ta-ma-shae bi-ta-ree'
ta-weel fee reef ⓜ/⒡
holiday إجازة 'i-jae-ze ⒡
homosexual a لوطي /سحاقية
loo-tee/su-hae-'ee-ye ⓜ/⒡
hospital مستشفى mus-tash-fa ⒡
hot حار/حارة haar/haa-re ⓜ/⒡
hotel فندق fun-ku' ⓜ
hungry جوعانة/جوعانة jaw-'aen/jaw-'ae-ne ⓜ/⒡
husband زوج zawj ⓜ

I

identification (card) شخصية shakh-see-ye ⒡
ill مريض/مريضة ma-reed/ma-ree-de ⓜ/⒡
important مهم/مهمة
mu-him/mu-him-me ⓜ/⒡
included محتوى/محتوية
muh-ta-wee/muh-ta-wee-ye ⓜ/⒡
injury ضرر da-rar
insurance تأمين ta'-meen ⓜ
internet الانترنت il-'in-ter-net ⓜ
interpreter مترجم/مترجمة
mu-tar-jim/mu-tar-ji-me ⓜ/⒡

J

jewellery مجوهرات mu-jaw-hi-raet ⒡
job شغل shaghl ⓜ

K

key مفتاح mif-taeh ⓜ
kilogram كيلوغرام kee-loo-ghraem ⓜ
kitchen مطبخ mat-bakh ⓜ
knife سكين sik-keen ⓜ

L

laundry (place) مغسل magh-sel ⓜ
lawyer محامي/محامية
mu-hae-mee/mu-hae-mee-ye ⓜ/⒡
left (direction) يسار ya-saer

left-luggage office مكتب الاحتفاظ بالأمتعة
mak-tab il-'ih-ti-faez bil-'am-ti-'e ⓜ
leg رجل rijl ⓜ
lesbian a سحاقية su-hae-'ee-ye ⒡
less أقل 'a-'al
letter (mail) رسالة ri-sae-le ⒡
lift (elevator) مصعد mas-'ad ⓜ
light n ضوء daw' ⓜ
like v بيحب/بتحب byu-hib/bit-hib ⓜ/⒡
lock n قفل 'ifl ⓜ
long طويل/طويلة ta-weel/ta-wee-le ⓜ/⒡
lost ضائع/ضائعة dae-'e'/dae-'e-'a ⓜ/⒡
lost-property office مكتب الأغراض الضائعة
mak-tab il-'agh-raed il-dae-'e-'a ⓜ
love v بيحب/بتحب byu-hib/bit-hib ⓜ/⒡
luggage أمتعة 'am-ti-'a ⒡
lunch غداء gha-dae ⓜ

M

mail n بريد ba-reed ⓜ
man رجل ra-jul ⓜ
map خريطة kha-ree-te ⒡
market سوق soo' ⓜ
matches كبريت kib-reet ⓜ
meat لحم lahm ⓜ
medicine دواء da-wae
menu قائمة الطعام 'ae-'i-met it-ta-'aem ⒡
message رسالة ri-sae-le ⒡
milk حليب ha-leeb ⓜ
minute دقيقة da-'ee-'a ⒡
mobile phone موبيل moo-beel ⓜ
money مصاري msae-re ⓜ
month شهر shahr ⓜ
morning صبح su-beh ⓜ
mother أم 'im ⒡
motorcycle موتر بيك moo-ter bayk ⓜ
motorway اوتوستراد 'oo-too-straed ⓜ
mouth تم tim ⓜ
music موسيقى moo-see-'a ⒡

N

name اسم 'esm ⓜ
napkin محرمة mah-ra-me ⒡
nappy حفاظة طفل ha-fae-zet tifl ⒡
near قريب a-reeb
neck رقبة ru'-be ⒡
new جديد/جديدة 'ij-deed/'ij-dee-de ⓜ/⒡
news أخبار 'akh-baar ⓜ
newspaper جريدة je-ree-de ⒡
night ليلة lay-le ⒡

no ﻻ laa

noisy ﺿﺠﻴﺠﺔ/ﺿﺠﻴﺞ da-jeej/da-jee-je ⓜ/ⓕ

nonsmoking ﻏﻴﺮ ﺍﻟﻤﺪﺧﻨﻴﻦ
ghayr il-mu-dakh-khi-neen

north ﺷﻤﺎﻝ shi-mael ⓜ

nose ﻣﻨﺨﺎﺭ mun-khaer ⓜ

now ﻫﻠﻖ 'hal-la

number ﺭﻗﻢ ra'm ⓜ

O

oil (engine) ﺯﻳﺖ zayt ⓜ

old ﻗﺪﻳﻤﺔ/ﻗﺪﻳﻢ 'a-deem/'a-dee-me ⓜ/ⓕ

one-way ticket ﺗﺬﻛﺮﺓ ﺫﻫﺎﺏ taz-ki-ret za-haeb

open a ﻣﻔﺘﻮﺣﺔ/ﻣﻔﺘﻮﺡ
maf-tooh/maf-too-he ⓜ/ⓕ

outside ﺑﺮﻯ bar ra

P

package ﻃﺮﺩ tard ⓜ

paper ﻭﺭﻗﺔ war-'a ⓕ

park (car) v ﺑﻴﻮﻗﻒ/ﺑﺘﻮﻗﻒ byoo-'if/btoo-'if ⓜ/ⓕ

passport ﺟﻮﺍﺯ ﺳﻔﺮ ja-waez sa-fer ⓜ

pay ﺑﻴﺪﻓﻊ/ﺑﺘﺪﻓﻊ byad-ta'/btad-ta' ⓜ/ⓕ

pen ﻗﻠﻢ 'alm ⓜ

petrol ﺑﺘﺮﻭﻝ bit-rool ⓜ

pharmacy ﺻﻴﺪﻟﻴﺔ say-da-le-ye ⓕ

phonecard ﺑﻄﺎﻗﺔ ﺗﻠﻔﻮﻥ bi-tae-'et te-li-foon ⓕ

photo ﺻﻮﺭﺓ soo-re ⓕ

plate ﺻﺤﻦ sahn ⓜ

police ﺷﺮﻃﺔ shur-ta ⓕ

postcard ﺑﻄﺎﻗﺔ ﻣﻌﺎﻳﺪﺓ bi-tae-'et mu-'ae-ye-de ⓕ

post office ﻣﻜﺘﺐ ﺍﻟﺒﺮﻳﺪ mak-teb il-ba-reed ⓜ

pregnant ﺣﺎﻣﻞ hae-mil ⓕ

price ﻫﻖ ha' ⓜ

Q

quiet ﻫﺎﺩﻳﺔ/ﻫﺎﺩﻱ hae-dee/hae-dee-ye ⓜ/ⓕ

R

rain n ﻣﻄﺮ ma-ter ⓜ

razor ﻣﻮﺳﻰ moo-saa ⓕ

receipt n ﻭﺻﻞ wa-sil ⓜ

red ﺣﻤﺮﺍ/ﺃﺣﻤﺮ 'ah-mar/ham-rae ⓜ/ⓕ

refund n ﺇﻋﺎﺩﺓ ﻣﺎﻟﻲ 'i-'ae-det mae-lee ⓜ

registered mail ﺑﺮﻳﺪ ﻣﺴﺠﻞ ba-reed mu-saj-jel ⓜ

rent v ﺑﻴﺴﺘﺄﺟﺮ/ﺑﺘﺴﺘﺄﺟﺮ byas-ta'-jir/btas-ta'-jir ⓜ/ⓕ

repair v ﺑﻴﺼﻠﺢ/ﺑﺘﺼﻠﺢ byas-lah/btas-lah ⓜ/ⓕ

reservation ﺣﺠﺰ ha-jez ⓜ

restaurant ﻣﻄﻌﻢ mat-'em ⓜ

return v ﺑﻴﺮﺟﻊ/ﺑﺘﺮﺟﻊ byur-ji'/btur-ji' ⓜ/ⓕ

return ticket ﺗﺬﻛﺮﺓ ﺫﻫﺎﺏ ﻭﺇﻳﺎﺏ
taz-ki-re za-haeb ool-'ee-yaeb

right (direction) ﺷﻤﺎﻝ she-mael ⓜ

road ﻃﺮﻳﻖ ta-ree' ⓜ

room ﻏﺮﻓﺔ ghur-fe ⓕ

S

safe a ﺁﻣﻦ/ﺁﻣﻨﺔ 'aa-min/'aa-mi-ne ⓜ/ⓕ

sanitary napkin ﻣﻨﺪﻳﻞ ﻧﺴﺎﺋﻲ
men-deel ni-sae-'ee ⓜ

seat ﻣﻘﻌﺪ ma'-ad ⓜ

send ﺑﻴﻨﻌﺚ/ﺑﺘﻨﻌﺚ bynb-'at/btnb-'at ⓜ/ⓕ

service station ﻣﺤﻄﺔ ﺍﻟﺒﻨﺰﻳﻦ
ma-hat-tet il-bin-zeen ⓕ

sex ﺟﻨﺲ jins ⓜ

shampoo ﺷﺎﻣﺒﻮ shaem-boo ⓜ

share (a dorm etc) ﺑﻴﺸﺎﺭﻙ/ﺑﺘﺸﺎﺭﻙ
bya-shae-rik/bit-shae-rik ⓜ/ⓕ

shaving cream ﻣﻌﺠﻮﻥ ﺍﻟﺤﻼﻗﺔ
ma'-joon il-hal-lae-'e ⓜ

she ﻫﻲ hi-ye

sheet (bed) ﺷﺮﺷﻒ shar-shaf ⓜ

shirt ﻗﻤﻴﺺ 'a-mees ⓜ

shoes ﺑﻮﻁ ma-hal ⓜ

shop n ﻣﺤﻞ ma-hal ⓜ

short ﻗﺼﻴﺮﺓ/ﻗﺼﻴﺮ 'a-seer/'a-see-re ⓜ/ⓕ

shower n ﺩﻭﺵ doosh ⓜ

single room ﻏﺮﻓﺔ ﻟﺸﺨﺺ ﻭﺍﺣﺪ
ghur-fet li-shakh-es wae-hid ⓕ

skin ﺑﺸﺮﺓ ba-sha-re ⓕ

skirt ﺗﻨﻮﺭﺓ tan-noo-re ⓕ

sleep v ﺑﻴﻨﺎﻡ/ﺑﺘﻨﺎﻡ bya-naem/bit-naem ⓜ/ⓕ

slowly ﺷﻮﻱ ﺷﻮﻱ shway shway

small ﺻﻐﻴﺮﺓ/ﺻﻐﻴﺮ 'iz-gheer/'iz-ghee-re ⓜ/ⓕ

smoke (cigarettes) v ﺑﻴﺪﺧﻦ/ﺑﺘﺪﺧﻦ
bya-dakh-khin/bit-dakh-khin ⓜ/ⓕ

soap ﺻﺎﺑﻮﻥ saa-boon ⓜ

some ﺷﻮﻱ shway

soon ﻗﺮﻳﺐ a-reeb'

south ﺟﻨﻮﺏ 'ij-noob ⓜ

souvenir shop ﻣﺤﻞ ﺍﻟﺘﺬﻛﺎﺭﺍﺕ
ma-hal it-tiz-kae-raet ⓜ

speak v ﺑﻴﺤﻜﻲ/ﺑﺘﺤﻜﻲ byah-kee/btah-kee ⓜ/ⓕ

spoon ﻣﻌﻠﻘﺔ ma'-la-'e ⓕ

stamp ﻃﺎﺑﻊ tae-bi' ⓜ

stand-by ticket ﺗﺬﻛﺮﺓ ﺑﺪﻳﻠﺔ taz-ki-ret ba-dee-le ⓕ

station (train) ﻣﺤﻄﺔ ma-hat-tet ⓕ

stomach ﻣﻌﺪﺓ mi'-de ⓕ

stop v يقف/يتقف bya-'if/bta-'if ⓜ/ⓕ
stop (bus) n موقف maw-'if ⓜ
street شارع shae-ri' ⓜ
student طالب/طالبة tae-lib/tae-li-be ⓜ/ⓕ
sun شمس shams ⓕ
sunscreen معجون واقي في الشمس
ma'-joon waa-'ee fee ish-shams ⓜ
swim v يسبح/يتسبح byas-bah/btas-bah ⓜ/ⓕ

T

tampons الصمام النسائي
is-sa-maem in-ni-sae-ee ⓜ
taxi تكسي tak-see
teaspoon ملعقة شاي ma'-la-'et shaa-ee ⓕ
teeth أسنان 'is-naen ⓕ
telephone n تلفون te-li-foon ⓜ
television تلفسيون te-le-fi-see-yoon ⓜ
temperature (weather) درجة da-ra-jet ⓕ
tent خيمة khay-me ⓕ
that (one) ذالك (الواحد/الواحدة) zae-lik (il-wae-hid/il-waeh-de) ⓕ
they هن hun-ne ⓜ&ⓕ
thirsty عطشان/عطشانة
'at-shaen/'at-shae-ne ⓕ
this (one) هيدا/هيدي (الواحد/الواحدة)
hay-dae/hay-dee (il-wae-hid/il-waeh-de)
throat حلق hal' ⓜ
ticket تذكرة ta-zki-re ⓕ
time وقت wa-'et ⓕ
tired تعبان/تعبانة ta'-baen/ta'-bae-ne ⓜ/ⓕ
tissues محارم ma-ha-rem ⓕ
today اليوم il-yawm ⓜ
toilet حمامات ham-mae-maet ⓕ
tomorrow بكرة buk-ra ⓕ
tonight ليلة اليوم lay-let il-yawm ⓕ
toothbrush فرشاة الأسنان far-shaeh il-'is-naen ⓕ
toothpaste معجون الأسنان ma'-joon il-'is-naen ⓜ
torch (flashlight) مشعل كهربائي
mish-'al kah-ra-bae-'ee ⓜ
tour n دورة daw-re ⓕ
tourist office مكتب السياحة
mak-teb is-see-yae-he ⓜ
towel منشفة man-sha-fe ⓕ
train قطار 'i-taer ⓜ
translate يترجم/بترجم
byu-tar-jem/bit-tar-jem ⓜ/ⓕ
travel agency وكالة السفر wi-kae-let is-sa-fer ⓕ
travellers cheque شيك سياحي
sheek see-yae-he ⓜ
trousers بنطلون bin-ta-loon ⓜ
twin beds تختين منفردين
takh-tayn mun-fa-ri-dayn ⓜ
tyre إطار السيارة 'i-taer is-say-yae-re ⓜ

U

underwear لباس تحتية li-baes tah-tee-ye ⓕ
urgent مستعجل/مستعجلة
mus-ta'-jal/mus-ta'-ja-le ⓜ/ⓕ

V

vacant فاضي/فاضية fae-dee/fae-dee-ye ⓜ/ⓕ
vacation عطلة 'ut-le ⓕ
vegetable n خضروات khad-ra-waet ⓕ
vegetarian a نباتي/نباتية
na-bae-tee/na-bae-tee-ye ⓜ/ⓕ
visa فيسا fee-saa ⓕ

W

waiter غرسن ghar-son ⓜ
walk v يمشي/بتمشي
byam-shee/btam-shee ⓜ/ⓕ
wallet محفظة mah-fa-ze ⓕ
warm a دافع/دافعة dae-fi'/dae-fi'-e ⓜ/ⓕ
wash (something) يغسل/بتغسل
byagh-sel/btagh-sel ⓜ/ⓕ
watch n ساعة يد sae-'et yad ⓕ
water ماء maay ⓜ
we نحنا nah-nae
weekend نهاية الأسبوع ni-hae-yet il-'us-boo' ⓜ
west غرب gharb ⓜ
wheelchair كرسي المقعدين
kur-see il-mu'-'a-deen ⓜ
when امتى 'em-ta
where وين wayn
white أبيض/بيضة 'ib-yad/bay-dae ⓜ/ⓕ
who مين meen
why ليش leesh
wife زوجة zaw-je ⓕ
window شباك shub-baek ⓜ
wine نبيذ nbeez ⓜ
with مع ma-'a
without بدون bi-doon
woman مراة ma-ra ⓕ
write يكتب/بتكتب byak-tub/btak-tub ⓜ/ⓕ

Y

yellow أصفر/صفرا 'is-far/saf-rae ⓜ/ⓕ
yes إيه 'eeh
yesterday مبارح mbae-reh
you sg أنت/أنتي 'en-te/'en-tee ⓜ/ⓕ
you pl أنتوا 'en-too ⓜ&ⓕ

T

Tunisian
Arabic

language difficulties

Note that, unlike Modern Standard Arabic or the other varieties of Arabic included in this phrasebook, Tunisian Arabic doesn't distinguish between the masculine and feminine gender in the second-person singular verb forms (ie with the 'you' pronoun) – all people are addressed the same way, regardless of their gender.

Do you speak English?

تتكلم بالانجليزية؟   *tit*·kal·am bil·in·glee·zee·*ya*

Do you understand?

فهمت؟   fa·*himt*

I understand.

فهمت.   fa·*himt*

I don't understand.

ما فهمتش   ma fa·*himt*·ish

Could you please ...?   برني ...؟   *brab*·ee ...
    repeat that   عودها   aw·*wid*·ha
    speak more slowly   اتكلم بشوية   it·*kal*·im bi·*shway*·a
    write it down   اكتبهالي   ik·tib·*haa*·lee

numbers

0	صفر	*si*·fur	20	عشرين	'*ash*·reen
1	واحد	*waa*·hid	30	ثلاثين	thlaa·*theen*
2	زوز	zooz	40	اربعين	ar·bai·*een*
3	ثلاثة	thlaa·tha	50	خمسين	*kham*·seen
4	اربعة	ar·*ba*'	60	ستين	sit·*een*
5	خمسة	*kham*·sa	70	سبعين	sa·ba·'*een*
6	ستة	sit·a	80	ثمنين	tha·ma·*neen*
7	سبعة	sa·ba'	90	تسعين	ti·sa'·*een*
8	ثمانية	the·*maan*·ya	100	مية	*mee*·ya
9	تسعة	tis·a'	1000	الف	alf
10	عشرة	'*ash*·ra	1,000,000	مليون	mel·*yoon*

For Arabic numerals, see the box on page 14.

time & dates

What time is it?	قداش الوقت؟	ka-*daysh* il-*wokt*
It's one o'clock.	ماضي ساعة.	maa-*dhee saa*-a'
It's four o'clock.	لاربعة.	*ler*-ba'
Quarter past (four).	(لاربعة) و ربع.	(*ler*-ba') wi re-*ba*'
Half past (four).	(لاربعة) و نص.	(*ler*-ba') wi nus
Quarter to (four).	(لاربعة) غير اربعة.	(*ler*-ba') gheer *ar*-ba'
At what time ...?	مع اما وقت ...؟	ma' *aa*-ma wokt ...
At ...	مع ...	ma' ...

| am | متاع صباح | im-*taa*'se-*baah* |
| pm | متاع لعشية | im-*taa*'l'ash-*ee*-ya |

Monday	النهار الاثنين	in-*haar* lith-*neen*
Tuesday	النهار الثلاثة	in-*haar* ith-*laa*-tha
Wednesday	النهار الاربعة	in-*haar* lur-ba'
Thursday	النهار الخميس	in-*haar* il-kham-*ees*
Friday	النهار الجمع	in-*haar* a-*jum*-a'
Saturday	النهار السبت	in-*haar* a-*sibt*
Sunday	النهار الاحد	in-*haar* la-*had*

last ...	الي فات ...	*i*-lee faat ...
next ...	القادم ...	il-*kaa*-dim ...
night	البلة	i-*lee*-la
week	الجمعة	i-*ji*-ma'
month	الشهر	a-*shahr*
year	السنة	a-*snaa*

yesterday ...	البارح ...	il-*baa*-rih ...
tomorrow ...	غدوة ...	*ghud*-wa ...
morning	في الصباح	fis-*baah*
afternoon	في العشية	fil-'ash-*ee*-ya
evening	في ليل	fi-*leel*

What date is it today?

شنوة التاريخ اليوم؟   shnoo-wa it-*taa*-reekh il-*yoom*

It's (15 December).

اليوم (خمسطاش ديسامبر).   il-*yoom* (kha-ma-staa-shin dee-*sam*-bur)

border crossing

I'm here ...	انا هوني ...	aa·na hoo·nee ...
in transit	في ترنست	fee tran·sit
on business	في الخدمة	fil·khid·ma
on holiday	في الكونجي	fil·koon·jee

I'm here for ...	بش نقعد ...	bish no·ko'd ...
(10) days	(عشرة) ايام	('ash·rat) ay·aam
(three) weeks	(ثلاثة) جمعات	(thlaa·tha) jim·a'·aat
(two) months	(خمسة) شهور	(kham·sa) she·hoor

I'm going to (Susa).
نمشي لـ(سوسة). — nim·shee li·(soo·sa)

I'm staying at the (Hotel Africa).
نبات في (اوتيل افريقا). — in·baat fee (oo·teel af·ree·ka)

I have nothing to declare.
ما عندي شي بش نخبرك. — ma 'and·ee shay bish in·kha·bar·ik

I have something to declare.
عندي هاجة بش نعلم عليها. — 'and·ee haa·ja bish na'·lim 'a·lee·ha

That's (not) mine.
هاذاك (مش) متعاي. — haa·dhaa·ka (mush) im·taa·'ee

tickets & luggage

Where can I buy a ticket?
وين نجم نشري تذكرة؟ — ween na·jam nish·ree tiz·ki·ra

Do I need to book a seat?
يلزمني نحجز بلاصة؟ — yel·zim·nee nah·jiz blaa·sa

One ... ticket	بربي عطني ...	brab·ee 'a·tee·nee ...
(to Sfax), please.	تذكرة (لصفاكس).	tiz·ki·ra (li·sfa·kis)
one-way	ماشي	maa·shee
return	ماشي و جاي	maa·shee oo jay

I'd like to ... my ticket, please.	نحب ... تذكرتي.	in-heb ... tiz-ki-ra-tee
cancel	نلغا	nal-gha
change	نحاول	in-haa-wil
collect	نتسلم	nit-sa-lim

I'd like a ... seat, please.	نحب بلاصة ...	in-heb blaa-sa ...
nonsmoking	ممنوع فيها تدخين	mam-noo-'a fee-ha tad-kheen
smoking	وين نجم نتخيف	ween na-jam nit-khay-if

Is there air conditioning?

فم اكليمتيسر؟   fa-ma ak-lee-ma-tee-ser

Is there a toilet?

فم توالت؟   fa-ma twa-let

How long does the trip take?

قداش تاخذ وقت الرحلة؟   ka-daysh taa-khudh wokt i-rah-la

Is it a direct route?

تمشي ديركت؟   tim-shee dee-rekt

My luggage has been ...	بقاج متاعي ...	ba-gaaj im-taa-'ee ...
damaged	متكسر	mit-kas-er
lost	مضيع	im-dhee-a'
stolen	سرقولي	sir-koo-lee

transport

Where does flight (number 20) arrive/depart?

وين يوصل/يطلع طيارة (نومرو عشرين)؟   ween yoo-sil/yat-la' tay-aa-ra (noom-roo 'ash-reen)

Is this the ... (to Kerkenna)?	هاذا ال ... (لقرفنة)؟	haa-dha il ... (li-kar-ka-na)
boat	فلوكة	floo-ka
bus	كار	kaar
plane	طيارة	tay-aa-ra
train	ترن	tren

What time's the ... bus?	وقتاش الكار ...؟	wok·*taysh* il·*kaar* ...
first	الاول	il·*aw*·il
last	الاخر	il·*aa*·khir
next	الجاي	i·*jay*

How long will it be delayed?

قداش ساعة يتاخر؟   ka·*daysh* saa·a' yit·*aa*·kher

What station/stop is this?

شسمها هاذي المحطة؟   shism·ha haa·*dhee* lim·*ha*·ta

Please tell me when we get (to Guellala).

بري قلي وقتلي   brab·ee *kul*·ee wok·*til*·ee
نوصلو (لقلالة).   *noo*·sil·oo (li·ga·*laa*·la)

Is this seat available?

بلاصة هاذا فارغة؟   blaa·sa haa·dha faa·ri·gha

That's my seat.

هاذيكا بلاصتي.   haa·*dhee*·ka *blaa*·stee

I'd like a taxi ...	نحب تكسي ...	in·*heb* tak·*see* ...
at 9am	تسعة متاع الصباح	*tis*·a' im·*taa'* sbaah
now	توة	*taw*·a
tomorrow	غدوة	*ghud*·wa

How much is it to ...?

قداش توصلني ل ...؟   ka·*daysh* twa·*sil*·nee li ...

Please put the meter on.

بري حل الكنتر.   brab·ee hil il·kon·tur

Please take me to (this address).

بري وصلني   brab·ee wa·*wil*·nee
(للادريسة هاذي).   (lil·ad·*ree*·sa haa·*dhee*)

Please ...	بري ...	brab·ee ...
stop here	وقف هنا	*wok*·if hi·*naa*
wait here	ستناني هنا	sta·*naa*·nee hi·*naa*

I'd like to hire a ...	نحب نكري ...	in·*heb* nik·*ree* ...
car	كرهبة	*kar*·ha·ba
4WD	كتر كتر	*ka*·tra *ka*·tra

with ...	... مع	ma' ...
a driver	شيفور	shee·*foor*
air conditioning	بالاكليمتيسر	bil·ak·*lee*·ma·tee·ser

How much for ... hire?	... قداش؟ يكري	yik·ree ... ka·*daysh*
daily	باليوم	bil·*yoom*
weekly	بالجمعة	bil·*jim*·a'

I need a mechanic.

حاجتي بالمكنيك   *haaj*·tee bil·*mee*·ka·neek

I've run out of petrol.

البنزين وفاتني   il·ben·*zeen* oo·*faat*·nee

I have a flat tyre.

العجلة مفشوشة.   *la'j*·la maf·*shoo*·sha

directions

Where's the ...?	... جاء وين؟	ween jaa ...
bank	البنكة	il·*ban*·ka
market	المرشي	il·*mar*·shee
post office	بوسطة	il·*boo*·sta

Is this the road (to Mahdia)?

الثنية هاني تمشي (المهدية؟)   ith·*nee*·ya *haa*·dhee *tim*·shee (li·mah·*dee*·ya)

Can you show me (on the map)?

وريني (فالخريطة؟)   wa·*ree*·nee (fil·kha·*ree*·ta)

What's the address?

شنية الادريسة؟   *shnoo*·wa la·*dree*·sa

How far is it?

قداش كلومتر؟   ka·*daash* kee·loo·*me*·tra

How do I get there?

كيفاش نمشي غادي؟   kee·*faysh* *nim*·shee *ghaa*·dee

Turn left/right.

دور اليسار/اليمين.   door a·lee·*saar*/a·lee·*meen*

It's ...	... جاء	jaa ...
behind ...	ورا ...	we-raa ...
in front of ...	قدام ...	ku-daam ...
near to ...	قريب من ...	kreeb min ...
next to ...	بحضة ...	bah-dha ...
on the corner	في الكوان	fil-kwan
opposite ...	قدام ...	ku-daam ...
straight ahead	طول طول	tool tool
there	غادي	ghaa-dee
north	شمال	she-maal
south	جنوب	je-noob
east	شرق	shark
west	غرب	gharb

signs

دخول	de-khool	**Entrance**
خروج	khe-rooj	**Exit**
محلول	mah-lool	**Open**
مغلق	mugh-lak	**Closed**
معلومات	ma'-loo-maat	**Information**
مركز الشرطة	mar-kaz i-shur-ta	**Police Station**
ممنوع	mam-noo-a'	**Prohibited**
مرحاض	mir-haadh	**Toilets**
رجال	re-jaal	**Men**
نساء	in-saa	**Women**

accommodation

Where's a ...?	وين فم ...؟	ween fa·ma ...
camping ground	كمبين	kom-peen
hotel	وتيل	oo-teel
youth hostel	دار الشباب	daar ash-baab

Can you recommend somewhere ...?	تنجمشي تنصحني لبلاصة ...؟	it-na-jam-shee tin-sah-nee blaa-sa ...
cheap	رخيص	re-khees
good	باهي	baa-hee
nearby	قريب	kreeb

I'd like to book a room, please.

نحب نحجز بيت.   in·heb nah·jiz beet

I have a reservation.

عندي حجز.   'and·ee ha·jiz

Do you have	عندكمشي	'and·kum·shee
a ... room?	بيت ...؟	beet ...
single	للواحد	lil·waa·hid
double	دوبل	doo·bal
twin	بزوز فرش	bi·zooz farsh

How much is it per ...?	بقداش كل ...؟	bi·ka·daysh kul ...
night	ليلة	lee·la
person	شخص	shakhs

I'd like to stay for (three) nights.

نحب نقعد (ثلاثة) ليالي.   in·heb no·ko'd (thlaa·tha) lay·aa·lee

Am I allowed to camp here?

نجم نخيم هوني؟   na·jam in·khay·im hoo·nee

Could I have my key, please?

بربي عطيني مفتاحي؟   brab·ee 'a·tee·nee mif·taa·hee

Can I get another (blanket)?

بربي زيدني (فرشية)؟   brab·ee zeed·nee (fa·ra·shee·ya)

The (air conditioning) doesn't work.

(الاكليمتيسر) ما يمشيش.   (lak·lee·ma·tee·ser) ma yim·sheesh

This (sheet) isn't clean.

هادي (الملحفة) مش نظيفة.   haa·dhee (il·mal·ha·fa) mish na·dhee·fa

Is there an elevator/a safe?

فم اسنسر/كشة؟   fa·ma a·son·sur/ka·sha

What time is checkout?

وكتاش يلزمني نمشي؟   wok·taysh yel·zim·nee nim·shee

Could I have my ..., please?	بربي عطيني ؟...	brab·ee 'a·tee·nee ...
deposit	ضمد	dhe·mud
passport	باسبور	pas·por
valuables	دباشي	de·baa·shee

banking & communications

Where's a/an ...?	وين فم ؟...	ween fa·ma ...
ATM	دستربوتر	dis·tri·boo·tur
foreign exchange office	صراف	sa·raaf

I'd like to ...	نحب ...	in·heb ...
arrange a transfer	نعمل تحويل	na'·mel tah·weel
cash a cheque	نصرف شك	in·sa·rif shek
change a travellers cheque	نصرف شك	in·sa·rif shek
	سياحي	see·yaa·hee
change money	نصرف فلوس	in·sa·rif floos
withdraw money	نجبد فلوس	nij·bid floos

What's the ...?	قداش هاذا ؟...	ka·daysh haa·dha ...
charge for that	السوم	i·soom
exchange rate	كورت د شانج	koor de shanj

Where's the local internet café?

وين فم بوبلينت؟   ween fa·ma poo·blee·net

How much is it per hour?

بقداش ساعة؟   bi·ka·daysh saa·a'

I'd like to ...	نحب ...	in·heb ...
check my email	نشوف يمايل	in·shoof ee·mayl
get internet access	نشوف لانترنت	in·shoof lin·ter·net
use a printer	نطبع اوراق	nut·ba' aw·raak
use a scanner	نعمل سكنر	na'·mel ska·nur

I'd like to hire a ...	نحب نكري ...	in·heb nik·ree ...
mobile/cell phone	برتابل	por·taa·bel
SIM card for your network	بوس تونسيانة	poos too·nis·yaan

What's your phone number?

عطيني نومرو متاعك؟   'a·*tee*·nee *noom*·roo im·taa·'*ik*

The number is ...

... النومرو هو   i·*noom*·roo *hoo*·wa ...

Where's the nearest public phone?

وين فم تكسيفون؟   ween *fa*·ma tak·see·*foon*

I'd like to buy a phonecard.

نحب نشري كرت لتلفون.   in·*heb* nish·ree kart li·tel·*foon*

How much does a (three)-minute call cost?

بقداش مكلمة   bi·ka·*daysh* moo·*kal*·ma
(ثلاثة) دقايق؟   (*thlaa*·tha) de·*kaa*·yik

What are the rates?

بقداش؟   bi·ka·*daysh*

I want to ...	... نحب نكلم	in·*heb* in·*kal*·im ...
call (Canada)	(كندا)	(*ka*·na·da)
make a local call	تونس	*too*·nis
reverse the	نعمل بي	na·'·mel pay
charges	سي في	say vay
I want to send a ...	... نحب نبعث	in·*heb* nib·'·*ath* ...
fax	فاكس	faks
parcel	كولي	koo·*lee*
I want to buy a/an ...	... نحب نشري	in·*heb* nish·ree ...
envelope	جواب	je·*waab*
stamp	تمبري	*tim*·bree
Please send it	بريي بعثهالي	*brab*·ee ba·'ath·*haa*·lee
(to Australia) by ...	... (لاستراليا)	(los·traa·*lee*·ya) ...
airmail	بار افيون	par av·*yon*
surface mail	اردنار	or·din·*aar*

sightseeing

What time does it open/close?

وقتاش يحل/يسكر؟   wok·*taysh* ye·*hil*/ye·sa·*kar*

What's the admission charge?

بقداش الدخول؟   bi·ka·*daysh* i·de·*khool*

Is there a discount for students/children?

فم تخفيذ للطالبة/اولاد؟   fa·ma takh·*feedh* lil·*taa*·li·ba/oo·*laad*

I'd like to see ...

نحب نشوف ...   in·*heb* in·*shoof* ...

I'd like a ...	نحب ...	in·*heb* ...
catalogue	كتالوق	ka·ta·*loog*
guide	قيد	geed
local map	خريطة محلية	kha·*ree*·ta ma·ha·*lee*·ya

When's the next ...?	وقتاش ال ... الجاي؟	wok·*taysh* il ... i·*jay*
day trip	الرحلة	i·*rah*·la
tour	الجولة	i·*jaw*·la

Is ... included?	... داخلة في الحساب؟	... *daa*·khil·a feel hi·*saab*
accommodation	سكن	i·*skan*
the admission charge	الدخول	i·de·*khool*
food	الماكلة	il·*maa*·kla
transport	ترانسبور	trans·*por*

How long is the tour?

الجولة قداش من ساعة؟   i·*jaw*·la ka·*daysh* min saa·'a

What time should we be back?

وقتاش نرجعو؟   wok·*taysh* nar·ja·'oo

What's that?

شنوة هاذا؟!   shnoo·wa haa·dha

Can I take a photo?

نجم نصور؟   na·jam in·*saw*·er

castle	قصر	ke·*sar* m
church	كنيسة	ke·*nee*·sa f
main square	الساحة الرسمية	i·*saa*·ha i·ras·*mee*·ya f
mosque	جامع	*jaa*·ma' m
old city	المدينة	lim·*dee*·na f
palace	قصر	ke·*sar* m
ruins	اثار	a·*thaar* f

shopping

Where's a ...?	وين فم ...؟	ween *fa*·ma ...
bookshop	مكتبة	*mak*·ta·ba
camera shop	مصور	moo·*saw*·ir
department store	قراند سرفاس	grand ser·*fas*
grocery store	عطار	'a·*taar*
newsagency	قمرق	*gum*·rug
souvenir shop	حنوت تورستيك	ha·*noot* too·ris·*teek*
supermarket	سوبرمارشي	soo·per mar·*shee*

I'm looking for ...

نلوج في ...   in·*law*·ij fee ...

Can I look at it?

نجم نشوفه؟   *na*·jam in·*shoo*·foo

Do you have any others?

عندكمشي اخرين؟   'and·*kum*·shee ukh·*reen*

Does it have a guarantee?

عنده مضمونة؟   'and·oo madh·*moo*·na

Can I have it sent overseas?

تنجمشي تبعثهلي البرة؟   it·na·*jam*·shee ta·ba'th·*hoo*·lee il·*bu*·ra

Can I have my ... repaired?

تنجمشي اتصلي ...؟   it·na·*jam*·shee it·*sal*·ee ...

It's faulty.

ما تخدمش   ma tikh-*dimsh*

I'd like a bag, please.

بربي عطيني شكارة.   *brab*-ee a-*tee*-nee *shkaa*-ra

How much is it?

بقداش؟   bi-ka-*daysh*

Can you write down the price?

بربي اكتبلي سومها؟   *brab*-ee ik-*tib*-lee *soom*-ha

That's too expensive.

غالي ياسر.   *ghaa*-lee *yaa*-ser

What's your lowest price?

شنوة الاخر سوم؟   *shnoo*-wa *laa*-kher soom

I'll give you (10 dinar).

نعطيك (عشرة دينار).   na'-*teek* ('*ash*-ra dee-*naar*)

There's a mistake in the bill.

الحسبة غالطة.   il-*his*-ba *ghaal*-ta

Do you accept ...?	تاخذ ...؟	taa-khudh ...
credit cards	كرت كريدي	kart kre-*dee*
debit cards	كرت متاع بنكة	kart im-*taa'* ban-ka
travellers cheques	شيكات سياحية	shee-*kaat* say-aa-*hee*-ya

I'd like ..., please.	بربي جيبلي ...؟	*brab*-ee *jeeb*-lee ...
my change	باقية فلوسي	*baa*-kee-yat floo-*see*
a receipt	توصيل	taw-*seel*

I'd like ...	عطيني ...	'a-*tee*-nee ...
(100) grams	(مية) قرام	(*mee*-yat) gram
(two) kilos	(زوز) كيلو	(zooz) *kee*-loo
(three) pieces	(ثلاثة) كعبات	(*thlaa*-tha) ka-'ib-*aat*
(six) slices	(ستة) قدمات	(*sit*-a) gid-*maat*

Less.	اقل.	a·kul
Enough.	يزيني.	yi·zee·nee
More.	زيدني.	zeed·nee

photography

Can you ...?	تنجم ...؟	it·na·jam ...
burn a CD	تعملي نسخة من	ta'·mel·ee nus·kha min
from my	كرت مموار	kart mem·waar
memory card		
develop this film	طلعلي التصوير	ta·la'·lee it·saw·ir
load my film	حطلي الفلم في	hut·lee feelm fee
	مصورة	moo·saw·ir·a

I need a/an ... film	حاجتي فلم ...	haaj·tee feelm ...
for this camera.	المصورة هاذي.	lil·moo·saw·ir·a haa·dhee
APS	ا ب س	aa pay es
B&W	ابيض و اكحل	ab·yadh oo ak·hil
colour	ملون	moo·law·an
slide	برجكتر	pro·jek·tur
200 speed	ميتين	mee·teen

| When will it be ready? | وقتاش نرجع؟ | wok·taysh nar·ja' |

making conversation

Hello.	عسلامة.	'a·slaa·ma
Good night.	تسبح على خير.	tis·bah·la kheer
Goodbye.	بسلامة.	bi·slaa·ma

Mr	سي	see
Mrs	مدام	ma·daam
Miss	انيسة	aa·nee·sa

How are you?

شنوة حوالك؟ shnoo·wa haw·aa·lik

Fine, thanks. And you?

لا باس و انت؟ la·baas win·tee

What's your name?

شسمك؟   *shis·*mik

My name is ...

اسمي ...   *is·*mee ...

I'm pleased to meet you.

نتشرفو.   nit·sha·ra·*foo*

This is my ...	هاذا/هاذي ...	haa·dha/haa·dhee ... m/f
brother	خويا	*khoo·*ya
daughter	بنتي	*bin·*tee
father	بويا	*boo·*ya
friend	صاحبي	*saah·*bee m
	صاحبتي	saa·*hib·*tee f
husband	راجلي	*raaj·*lee
mother	امي	*u·*mee
sister	اختي	*ukh·*tee
son	ولدي	*wil·*dee
wife	مرتي	*mar·*tee
Here's my ...	هاذا ... متاعي.	haa·dha ... im·*taa·*'ee
What's your ...?	شنوة ... متاعك؟	*shnoo·*wa ... im·*taa·*'ik
address	اديسة	ad·*ree·*sa
email address	يميل	ee·*mayl*
phone number	نومرو تلفون	*noom·*roo tel·*foon*
Where are you from?	انت منين؟	*in·*tee mi·*neen*
I'm from ...	انا من ...	*aa·*na min ...
Australia	استراليا	as·*traa·*lee·ya
Canada	كندا	*ka·*na·da
New Zealand	نيوزيلاندا	noo zee·*lan·*da
the UK	المملكة المتحدة	il·*mam·*la·ka il·moo·*ta·*hi·da
the USA	الولايات المتحدة	il·wu·*lay·aat* il·moo·*ta·*hi·da
What's your occupation?	فاش تخدم؟	faash *tikh·*dim

I'm a/an ...	... انا نخدم	aa·na nikh·dim ...
businessperson	راجل عمال	raa·jil 'um·aal
office worker	موظف/	moo·wadh·af/
	موظفة	moo·wadh·fa m/f
tradesperson	صناعي/	sa·naa·'ee/
	صنابة	sa·naa·'ee·ya m/f

Do you like ...?	...؟ نحب	te·heb ...
I (don't) like ...	(ما) نحبش ...	(ma) in·heb·ish ...
art	فن	fan
movies	سينيما	see·nee·ma
music	موسيقى	moo·see·ka
reading	قراء	ki·raa
sport	سبور	spor

eating out

Can you	تنحمشي	it·na·jam·shee
recommend a ...?	تنصحني ...؟	tin·sah·nee ...
bar	بار	baar
café	قهوة	kah·wa
restaurant	مطعم	ma·ta'm

I'd like ..., please.	نحب ...	in·heb ...
a table for (four)	طاولة (أربعة)	taa·wi·la (lar·ba')
	برسون	per·son
the (non)smoking	بلاصة (ممنوع)	blaa·sa (mam·noo·a')
section	تدخين	tad·kheen

breakfast	فطور الصباح	if·toor is·bah m
lunch	الفطور	if·toor m
dinner	العشاء	la·shaa m

What would you recommend?

شنوة تنصح به؟ shnoo·wa tin·sah bee

What's the local speciality?

شنية الماكلة محلية؟ shnee·ya il·maa·ki·la mah·lee·ya

What's that?

شنوة هاذا؟ shnoo·wa haa·dha

I'd like (the) ..., please.	بريني جيبلي ...	*brab·ee jeeb·lee* ...
bill	الحسبة	*il·his·ba*
drink list	قائمة	*kaa·im·at*
	المشروبات	*il·mash·roo·baat*
menu	المنو	*il·me·noo*
that dish	الصحن هاذاكا	*i·sa·han haa·dhee·ka*

drinks

I'll have ...	... ناخذ	*naa·kudh* ...

I'll buy you a drink.

نشريلك مشروبة.   *nish·ree·lik mash·roo·ba*

What would you like?

اش تشرب؟   *aash tush·rub*

(cup of) coffee ...	(كاس) قهوة ...	*(kaas) kah·wa* ...
(cup of) tea ...	(كاس) تاي ...	*(kaas) tay* ...
with milk	بالحليب	*bil·ha·leeb*
without sugar	بلاش سكر	*blaash su·kur*

(orange) juice	عصير (برقدان)	*'a·seer (bor·ge·daan)* m
soft drink	قزوز	*ga·zooz* m

... water	ما ...	*maa* ...
boiled	مغلي	*mugh·lee*
mineral	معدني	*ma'd·nee*

a bottle/glass of beer	دبوزة/كاس بيرة	*da·boo·za/kaas bee·ra*
a shot of whisky	ويسكي	*wee·skee*

a bottle/glass	دبوزة/كاس	*da·boo·za/kaas*
of ... wine	الشراب ...	*shraab* ...
red	احمر	*ah·mir*
sparkling	بالغاز	*bil·gaaz*
white	ابيض	*ab·yadh*

special diets & allergies

Is there a vegetarian restaurant near here?
فم مطعم فجتاريان قريب؟   fa·ma ma·*ta'm* ve·je·taar·*yaan* kreeb

Do you have ...	عندكمشي	'and·*kum*·shee
food?	ماكلة ...؟	maa·ki·la ...
halal	حلال	ha·*laal*
vegetarian	فجتاريان	ve·je·taar·*yaan*
Could you	تنجمشي طيبلي	it·na·*jam*·shee ta·*yib*·lee
prepare a meal	ماكلة بلاش ...؟	maa·ki·la blaash ...
without ...?		
butter	زيدة	*zib*·da
eggs	عضم	'·*dham*
meat stock	مرقة باللهم	mar·ka bil·*ham*
I'm allergic to ...	عندي	'·*and*·ee
	حساسية ل ...	ha·saa·*see*·ya ll ...
dairy produce	الحليب و	il·ha·*leeb* oo
	مشتقاته	mush·ta·*kaa*·too
gluten	قمح	*ka*·mah
nuts	لوز	looz
seafood	فرو د مار	froo·de·*maar*

emergencies

Help!	نجدة!	*naj*·da
Stop!	اقف!	*aa*·kif
Go away!	ابعد عليا!	i·ba'd·'a·*lay*·a
Thief!	سارق!	*saa*·rik
Fire!	حريقة!	ha·*ree*·ka
Watch out!	رد بالك!	rud *baal*·ik
Call ...!	كلملي...!	ka·*lem*·lee ...
a doctor	طبيب	ta·*beeb*
an ambulance	اميولانس	am·boo·*lans*
the police	الشرطة	i·*shur*·ta

Could you help me, please?

تنجمشي تعاوني؟   it·na·*jam*·shee t'aa·*wu*·nee

I have to use the phone.

يلزمني نعمل تلفون   yel·*zim*·nee n'a·mel til·*foon*

I'm lost.

انا ضعت.   *aa*·na dhu't

Where are the toilets?

وين التوالت؟   ween it·*wol*·et

Where's the police station?

وين مركز الشرطة؟   ween *mar*·kaz i·*shur*·ta

I want to report an offence.

نحب نخبرك على محظر.   in·*heb* in·kha·ba·rik 'a·la *mah*·dher

I have insurance.

عندي اسورانس   'and·ee a·sur·*ans*

I want to contact my embassy.

نحب نتكلم سفارتي.   in·*heb* it·ka·lam si·*far*·tee

I've been ...	... فم شكون	*fa*·ma shkoon ...
assaulted	ضربني	dhar·*boo*·nee
raped	اغتصبني	igh·*ta*·sab·nee
robbed	سرقني دباشي	se·*rik*·nee de·*baa*·shee
I've lost my ...	... طحت مني.	... tuht *min*·ee
My ... was/were stolen.	... سرقولي.	sir·*koo*·lee ...
bag	ساك	saak
credit card	كرت كريدي	kart kre·*dee*
money	فلوس	floos
passport	باسبور	pas·*por*
travellers cheques	شيكات سياحية	shee·*kaat* say·aa·*hee*·ya

health

Where's the nearest ...?	وين الاقرب ...؟	ween lak·rab ...
dentist	دنتيست	don·teest
doctor	طبيب/طبيبة	ta·beeb/ta·bee·ba m/f
hospital	صبيطار	sbee·taar
(night)	صيدلية	say·da·lee·ya
pharmacist	(محلولة في)	(mah·loo·la fee leel)

I need a doctor (who speaks English).

حاجتي بطبيب/بطبيبة (اللي
يتكلم/تتكلم انجليزية).

haaj·tee bi·ta·beeb/bi·ta·bee·ba (il·ee
yil·kal·im/tit·kal·im bil·in·glee·zee·ya) m/f

Could I see a female doctor?

نحب نشوف طبيبة؟

in·heb in·shoof ta·bee·ba

I've run out of my medication.

وفالي دوا.

oo·faa·lee dwaa

I'm sick.

انا مريض.

aa·na im·reedh

It hurts here.

يوجعني هوني.

yoo·ja'·nee hoo·nee

I have (a) ...	انا مريض ب ...	aa·na im·reedh bi ...
asthma	الفدة	il·fa·da
constipation	الامساك	lim·saak
diarrhoea	الاسهال	lis·haal
fever	السخانة	is·khaa·na
headache	راسي يوجع فيا	raa·see yoo·ja' fee·ya
heart condition	القلب	il·kalb
nausea	الردانة	il·ru·daa·na
pain	وجيع	oo·jee·a'
sore throat	القرجومة	il·gar·joo·ma
toothache	الاسنان	lis·naan

I'm allergic to ...	عندي حساسية ل ...	'and·ee ha·saa·see·ya li ...
antibiotics	انتي بيوتيك	on·tee bee·yo·teek
anti-inflammatories	انتي فلاماتوار	on·tee fla·ma·twaar
aspirin	اسبيرين	as·pi·reen
bees	نحل	na·hal
penicillin	بنيسيلين	pen·ee·si·lin

english–tunisian arabic dictionary

Words in this dictionary are marked as n (noun), a (adjective), v (verb), sg (singular), pl (plural), ⓜ (masculine) and ⓕ (feminine) where necessary. Verbs are given in the present tense in the third-person singular ('he/she'), in both masculine and feminine forms.

A

accident اكسيدان *ak-si-don* ⓜ
accommodation سكن *skan* ⓜ
adaptor اداپتاتور *a-dap-ta-tur* ⓜ
address n ادريسة *a-dree-sa* ⓕ
after بعد *ba'd*
air-conditioned بالاكليماتيسر *bil-ak-lee-ma-tee-ser*
airplane طيارة *tay-aa-ra* ⓕ
airport مطار *ma-taar* ⓜ
alcohol الكول *al-kool* ⓜ
all كل *kul*
allergy حساسية *ha-saa-see-ya* ⓕ
ambulance اميولانس *am-boo-lans* ⓜ
and و *wi*
ankle كعبة *ka'-ba* ⓕ
arm يد *yid* ⓜ
ashtray طقطوقة *tak-too-ka* ⓕ
ATM دستريبوتور *dis-tri-boo-tur* ⓜ

B

baby صغير/صغيرة *sgheer/sghee-ra* ⓜ/ⓕ
back (body) ضهر *dhe-har* ⓜ
backpack سكادو *sak-a-do* ⓜ
bad خيب/خيبة *khai-yib/khai-ba* ⓜ/ⓕ
bag ساك *sak* ⓜ
baggage claim ايداع الامتعة *ee-daa' al-im-ti-'a* ⓜ
bank بنكة *ban-ka* ⓕ
bar بار *baar* ⓜ
bathroom بيت بانو *beet ba-noo* ⓜ
battery بيلة *pee-la* ⓕ
beautiful مزيان/مزيانة *miz-yaan/miz-yaa-na* ⓜ/ⓕ
bed فرش *farsh* ⓜ
beer بيرة *bee-ra* ⓕ
before قبال ما *ke-bal ma*
behind ورا *we-ra*
bicycle بيسكلات *bees-klaat* ⓕ
big كبير/كبيرة *ke-beer/ke-bee-ra* ⓜ/ⓕ
bill حسبة *his-ba* ⓕ
black اكحل/كحلة *ak-hil/kah-la* ⓜ/ⓕ
blanket فرشية *far-a-shee-ya* ⓕ
blood group نوع دم *noo-wa' dam* ⓜ
blue ازرق/زرقة *az-rak/zar-ka* ⓜ/ⓕ

boat فلوكة *floo-ka* ⓕ
book (make a reservation) v يحجز *yah-jiz/tah-jiz* ⓜ/ⓕ
bottle دابوزة *da-boo-za* ⓕ
bottle opener حلال الدابوزة *ha-laal id-da-boo-za* ⓜ
boy ولد *oo-lad* ⓜ
brakes (car) فرينوات *free-noo-waat* ⓜ
breakfast فطور الصباح *fe-toor is-sbah* ⓜ
broken (faulty) مكسر/مكسرة *im-kas-ar/im-kas-ra* ⓜ/ⓕ
bus كار *kaar* ⓕ
business خدمة *khid-ma* ⓕ
buy يشري/تشري *yish-ree/tish-ree* ⓜ/ⓕ

C

café قهوة *kah-wa* ⓕ
camera مصورة *moo-saw-ra* ⓕ
camp site كمپين *kom-peen* ⓜ
cancel يلغي/تلغي *yul-ghee/tul-ghee* ⓜ/ⓕ
can opener حلالة حكة *ha-laa-lat hu-ka* ⓕ
car كرهبة *kar-ha-ba* ⓕ
cash n فلوس *floos* ⓜ
cash (a cheque) v يصرف/تصرف *yi-sar-if/ti-sar-if* ⓜ/ⓕ
cell phone پورتابل *por-taa-bel* ⓜ
centre n وسط *wist* ⓜ
change (money) v يصرف/تصرف *yi-sar-if/ti-sar-if* ⓜ/ⓕ
cheap رخيص/رخيصة *re-khees/re-khee-sa* ⓜ/ⓕ
check (bill) حسبة *his-ba* ⓕ
check-in n مراقبة *moo-raa-ki-ba* ⓕ
chest صدر *is-dir* ⓜ
child ولد/بناية *oo-lid/bnay-a* ⓜ/ⓕ
cigarette سيڤارو *si-gaa-roo* ⓜ
city مدينة *im-dee-na* ⓕ
clean a نظيف/نظيفة *in-dheef/in-dhee-fa* ⓜ/ⓕ
closed مسكر/مسكرة *msa-kar/msa-ka-ra* ⓜ/ⓕ
coffee قهوة *kah-wa* ⓕ
coins صرف *sarf* ⓜ
cold بارد/باردة *baa-rid/baar-da* ⓜ/ⓕ
collect call مكلمة بي سي في *moo-kal-ma pay say vay* ⓕ
come يجي/تجي *yi-jee/ti-jee* ⓜ/ⓕ

computer كمبيوتر or-di-na-*tur* ⓜ
condom واقي ذكري/بريسرفاتيف pre-ser-va-*teef* ⓜ
contact lenses عدسات لاصقة
len-*teel* de *kon*-takt ⓜ
cook v يطيب/تطيب yit-*tai*-yib/tit-*tai*-yib ⓜ/①
cost n سوم soom ⓜ
credit card كرت كريدي kart kre-*dee* ⓜ
cup كاس kaas ⓜ
currency exchange صرف se-*raf* ⓜ
customs (immigration) ديوان dee-*waan* ⓜ

D

dangerous خطير/خطيرة
khe-*teer*/khe-*tee*-ra ⓜ/①
date (time) تاريخ taa-*reekh* ⓜ
day نهار in-*haar* ⓜ
delay n وخر wa-*khir* ⓜ
dentist دنتيست don-*teest* ⓜ & ①
depart يمشي/تمشي yim-*shee*/tim-*shee* ⓜ/①
diaper كوش koosh ⓜ
dictionary منجد mun-*jid* ⓜ
dinner عشاء 'ash-*aa* ⓜ
direct ديركت dee-*rekt*
dirty مسخ/مسخة mas-*akh*/mas-*kha* ⓜ/①
disabled عاجز/عاجزة 'a-*jiz*/'uj-*za* ⓜ/①
discount n انخفاض in-*khif-aadh* ⓜ
doctor طبيب/طبيبة te-*beeb*/te-bee-*ba* ⓜ/①
double bed فرش بالاستين farsh bi-*blaas*-teen ⓜ
double room بيت لزوز من ناس
beet li-*zooz* min naas ①
drink n شربة shar-ba ①
drive v يسوق/تسوق yi-*sook*/ti-*sook* ⓜ/①
drivers licence بطاقة السوس
bi-*taa*-kat a-see-*waa*-ka ①
drug (illicit) دروق droog ⓜ
dummy (pacifier) سوست . soo-*set* ⓜ

E

ear ودن wi-*dhin* ⓜ
east شرق shark ⓜ
eat ياكل/تاكل yaa-*kil*/taa-*kil* ⓜ/①
economy class درجة الثانية daar-ja a-thaan-ya ①
electricity ضو dhaw ⓜ
elevator اسنسر a-son-*sur* ⓜ
email ميل ee-*mayl* ⓜ
embassy سفارة si-faa-ra ①
emergency طاري taa-ree-'a ⓜ
English (language) الجليزية in-glee-*zee*-ya ①
entrance دخول du-*khool* ⓜ
evening ليل leel ⓜ

exchange rate شانج كورد kor de shanj ⓜ
exit n خروج khu-*rooj* ⓜ
expensive غالي/غالية ghuu-*lee*/ghaa-*lee*-ya ⓜ/①
express mail بريد السريع 'ba-*reed* is-*sar*-ee ⓜ
eye عين 'een ⓜ

F

far بعيد/بعيدة ba-'*eed*/ba-'*ee*-da ⓜ/①
fast سريع/سريعة si-*ree*-a'/si-*ree*-'a ⓜ/①
father بو boo ⓜ
film (camera) فلم feelm ⓜ
finger اصبع is-*boo*-a' ①
first-aid kit صندوق السعف sun-*dook* is-sa-'*af* ⓜ
first class درجة الولة daar-ja loo-la ①
fish n حوت hoot ⓜ
food ماكلة maa-kla ①
foot ساق saak ⓜ
fork فرقيطة far-*gee*-ta ①
free (of charge) بلاش blaash
friend صاحب/صاحبة
saa-heb/*sah*-ha ⓜ/①
fruit غلة ghal-la ①
full معبي/معبية m'ab-ee/m'ab-ee-ya ⓜ/①
funny ضحك/ضحكة dha-*hik*/dhah-ka ⓜ/①

G

gift هدية ih-*dee*-ya ①
girl طفلة tuf-la ①
glass (drinking) كاس kaas ⓜ
glasses (eyesight) مرايات mray-*yaat* ①
go يمشي/تمشي yim-*shee*/tim-*shee* ⓜ/①
good باهي/باهية baa-hee/baa-hee-ya ⓜ/①
green اخضر/اخضرة akh-dher/khadh-ra ⓜ/①
guide n فيد geed ⓜ & ①

H

half n شطر ish-*taar* ⓜ
hand يد yid ①
handbag سك sak ①
happy فرحان/فرحانة fir-*haan*/fir-*haa*-na ⓜ/①
have عند 'and
he هو hoo-wa
head راس raas ⓜ
heart قلب galb ⓜ
heat n سخانة is-*khaa*-na ①
heavy زين/زينة ir-*zeen*/ir-*zee*-na ⓜ/①
help v يعاين/تعاون yi-'*aa*-win/ti-'*aa*-win ⓜ/①
here هوني hoo-nee
high عالي/عالية 'aa-*lee*/'aa-*lee*-ya ⓜ/①

highway اوطوروت *aw*-taw-root ⓜ
hike v يمشي/تمشي *yim-shee/tim-shee* ⓜ/ⓕ
holiday كوجي *koon-jee* ⓜ
homosexual لوطي *loo-tee* ⓜ
hospital صبيطار *sbee-taar* ⓜ
hot سخون/سخونة *is-khoon/skhoo-na* ⓜ/ⓕ
hotel وطيل *oo-teel* ⓜ
hungry جيعان/جيعانة *jee-'aan/jee-'aa-na* ⓜ/ⓕ
husband راجل *raa-jil* ⓜ

I

I انا *aa-na*
identification (card) بطاقة تعريف
bi-*taa-*ka ta-*'reef*
ill مريض/مريضة *im-reedh/im-ree-dha* ⓜ/ⓕ
important هم/همة *ham/ha-ma* ⓜ/ⓕ
included داخلة *daa-khi-la*
injury جرح *jurh* ⓜ
insurance اسيورانس *as-yoo-rans* ⓜ
internet انترنت *in-ter-net* ⓜ
interpreter مترجم/مترجمة
moo-taar-jim/moo-taarj-ma ⓜ/ⓕ

J

jewellery صياغة *see-yaa-gha* ⓕ
job خدمة *khid-ma* ⓕ

K

key مفتاح *mif-taah* ⓜ
kilogram كيلو *kee-loo* ⓜ
kitchen كوجينة *koo-jee-na* ⓕ
knife سكينة *sik-kee-na* ⓕ

L

laundry (place) بلاصة صابون *blaa-*sat *is-sa-boon* ⓕ
lawyer محامي/محامية
mo-haa-mee/mo-haa-mee-ya ⓜ/ⓕ
left (direction) ليسار *lee-saar*
left-luggage office باقاجاري *ba-gaa-jaa-ree* ⓜ
leg ساق *saak* ⓜ
lesbian ساحاقية *sa-haa-kee-ya* ⓕ
less اقل *a-kal*
letter (mail) جواب *je-waab* ⓜ
lift (elevator) اسنسر *a-son-sur* ⓜ
light n ضو *dhaw* ⓜ
like v يحب/تحب *yi-hib/ti-hib* ⓜ/ⓕ
lock n كوبة *koo-ba* ⓕ

long طويل/طويلة *tweel/twee-la* ⓜ/ⓕ
lost مضيع/مضيعة
im-*dhee-*ya'/im-*dhee-*ya'a ⓜ/ⓕ
lost-property office مفر ضيع الامتعة
ma-*kar dhee-*ya' al-im-ti-*'a*
love v يحب/تحب *yi-hib/ti-hib* ⓜ/ⓕ
luggage بقاج *bag-gaaj* ⓜ
lunch فطور *fe-toor* ⓜ

M

mail بوسطة *boo-sta* ⓕ
man راجل *raa-jil* ⓜ
map خريطة *khaa-ree-ta* ⓕ
market مرشي *mar-shee* ⓜ
matches وقيد *oo-keed* ⓜ
meat لحم *il-ham* ⓜ
medicine دوا *da-waa* ⓜ
menu مينو *mee-noo* ⓜ
message وسيعة *oo-see-a'* ⓕ
milk حليب *he-leeb* ⓜ
minute دقيقة *de-kee-ka* ⓕ
mobile phone بورتابل *por-taa-bel* ⓜ
money فلوس *floos* ⓜ
month شهر *she-har* ⓜ
morning صباح *se-baah* ⓜ
mother ام *um* ⓕ
motorcycle موطور *moo-toor* ⓜ
motorway اوطوروت *aw-taw-root* ⓜ
mouth فم *fum* ⓜ
music موسيقى *moo-see-ka* ⓕ

N

name اسم *ism* ⓜ
napkin منديلة *man-dee-la* ⓕ
nappy كوش *koosh* ⓜ
near كريب/قريبة *kreeb/kree-ba* ⓜ/ⓕ
neck رقبة *rak-ba* ⓕ
new جديد/جديدة *je-deed/je-dee-da* ⓜ/ⓕ
news خبار *khe-baar* ⓜ
newspaper جريدة *je-ree-da* ⓕ
night الليلة *lee-la* ⓕ
no لا *x la*
noisy برشة حس *bar-sha his*
nonsmoking منوع تدخين
mam-*noo-*wa' tad-*kheen*
north شمال *she-maal* ⓜ
nose خشم *khe-sham* ⓜ
now توة *taw-wa*
number نومرو *noom-roo* ⓜ

O

oil (engine) زيت zeet ⓜ
old قديمة/قديم ke-deem/ke-dee-ma ⓜ/ⓕ
one-way ticket تذكرة ماشي برك
tiz-ki-ra maa-shee bark ⓕ
open a محلولة/محلول
mah-lool/mah-loo-la ⓜ/ⓕ
outside برة ber-ra

P

package كولي koo-lee ⓜ
paper ورقة war-ka ⓕ
park (car) v بوقف/توقف
yi-wak-kif/ti-wak-kif ⓜ/ⓕ
passport باسبور pas-por ⓜ
pay v يخلص/تخلص yi-khal-is/ti-khal-is ⓜ/ⓕ
pen ستيلو stee-loo ⓜ
petrol قاز gaaz ⓜ
pharmacy صيدلية say-da-lee-ya ⓕ
phonecard كارت متاع تلفون kart im-taa' tel-foon ⓕ
photo تصويرة tas-wee-ra ⓕ
plate صحن is-han ⓜ
police بوليسية boo-lee-see-ya ⓕ
postcard كرت بوستال kart po-staal ⓜ
post office بوسطة boo-sta ⓕ
pregnant حبلة heb-la ⓕ
price سوم soom ⓜ

Q

quiet رايض/رايضة ray-idh/ray-dha ⓜ/ⓕ

R

rain n شتا ish-taa ⓜ
razor موس moos ⓜ
receipt n توصيل taw-seel ⓜ
red احمر/حمرة ah-mir/ham-ra ⓜ/ⓕ
refund n ارجع لي فلوسي re-ja'-lee floo-see ⓜ
registered mail بريد مسجل ba-reed moo-sa-jil ⓜ
rent v يكري/تكري yik-ree/tik-ree ⓜ/ⓕ
repair v يصلي/تصلي yi-sal-lee/ti-sal-lee ⓜ/ⓕ
reservation حجز hu-juz ⓜ
restaurant مطعم mat-'am ⓜ
return v يرجع/ترجع yar-ja'/tar-ja' ⓜ/ⓕ
return ticket تذكرة ماشي و جاي
tiz-ki-ra maa-shee oo jay ⓕ

S

safe a سالم/سالمة saa-lim/saal-ma ⓜ/ⓕ
sanitary napkin فوطة صحية foo-ta se-hee-ya ⓕ
seat بلاصة blaa-sa ⓕ
send v يبعث/تبعث yab-'ith/tab-'ith ⓜ/ⓕ
service station كيوسك kee-yosk ⓜ
sex جنس jins ⓜ
shampoo شمبوان shamp-wan ⓜ
share (a dorm etc) يشارك/تشارك
yi-shaa-rik/ti-shaa-rik ⓜ/ⓕ
shaving cream صبون متاع حجامة
sa-boon im-taa' ha-jaa-ma ⓜ
she هي hee-ya
sheet (bed) ملحفة mel-ha-fa ⓕ
shirt سورية soo-ree-ya ⓕ
shoes صباط sa-baat ⓜ
shop n حنوت ha-noot ⓜ
short قصيرة/قصير ke-seer/ke-see-ra ⓜ/ⓕ
shower n دوش doosh ⓜ
single room بيت للواحد beet lil-waa-hid ⓜ
skin جلدة jil-da ⓕ
skirt جوب joop ⓕ
sleep v يرقد/ترقد yur-kud/tur-kud ⓜ/ⓕ
slowly بشوية bi-shway-ya
small صغير/صغيرة se-gheer/se-ghee-ra ⓜ/ⓕ
smoke (cigarettes) v يتكيف/تتكيف
yit-kay-if/tit-kay-if ⓜ/ⓕ
soap صابون sa-boon ⓜ
some شوية shway-ya
soon قرب kreeb
south جنوب je-noob ⓜ
souvenir shop داكر متاع حنوت
ha-noot im-taa' ta-dhaa-kir ⓜ
speak v يتكلم/تتكلم yit-kal-lim/tit-kal-lim ⓜ/ⓕ
spoon مغرفة im-ghar-fa ⓕ
stamp تنبري tin-bree ⓜ
stand-by ticket تذكرة الانتظار
tiz-ki-rat lin-tee-dhaar ⓕ
station (train) محطة im-hat-ta ⓕ
stomach كرش kirsh ⓜ
stop v يوقف/نوقف yi wak-kif/ti-wak-kif ⓜ/ⓕ
stop (bus) محطة الكار im-hat-at il-kaar ⓕ
street شارع shaa-ra' ⓜ
student طالب/طالبة taa-lib/taa-li-ba ⓜ/ⓕ

sun شمس shams ⓕ
sunscreen كريمة ضد الشمس
kree-ma dud ish-*shams* ⓕ
swim v يعوم/تعوم yi-*'oom*/ti-*'oom* ⓜ/ⓕ

T

tampons تمبكس *tam*-paks ⓜ
taxi تكسي tak-*see* ⓕ
teaspoon مغرفة قهوة im-*ghar*-fit *kah*-wa ⓕ
teeth اسنان as-*naan* ⓕ
telephone n تلفون tel-*foon* ⓜ
television تلفزة tal-va-za ⓕ
temperature (weather) حرارة he-*raa*-ra ⓕ
tent خيمة *khee*-ma ⓕ
that (one) هاذاك/هاذيك
haa-*dhaa*-ka/haa-*dhee*-ka ⓜ/ⓕ
they هوم *hoo*-ma ⓜ&ⓕ
thirsty عطشان/عطشانة
'ut-shaan/*'ut*-shaa-na ⓜ/ⓕ
this (one) هاذا/هاذي haa-*dha*/haa-*dhee* ⓜ/ⓕ
throat قرجومة gar-*joo*-ma ⓕ
ticket تذكرة *tiz*-ki-ra ⓕ
time وقت wokt ⓜ
tired طايب/طايبة taa-*'ib*/taa-*'i*-ba ⓜ/ⓕ
tissues كلينكس klee-*neks* ⓕ
today النهار in-*haar* ⓜ
toilet توالت twa-*let* ⓜ
tomorrow غدوة *ghud*-wa
tonight الليلة al-*lee*-la ⓕ
toothbrush فرشة الاسنان *fer*-shat las-*naan* ⓕ
toothpaste دنتيفريس don-*tee*-frees ⓜ
torch (flashlight) مصباح mis-*bah* ⓜ
tour n جولة *jaw*-la ⓕ
tourist office مكتب السياحي
mak-tib a-*see*-*yaa*-hee ⓜ
towel منشفة *man*-sha-fa ⓕ
train ترينو *tree*-noo ⓜ
translate v يترجم/تترجم
yi-*tar*-jim/ti-*tar*-jim ⓜ/ⓕ
travel agency وكالة السفر we-*kaa*-lit a-*sa*-far ⓕ
travellers cheque شك سياحي
shek see-*yaa*-hee ⓜ
trousers سروال ser-*waal* ⓜ
twin beds زوز فرارش *zooz fraa*-rish ⓜ
tyre عجلة *'aj*-la ⓕ

U

underwear كلصون kal-*soon* ⓜ
urgent مستعجل/مستعجلة
mist-*'a*-jil/mist-*'aj*-la ⓜ/ⓕ

V

vacant فارغ/فارغة faa-*righ*/faa-*ri*-gha ⓜ/ⓕ
vacation كوني *koon*-jee ⓕ
vegetable n خضرة *khudh*-ra ⓕ
vegetarian a فجتاريان ve-je-taar-*yaan* ⓜ&ⓕ
visa فيزة *vee*-sa ⓕ

W

waiter قرصون gar-*soon* ⓜ
walk v يمشي/تمشي yim-*shee*/tim-*shee* ⓜ/ⓕ
wallet ستوش *stoosh* ⓜ
warm a دافعة daa-*fee'*/daa-*fee*-'a ⓜ/ⓕ
wash (something) يغسل/تغسل
yagh-*sel*/tagh-*sel* ⓜ/ⓕ
watch n منقالة mun-*gaa*-la ⓕ
water ما maa ⓜ
we احن *ah*-na
weekend سبت والاحد sibt wi-la-*had* ⓜ
west غرب gharb ⓜ
when وقتاش wok-*taash*
where وين ween ⓜ
white ابيض/بيضة ab-*yadh*/*bee*-dha ⓜ/ⓕ
who شكون shkoon
why علاش a-*laysh*
wife مرا *mra* ⓕ
window شباك shi-*baak* ⓜ
wine شراب shrab ⓜ
with مع ma'a
without بلاش blaash
woman مرا *mra* ⓕ
write v يكتب/تكتب yik-*tib*/tik-*tib* ⓜ/ⓕ

Y

yellow اصفر/صفرة as-*far*/*saf*-ra ⓜ/ⓕ
yes اي ay
yesterday البارح il-*baa*-rih
you sg انت in-*tee* ⓜ&ⓕ
you pl انتوما in-*too*-ma ⓜ&ⓕ

Farsi

word-final	word-medial	word-initial	alone	letter
‍ـا	‍ـا	‍ا	ا	alef
‍ـب	‍ـبـ	‍بـ	ب	be
‍ـپ	‍ـپـ	‍پـ	پ	pe
‍ـت	‍ـتـ	‍تـ	ت	te
‍ـث	‍ـثـ	‍ثـ	ث	se
‍ـج	‍ـجـ	‍جـ	ج	je
‍ـچ	‍ـچـ	‍چـ	چ	che
‍ـح	‍ـحـ	‍حـ	ح	he
‍ـخ	‍ـخـ	‍خـ	خ	khe
‍ـد	‍ـد	‍د	د	daal
‍ـذ	‍ـذ	‍ذ	ذ	zaal
‍ـر	‍ـر	‍ر	ر	re
‍ـز	‍ـز	‍ز	ز	ze
‍ـژ	‍ـژ	‍ژ	ژ	zhe
‍ـس	‍ـسـ	‍سـ	س	se
‍ـش	‍ـشـ	‍شـ	ش	she
‍ـص	‍ـصـ	‍صـ	ص	saad
‍ـض	‍ـضـ	‍ضـ	ض	zaad
‍ـط	‍ـطـ	‍طـ	ط	taa
‍ـظ	‍ـظـ	‍ظـ	ظ	zaa
‍ـع	‍ـعـ	‍عـ	ع	eyn
‍ـغ	‍ـغـ	‍غـ	غ	gheyn
‍ـف	‍ـفـ	‍فـ	ف	fe
‍ـق	‍ـقـ	‍قـ	ق	ghaaf
‍ـك	‍ـكـ	‍كـ	ك	kaaf
‍ـگ	‍ـگـ	‍گـ	گ	gaaf
‍ـل	‍ـلـ	‍لـ	ل	laam
‍ـم	‍ـمـ	‍مـ	م	meem
‍ـن	‍ـنـ	‍نـ	ن	noon
‍ـو	‍ـو	‍و	و	ve
‍ـه	‍ـهـ	‍هـ	ه	he
‍ـى	‍ـيـ	‍يـ	ى	ye

introduction

Did you know that 'Persian' and 'Farsi' (فارسی faar·see) are both names for the language of Iran? 'Persian' is commonly used in the West , but its native speakers call the language 'Farsi', a term which owes its existence to the Arab conquest of Iran in the 7th century. As Arabic doesn't have a 'p' sound, 'Pars' (originally the name of the southern Iranian province) became known as 'Fars' to the conquerors.

It might come as a surprise that Arabic and Farsi don't have the same roots. Farsi is an Indo-European language and belongs to the West Iranian branch of the Indo-Iranian language family. It's related to Kurdish, Baloshi and Pashto and, more distantly, Urdu. As the language of Iran, Afghanistan and Tajikistan, Farsi has around 70 million speakers, although only about 50 million claim it as their first language. The dialect of Farsi spoken in Afghanistan (known as Dari) is very similar to the standard Farsi of Iran, based on the speech of the capital Teheran. However, Tajik – the variety spoken in Tajikistan – has become quite different and is now usually considered a separate language.

The ancestor of modern Farsi is Old Persian, which was spoken by the Parsa tribe during the time of the Achaemenian Empire (550–300 BC). Related to Sanskrit, Old Persian was recorded in the cuneiform inscriptions of the time. It evolved into Middle Persian during the time of the Sassanian Empire (AD 220–650) , when it was written in Pahlavi script, a modified version of the Aramaic alphabet. After the Arab conquest, a huge number of words from Arabic entered Farsi's vocabulary. By the 9th century Modern Persian was emerging, and the Pahlavi script was replaced by Perso-Arabic script, based on the Arabic alphabet but with the addition of four letters to represent Farsi sounds that didn't occur in Arabic. Interestingly, Perso-Arabic script later served as the basis for Urdu's writing system. Farsi's influence on Hindi, Urdu and Bengali was huge, as it was the official language of the Islamic Mughal Empire in northern India from the 16th century until the establishment of the British Raj in the mid-19th century.

For arguably the best examples of Farsi's elegance, check out the mystical religious writings of Sufism and its rich stock of poetry by renowned authors like Rumi, Sa'di and Hafiz. The contact between Farsi and English over the centuries is reflected in a vast number of Farsi loanwords – from *arsenic* to *bezoar*, from *algorithm* and *chess* to *magic* and *serendipity*, from *baksheesh* and *bazaar* to *cheque* and *kiosk*, from *sandal* to *shawl*, and from *satrap* to *paradise* – a testament to the vitality of Persian culture through history.

vowel sounds

The vowel system in Farsi is fairly simple as it consists of only six vowels. Interestingly, all vowel sounds are represented by one letter – ا alef. In most cases you can only tell how to pronounce a vowel sound by its context. You don't need to worry about this though, as the correct pronunciation of each word or phrase is always given in our coloured pronunciation guides, next to the Arabic script throughout this chapter.

symbol	english equivalent	farsi example	transliteration
a	act	اسب	asb
aa	father	ماه	maah
e	bet	سه	se
ee	see	سیب	seeb
o	tone	گل	gol
oo	zoo	توپ	toop

word stress

Stress in Farsi is generally placed on the last syllable of a word – except for proper names, in which it falls on the first syllable (eg احمد *ah*·mad). You'll be fine if you follow our coloured pronunciation guides, in which the stressed syllable is always in italics.

consonant sounds

Most consonant sounds in Farsi are pronounced just like in English. You might need some practice with the gh and the kh – both are guttural sounds, pronounced at the back of the mouth. The glottal stop (marked in our pronunciation guides with an apostrophe) is pronounced in the throat, ie as a break in the flow of speech. Note also that if a consonant is written twice, it should be pronounced twice.

symbol	english equivalent	farsi example	transliteration
b	**b**ed	بز	boz
ch	**ch**eat	چوب	choob
d	**d**og	دست	dast
f	**f**un	فیل	feel
g	**g**o	گاو	gaav
gh	a guttural sound, like the Parisian French 'r'	قلب	ghalb
h	**h**at	هوا	ha·*vaa*
j	**j**ar	جو	jo
k	**k**it	کره	ka·*re*
kh	as the 'ch' in the Scottish *loch*	خر	khar
l	**l**ot	لب	lab
m	**m**an	مرد	mard
n	**n**ot	نان	naan
p	**p**et	پول	pool
r	**r**un (rolled)	رنگ	rang
s	**s**un	سر	sar
sh	**sh**ot	شیر	sheer
t	**t**op	تو	to
v	**v**ery	میوه	mee·*ve*
y	**y**es	یا	yaa
z	**z**ero	زبان	za·*baan*
zh	plea**s**ure	ژله	zhe·*le*
'	glottal stop (like the pause in the middle of 'uh-oh')	شمع	sham'

language difficulties

Do you speak English?

شما انگلیسی حرف می زنید؟

sho·*maa* een·gee·lee·*see* harf *mee*·za·need

Do you understand?

می فهمید؟

mee·fah·meed

I understand.

می فهمم.

mee·fah·mam

I don't understand.

من نمی فهم.

man ne·*mee*·fah·mam

Could you please speak more slowly?

لطفا یواشتر حرف بزنید؟

lot·*fan* ya·vaash·*tar* harf *be*·za·need

Could you	لطفا	lot·*fan*
please ...?	می توانید ...؟	*mee*·ta·vaa·need ...
repeat that	آن را تکرار	aan raa tek·*raar*
	بکنید	*be*·ko·need
write it down	آن را بنویسید	aan raa *be*·ne·vee·seed

numbers

0	صفر	sefr	20	بیست	beest	
1	یک	yek	30	سی	see	
2	دو	do	40	چهل	che·*hel*	
3	سه	se	50	پنجاه	pan·*jaah*	
4	چهار	chaa·*haar*	60	شصت	shast	
5	پنج	panj	70	هفتاد	haf·*taad*	
6	شش	shesh	80	هشتاد	hash·*taad*	
7	هفت	haft	90	نود	na·*vad*	
8	هشت	hasht	100	صد	sad	
9	نه	noh	1000	هزار	he·*zaar*	
10	ده	dah	1,000,000	یک میلیون	yek meel·*yon*	

For Arabic numerals, which are also used in Farsi, see the box on page 14.

time & dates

What time is it?	ساعت چنده؟	saa-'at chan-de
It's one o'clock.	ساعت یک هست.	saa-'at yek hast
It's (two) o'clock.	ساعت (دو) هست.	saa-'at (do) hast
Quarter past (two).	(دو) و ربع.	(do) vo rob'
Half past (two).	(دو) و نیم.	(do) vo neem
Quarter to (two).	یک ربع به (دو).	yek rob' be (do)
At what time ...?	چه ساعتی ...؟	che saa-'a-tee ...
At ...	در ...	dar ...

am	صبح	sobh
pm	بعد از ظهر	ba'd az zohr

Monday	دو شنبه	do shan·be
Tuesday	سه شنبه	se shan·be
Wednesday	چهار شنبه	chaa·haar shan·be
Thursday	پنج شنبه	panj shan·be
Friday	جمعه	jom·'e
Saturday	شنبه	shan·be
Sunday	یک شنبه	yek shan·be

last ...	... گذشته	...go·zash·te
next ...	... بعد	...ba'd
night	شب	shab
week	هفته	haf·te
month	ماه	maah
year	سال	saal

yesterday ...	... دیروز	dee·rooz ...
tomorrow ...	... فردا	far·daa ...
morning	صبح	sobh
afternoon	عصر	asr
evening	شب	shab

What date is it today?

امروز چه روزی هست؟   em·rooz che roo·zee hast

It's (15 December).

(پانزده دسامبر) هست.   (poonz·da·he de·saamr) hast

border crossing

I'm here ...	من اینجا ... هستم.	man een-*jaa* ... has-*tam*
in transit	برای عبور	ba-raa-ye oo-*boor*
on business	برای تجارت	ba-raa-ye te-jaa-*rat*
on holiday	برای تعطیلات	ba-raa-ye ta'-tee-*laat*

I'm here for ...	من اینجا	man een-*jaa*
	برای ... هستم.	ba-raa-ye ... has-*tam*
(10) days	(ده) روز	(dah) rooz
(three) weeks	(سه) هفته	(se) haf-*te*
(two) months	(دو) ماه	(do) maah

I'm going to (Karaj).
من به (کرج) می روم.
man be (ka-*raj*) *mee*-ra-vam

I'm staying at the (Homa hotel).
من در (هتل هما)
می مانم.
man dar (ho-*tel* ho-*maa*)
mee-maa-nam

I have nothing to declare.
من چیزی برای
اطلاع دادن ندارم.
man chee-*zee* ba-raa-ye
et-te-*laa'* daa-dan na-*daa*-ram

I have something to declare.
من چیزی برای
اطلاع دادن دارم.
man chee-*zee* ba-raa-ye
et-te-*laa'* daa-dan *daa*-ram

That's (not) mine.
اون مال من (نیست) هست.
oon maa-*le* man (neest) hast

tickets & luggage

Where can I buy a ticket?
من از کجا می توانم
بلیط بخرم؟
man az ko-jaa *mee*-too-nam
be-*leet* be-kha-ram

Do I need to book a seat?
لازم هست که جا رزرو کنم؟
laa-*zem* hast ke jaa re-*zerv* ko-nam

One ... ticket	یک بلیط ...	yek be-*leet* ...
(to Shiraz), please.	(به شیراز) لطفا.	(be shee-*raaz*) lot-*fan*
one-way	یک سره	yek sa-*re*
return	دو سره	do sa-*re*

I'd like to ...	لطفا من می خواهم	lot·*fan* man mee·khaam
my ticket, please.	بلیطم را ...	be·leet·*am* ro ...
cancel	کنسل کنم	kan·*sel* ko·nam
change	عوض کنم	a·*vaz* ko·nam
collect	بگیرم	be·gee·*ram*

I'd like a ...	لطفا من یک جای	lot·*fan* man yek jaa·ye
seat, please.	... می خواهم.	... mee·khaam
nonsmoking	غیر سیگاری	ghey·re see·gaa·*ree*
smoking	سیگاری	see·gaa·*ree*

Is there air conditioning?

تهویه مطبوع هست؟   tah·vee·ye·ye mat·*boo'* hast

Is there a toilet?

توالت هست؟   too·vaa·*let* hast

How long does the trip take?

مسافرت چقدر طول می کشد؟   mo·saa·fe·*rat* che·ghadr tool mee·ke·shad

Is it a direct route?

این راه مستقیم هست   een raah mos·ta·*gheem* hast

My luggage has been ...	بار من ... شده.	baa·re man ... sho·de
damaged	خراب	kha·*raab*
lost	گم	gom
stolen	دزدیده	doz·dee·de

transport

Where does the flight (to Shiraz) arrive/depart?

پرواز (شیراز) به کجا می آید/   par·vaa·ze (shee·*raaz*) be ko·jaa mee·yaa·yad/
از کجا حرکت می کند؟   az ko·jaa ha·re·*kat* mee·ko·nad

Is this the ...	این ... برای	een ... ba·raa·ye
to (Rasht)?	(رشت) هست؟	(rasht) hast
boat	کشتی	kesh·*tee*
bus	اتوبوس	oo·too·*boos*
plane	هواپیما	ha·vaa·pey·*maa*
train	قطار	gha·*taar*

What time's	اتوبوس ...	oo·too·boo·se ...
the ... bus?	کی هست؟	key hast
first	اول	av·val
last	آخر	aa·khar
next	بعدی	ba'·dee

How long will it be delayed?

اون چقدر تاخیر دارد؟	oon che·ghadr ta'·kheer daa·re

What station/stop is this?

این کدام ایستگاه هست؟	een koo·doom eest·gaah hast

Please tell me when we get to (Sari).

لطفا وقتی به (ساری)	lot·fan vagh·tee be (saa·ree)
می رسیم به من بگویید.	mee·re·seem be man be·goo·yeen

Is this seat available?

این جا خالی هست؟	een jaa khaa·lee hast

That's my seat.

اون جای من هست.	oon jaa·ye man hast

I'd like a taxi ...	من یک تاکسی	man yek taak·see
	برای ... می خواهم.	ba·raa·ye ... mee·khaam
at (9am)	(نه صبح)	(no·he sobh)
now	الان	a·laan
tomorrow	فردا	far·daa

How much is it to ...?

برای ... چقدر می شود؟	ba·raa·ye ... che·ghadr mee·she

Please take me to (this address).

لطفا من را (به این آدرس) ببر.	lot·fan man ro (be een aad·res) be·bar

Please put the meter on.

لطفا تاکسیمتر را روشن کن.	lot·fan taak·si·metr ro ro·shan kon

Please ...	لطفا ...	lot·fan ...
stop here	اینجا توقف کن	een·jaa ta·vagh·ghof kon
wait here	اینجا منتظر باش	een·jaa mon·ta·zer baash

I'd like to	من می خواهم	man mee·khaam
hire a ...	... یک کرایه کنم.	... yek·ke·raa·ye ko·nam
car	ماشین	maa·sheen
4WD	چهار دبلیو دی	chaa·haar daa·bel·yoo dee

with ...	... با	baa ...
a driver	راننده	raa·nan·de
air conditioning	تهویه مطبوع	tah·vee·ye ye mat·boo'

How much for	... کرایه	ke·raa·ye·ye ...
... hire?	چقدر می شود؟	che·ghadr mee·she
daily	روزانه	roo·zaa·ne
weekly	هفتگی	haf·te·gee

I need a mechanic.

من یک مکانیک لازم دارم.
man yek me·kaa·neek laa·zem daa·ram

I've run out of petrol.

من بنزین تمام کرده ام.
man ben·zeen ta·moom kar·dam

I have a flat tyre.

چرخم پنچر شده.
char·kham pan·char sho·de

directions

Where's the ...?	... کجاست؟	... ko·jaast
bank	بانک	baank
market	بازار	baa·zaar
post office	اداره پست	e·daa·re·ye post

Is this the road to (Enghelab)?

این راه به (انقلاب) می رود؟
een raah be (en·ghe·laab) mee·re

Can you show me (on the map)?

می توانید (در نقشه) به
من نشان بدهید؟
mee·too·neen (dar nagh·she) be
man ne·shun be·deen

What's the address?

آدرس اش چی هست؟
aad·re·sesh chee hast

How far is it?

تا اونجا چقدر راه هست؟
taa oon·jaa che·ghadr raah hast

How do I get there?

چطور به اونجا بروم؟
che·tor be oon·jaa be·ram

Turn left/right.

بپیچ چپ/راست.
be·peech chap/raast

It's ...	اون ... هست.	oon ... hast
behind ...	پشت ...	posh·te ...
in front of ...	جلوی ...	je·lo·ye ...
near to ...	نزدیک ...	naz·dee·ke ...
next to ...	کنار ...	ke·naa·re ...
on the corner	گوشه	goo·she·ye
opposite ...	مقابل ...	mo·ghaa·be·le ...
straight ahead	مستقیم	mos·ta·gheem
there	اونجا	oon·jaa

north	شمال	sho·maal
south	جنوب	joo·noob
east	شرق	shargh
west	غرب	gharb

accommodation

Where's a ...?	... کجاست؟	... ko·jaast
camping ground	محل چادر زدن	ma·hal·le chaa·dor za·dan
guesthouse	مهمان پذیر	meh·maan·pa·zeer
hotel	هتل	ho·tel

Can you recommend somewhere ...?	می توانین جایی ... پیشنهاد کنید؟	mee·too·neen jaa·yee ... peesh·na·haad ko·neen
cheap	ارزان	ar·zoon
good	خوب	khoob
nearby	نزدیک	naz·deek

Do you have a ... room?	... شما اتاق دارید؟	sho·maa o·taa·ghe ... daa·reen
single	یک خوابه	yek khaa·be
double	دو خوابه	do khaa·be
twin	دو نفره	do na·fa·re

How much is it per ...?	برای هر ... چقدر هست؟	ba·raa·ye har ... che·ghadr hast
night	شب	shab
person	نفر	na·far

I'd like to book a room, please.
لطفا می خواهم یک اتاق رزرو کنم .
lot·fan mee·khaam yek o·taagh re·zerv ko·nam

I have a reservation.
من رزرو کرده ام.
man re·zerv kar·dam

I'd like to stay for (two) nights.
من می خواهم (دو) شب بمانم.
man mee·khaam (do) shab be·moo·nam

Am I allowed to camp here?
من اجازه دارم اینجا چادر بزنم؟
man e·jaa·ze daa·ram een·jaa chaa·dor be·za·nam

Could I have my key, please?
میشه لطفا کلیدم را بدهید؟
mee·she lot·fan ke·lee·dam ro be·deen

Can I get another (blanket)?
می توانم (پتوی) دیگربگیرم؟
mee·too·nam (pa·too) ye dee·ge be·gee·ram

The (air conditioning) doesn't work.
(تهویه مطبوع) کار نمی کند.
(tah·vee·ye·ye mat·boo') kaar ne·mee·ko·ne

This (sheet) isn't clean.
این (ملافه) تمیز نیست.
een (ma·laa·fe) ta·meez neest

| Is there an elevator/a safe? | اینجا آسانسور/ گاو صندوق هست؟ | een·jaa aa·saan·sor/ gaav·san·doogh hast |

What time is checkout?
وقت تخلیه اتاق کی هست؟
vagh·te takh·lee·ye·ye o·taagh key hast

Could I have my ..., please?	لطفا میشه ... ام را بگیرم؟	lot·fan mee·she ... am ro be·gee·ram
deposit	بیعانه	be·yaa·ne
passport	پاسپورت	paas·port
valuables	اشیای قیمتی	ash·yaa·ye ghey·ma·tee

banking & communications

Where's a/an ...?	... کجاست؟	... ko·*jaast*
ATM	خود پرداز	khod·par·*daaz*
foreign exchange office	صرافی	sar·raa·*fee*

I'd like to ...	من می خواهم به ...	man *mee*·khaam be ...
arrange a transfer	پول بفرستم	pool be·fe·res·tam
cash a cheque	چک نقد کنم	chek naghd *ko*·nam
change a travellers cheque	چک مسافرتی نقد کنم	che·ke mo·saa·fe·ra·tee naghd *ko*·nam
change money	پول خرد کنم	pool khord *ko*·nam
withdraw money	پول بگیرم	pool be·gee·ram

What's the ...?	... چی هست؟	... chee hast
charge for that	خرج اش	khar·*jesh*
exchange rate	نرخ ارز	ner·*khe* arz

Where's the local internet café?

کافی نت محلی کجاست؟   kaa·*fee* ne·te ma·hal·lee ko·jaast

How much is it per hour?

برای هر ساعت   ba·raa·ye har saa·'at
چقدر می شود؟   che·ghadr *mee*·she

I'd like to ...	می خواهم ...	*mee*·khaam ...
check my email	ایمیل ام را چک کنم	ee·*mey*·lam ro chek *ko*·nam
get internet access	اینترنت را بگیرم	een·ter·net ro be·gee·ram
use a printer	از پرینتر استفاده کنم	az pee·reen·ter es·te·faa·de *ko*·nam
use a scanner	از اسکنر استفاده کنم	az es·ka·ner es·te·faa·de *ko*·nam

I'd like a ...	من ... می خواهم.	man ... *mee*·khaam
mobile/cell phone for hire	تلفن همراه برای کرایه	te·le·fo·ne ham·*raah* ba·raa·ye ke·raa·ye
SIM card for your network	سیم کارت برای شبکه تون	seem kaart ba·raa·ye sha·ba·ke·toon

What's your phone number?

شماره تلفن تون چنده؟   sho·maa·*re*·ye te·le·fo·*ne*·toon *chan*·de

The number is ...

شماره ... هست.   sho·maa·*re* ... hast

Where's the nearest public phone?

نزدیکترین تلفن   naz·deek·ta·*reen* te·le·fo·*ne*
عمومی کجاست؟   oo·moo·*mee* ko·jaast

I'd like to buy a phonecard.

می خواهم یک کارت   *mee*·khaam yek kar·*te*
تلفن بخرم   te·le·*fon* be·*kha*·ram

How much does a (three)-minute call cost?

(سه) دقیقه تلفن   (se) da·ghee·*ghe* te·le·*fon*
چقدر می شود؟   che·ghadr *mee*·she

What are the rates?

نرخ چقدر هست؟   nerkh che·ghadr hast

I want to ...	من می خواهم ...	man *mee*·khaam ...
call (Canada)	به (کانادا)	be (kaa·naa·*daa*)
	تلفن بکنم	te·le·*fon* be·ko·nam
make a local call	یک تلفن	yek te·le·fo·*ne*
	داخلی بکنم	daa·khe·*lee* be·ko·nam
I want to send a ...	من می خواهم یک	man *mee*·khaam yek
	... بفرستم.	... *be*·fe·res·tam
fax	فکس	faks
parcel	بسته	bas·*te*
I want to buy	من می خواهم یک	man *mee*·khaam yek
a/an ...	... بخرم.	... *be*·kha·ram
envelope	پاکت	paa·*kat*
stamp	تمبر	tamr
Please send it	لطفا اون را	lot·*fan* oon ro
(to Australia) by ...	(به استرالیا)	(be os·taa·raa·lee·*yaa*)
	با ... بفرستید.	baa ... *be*·fe·res·teen
airmail	پست هوایی	pos·*te* ha·vaa·*yee*
surface mail	پست زمینی	pos·*te* za·mee·*nee*

sightseeing

What time does it open/close?

آن چه ساعتی باز/بسته می شود؟ — oon che saa·'a·*tee* baaz/bas·*te* mee·she

What's the admission charge?

ورودی چقدر هست؟ — voo·roo·*dee* che·ghad·re

Is there a discount for students/children?

برای دانش آموزها/ — ba·raa·ye daa·nesh·aa·mooz·*haa*/
بچه ها تخفیف هست؟ — bach·che·*haa* takh·*feef* hast

I'd like to see ...

من می خواهم ... را ببینم. — man *mee*·khaam ... ro *be*·bee·nam

I'd like a ...	من یک ... می خواهم.	man yek ... *mee*·khaam
catalogue	کاتالوگ	kaa·taa·*log*
guide	راهنما	raah·na·*maa*
local map	نقشه محلی	nagh·she·ye ma·hal·*lee*

When's the next ...?	... بعدی کی هست؟	... ba'·*dee* key hast
day trip	مسافرت روزانه	mo·saa·fe·ra·*te* roo·zaa·ne
tour	تور	toor

Is ... included?	آن شامل ... هم هست؟	oon shaa·me·*le* ... ham hast
accommodation	مسکن	mas·kan
the admission charge	ورودی	voo·roo·*dee*
food	غذا	gha·*zaa*
transport	حمل و نقل	ham·lo·*naghl*

How long is the tour?

تور چقدر طول می کشد؟ — toor che·ghadr tool mee·ke·she

What time should we be back?

ما چه ساعتی باید برگردیم؟ — maa che saa·'a·*tee* baa·*yad* bar·gar·deem

What's that?

آن چی هست؟ — oon chee·yee

Can I take a photo?

می توانم عکس بگیرم؟ — *mee*·too·nam aks *be*·gee·ram

sightseeing

castle	قلعه	ghal·'e
church	کلیسا	ke·lee·saa
main square	میدان اصلی	mey·daa·ne as·lee
mosque	مسجد	mas·jed
old city	شهر قدیمی	shah·re gha·dee·mee
palace	کاخ	kaakh
ruins	خرابه ها	kha·raa·be·haa

shopping

Where's a ...?	... کجاست؟	... ko·jaast
bookshop	کتاب فروشی	ke·taab foo·roo·shee
camera shop	دوربین فروشی	door·been foo·roo·shee
department	فروشگاه	foo·roosh·gaa·he
store	زنجیره ای	zan·jee·re·yee
grocery store	بقالی	bagh·ghaa·lee
newsagency	روزنامه فروشی	rooz·naa me foo·roo·shee
souvenir shop	کادو فروشی	kaa·do foo·roo·shee
supermarket	فروشگاه	foo·roosh·ghaah

I'm looking for ...

من دنبال ... می گردم. man don·baa·le ... mee·gar·dam

Can I look at it?

می توانم به آن نگاه کنم؟ mee·too·nam be oon ne·ghaah ko·nam

Do you have any others?

چیز دیگر هم دارید؟ chee·ze dee·ge ham daa·reen

Does it have a guarantee?

آن گارانتی دارد؟ oon gaa·raan·tee daa·re

Can I have it sent overseas?

می توانم آن را به خارج mee·too·neen un ro be khaa·rej
بفرستم؟ be·fe·res·teen

Can I have my ... repaired?

می توانید ... ام را تعمیر کنین؟ mee·too·neen ... am ro ta'·meer ko·neen

It's faulty.

آن خراب هست. oon kha·raa·be

I'd like a bag, please.

لطفا من یک کیسه می خواهم.

lot·*fan* man yek kee·*se* mee·khaam

I'd like a refund.

من می خواهم پولم

را پس بگیرم

man mee·khaam poo·*lam*

ro pas be·gee·ram

I'd like to return this.

من می خواهم این را پس بدهم.

man mee·khaam een ro pas be·dam

How much is it?

آن چقدر هست؟

oon che·ghadr hast

Can you write down the price?

می توانید قیمت را بنویسید؟

mee·too·neen ghey·*mat* ro be·ne·vee·seen

That's too expensive.

آن خیلی گران هست.

oon khey·*lee* ge·*roon* hast

What's your lowest price?

پایین ترین قیمت تون چند هست؟

paa·yeen·ta·*reen* ghey·ma·te·*toon* chan·de

I'll give you (1000 toman).

من به شما (ده هزار تومن)

می دهم.

man be sho·*maa* (dah he·zaar to·*man*)

mee·dam

There's a mistake in the bill.

در صورت حساب اشتباه شده.

dar soo·rat·he·*saab* esh·te·*baah* sho·de

Do you accept ...?	شما ... قبول می کنید؟	sho·*maa* ... gha·*bool* mee·ko·neen
credit cards	کارت اعتباری	kar·te e'·te·baa·*ree*
travellers cheques	چک مسافرتی	che·ke mo·saa·fe·ra·*tee*

I'd like ..., please.	لطفا من ... می خواهم.	lot·*fan* man ... mee·khaam
my change	بقیه پولم را	be·ghee·ye·ye *poo*·lam ro
a receipt	یک رسید	yek re·*seed*

I'd like ...	من ... می خواهم.	man ... mee·khaam
(100) grams	(صد) گرم	(sad) ge·*ram*
(two) kilos	(دو) کیلو	(do) kee·*lo*
(three) pieces	(سه) تکه	(se) teek·*ke*
(six) slices	(شش) تکه	(sheesh) teek·*ke*

Less.	کمتر.	kam·*tar*
Enough.	کافی.	kaa·*fee*
More.	بیشتر.	beesh·*tar*

photography

Can you ...?	می توانید ...؟	*mee*-too-neen ...
burn a CD from my memory card	از کارت حافظه من یک سی دی بزنید	az kar-te haa-fe-ze-ye man yek see-*dee* be-za-neen
develop this film	این فیلم را ظاهر کنید	een feelm ro zaa-her ko-neen
load my film	فیلم ام را جا بیاندازید	*feel*-mam ro jaa bee-yan-daa-zeen

I need a ... film for this camera.	من یک فیلم ... برای دوربین می خواهم.	man yek feel-*me* ... ba-raa-*ye* een door-*been* mee-khaam
B&W	سیاه و سفید	see-yaa-ho-se-*feed*
colour	رنگی	ran-*gee*
slide	اسلاید	es-*laayd*
(200) speed	با سرعت (دویست)	baa sor-'a-te (de-*veest*)

When will it be ready?	آن کی حاضر می شود؟	oon key haa-zer mee-she

making conversation

Hello.	سلام.	sa-*laam*
Good night.	شب بخیر.	shab be-*kheyr*
Goodbye.	خدا حافظ.	kho-daa-haa-*fez*

Mr	آقا	aa-*ghaa*
Mrs/Miss	خانم	khaa-*nom*

How are you?

حالتون چطور هست؟   haa-le-toon che-to-re

Fine, thanks. And you?

خوبم خیلی ممنون.   *khoo*-bam khey-lee mam-*noon*
شما چطور هستید؟   sho-*maa* che-to-reen

What's your name?

اسمتون چی هست؟   es·me·toon *chee*·ye

My name is ...

اسم من ... هست.   es·*me* man ... hast

I'm pleased to meet you.

از آشنایی تون خوشبختم.   az aa·she·naa·yee·ye·toon khosh·bakh·tam

This is my ...	این ... من هست.	een ... man hast
brother	برادر	ba·raa·*dar*
daughter	دختر	dokh·*tar*
father	پدر	pe·*dar*
friend	دوست	doost
husband	شوهر	sho·*har*
mother	مادر	maa·*dar*
sister	خواهر	khaa·*har*
son	پسر	pe·*sar*
wife	زن	zan

Here's my ...	این ... من هست.	een ... man hast
What's your ...?	... تون چی هست؟	... e·*toon* chee hast
address	آدرس	aad·*res*
email address	آدرس ایمیل	aad·re·*se* ee·*meyl*
phone number	شماره تلفن	sho·maa·re·*ye* te·le·*fon*

Where are you from?

شما کجایی هستید؟   sho·*maa* ko·jaa·yee has·*teen*

I'm from ...	من ... یی هستم؟	man ... yee has·*tam*
Australia	استرالیا	os·taa·raa·lee·*yaa*
Canada	کانادا	kaa·naa·*daa*
New Zealand	نیوزیلند	nee·yoo·zee·*land*
the UK	انگلیس	een·gee·*lees*
the USA	آمریکا	aam·ree·*kaa*

What's your occupation?

شغلتون چی هست؟   shogh·*le*·toon *chee*·ye

I'm a/an ...	من ... هستم.	man ... has·*tam*
businessperson	تاجر	taa·*jer*
office worker	کارمند	kaar·*mand*
tradesperson	کاسب	kaa·*seb*

Do you like ...?	شما ... دوست دارید؟	sho·*maa* ... doost daa·*reen*
I (don't) like ...	من ... دوست (نه) دارم.	man ... doost (na) daa·*ram*
art	هنر	ho·*nar*
movies	فیلم	feelm
music	موسیقی	moo·see·*ghee*
reading	خواندن	khaan·*dan*
sport	ورزش	var·*zesh*

eating out

Can you recommend a ...?	می توانید یک ... پیشنهاد کنید؟	*mee*·too·neen yek ... peesh·na·*haad* ko·neen
café	کافه	kaaf·*fe*
restaurant	رستوران	res·too·*raan*
I'd like ..., please.	لطفا من ... می خواهم.	lot·*fan* man ... *mee*·khaam
a table for (four)	یک میز برای (چهار نفر)	yek meez ba·raa·*ye* (chaa·*haar*)
the (non)smoking section	قسمت (غیر) سیگاری	ghes·ma·*te* (ghey·*re*) see·gaa·*ree*
breakfast	صبحانه	sob·haa·*ne*
lunch	ناهار	naa·*haar*
dinner	شام	shaam

What would you recommend?

شما چی پیشنهاد می کنید؟   sho·*maa* chee peesh·na·*haad* *mee*·ko·neen

What's the local speciality?

غذای مخصوص محلی چی هست؟   gha·zaa·*ye* makh·soo·*se* ma·hal·*lee* *chee*·ye

What's that?

آن چی هست؟   oon *chee*·ye

I'd like (the)	... لطفا من	lot·fan man ...
..., please.	را می خواهم.	ro mee·khaam
bill	صورت حساب	soo·rat he·saab
drink list	لیست نوشیدنی	lees·te noo·shee·da·nee
menu	منو	me·noo
that dish	آن غذا	oon gha·zaa

drinks

(cup of) coffee ...	(یک فنجان) قهوه ...	(yek fen·joon) ghah·ve ...
(cup of) tea ...	(یک فنجان) چای ...	(yek fen·joon) chaa·yee ...
with milk	با شیر	baa sheer
without sugar	بدون شکر	be·doo·ne she·kar
(orange) juice	آب (پرتقال)	aa·be (por·te·ghaal)
soft drink	نوشابه	noo·shaa·be
... water	آب ...	aa·be ...
boiled	جوش	joosh
mineral	معدنی	ma'·da·nee

I'll have ...

من ... می خورم.	man ... mee·kho·ram

I'll buy you a drink.

من برای شما یک	man ba·raa·ye sho·maa yek
نوشیدنی می خرم.	noo·shee·da·nee mee·kha·ram

What would you like?

چی میل دارید؟	chee meyl daa·reen

special diets & allergies

Is there a vegetarian restaurant near here?

این نزدیکی رستوران	een naz·dee·kee res·too·raa·ne
گیاه خواری هست؟	gee·yaah·khaa·ree hast

Do you have	شما غذای	sho·maa gha·zaa·ye
... food?	... دارید؟	... daa·reen
halal	حلال	ha·laal
kosher	کوشر	ko·sher
vegetarian	گیاه خواری	gee·yaah·khaa·ree

Could you prepare a meal without ...?	می توانید یک غذای بدون ...درست کنید؟	mee·too·neen yek gha·zaa·ye be·doo·ne ... do·rost ko·neen
butter	کره	ka·re
eggs	تخم مرغ	tokh·me·morgh
meat stock	آبگوشت	aab·goosht
I'm allergic to ...	من به ... حساسیت دارم.	man be ... has·saa·see·yat daa·ram
dairy produce	لبنیات	la·ba·nee·yaat
gluten	گلوتن	ge·lo·ten
nuts	آجیل	aa·jeel
seafood	غذای دریایی	gha·zaa·ye dar·yaa·yee

emergencies

Help!	کمک!	ko·mak
Stop!	ایست!	eest
Go away!	برو کنار!	bo·ro ke·naar
Thief!	دزد!	dozd
Fire!	آتش!	aa·teesh
Watch out!	مواظب باش!	mo·vaa·zeb baash

Call ...!	... صدا کنید !	... se·daa ko·neen
a doctor	یک دکتر	yek dok·tor
an ambulance	یک آمبولانس	yek aam·boo·laans
the police	پلیس	po·lees

Could you help me, please?

لطفا میشه به من کمک کنید؟ lot·fan mee·she be man ko·mak ko·neen

I have to use the phone.

من باید از تلفن استفاده کنم. man baa·yad az te·le·fon es·te·faa·de ko·nam

I'm lost.

من گم شده ام. man gom sho·dam

Where are the toilets?

توالت کجاست؟

too·vaa·*let ko*·jaast

Where's the police station?

اداره پلیس کجاست؟

e·daa·re·*ye* po·*lees ko*·jaast

I want to report an offence.

من می خواهم یک خلاف
را گزارش بدهم.

man *mee*·khaam yek khe·*laaf*
ro go·zaa·*resh* be·*dam*

I have insurance.

من بیمه دارم.

man bee·*me* daa·*ram*

I want to contact my embassy.

من می خواهم با سفارتم
تماس بگیرم.

man *mee*·khaam baa se·faa·ra·*tam*
ta·*maas* be·*gee*·ram

I've been assaulted.

مرا اذیت کرده اند.

ma·*no* a·zee·*yat* kar·*dan*

I've been raped.

به من تجاوز کرده اند.

be man ta·jaa·*voz* kar·*dan*

I've been robbed.

وسایل ام را دزدیده اند.

va·saa·ye·*lam* ro doz·dee·*dan*

I've lost my ...	من ... ام را	man ... am ro
	گم کرده ام.	gom kar·*dam*
My ... was/were	... ام دزدیده	... am doz·dee·*de*
stolen.	شد.	shod
bag	کیف	keef
credit card	کارت اعتباری	*kar*·te e'·te·baa·*ree*
money	پول	pool
passport	گذرنامه	go·*zar* naa·*me*
travellers cheques	چک مسافرتی	che·*ke* mo·saa·fe·ra·*tee*

health

Where's the	نزدیکترین ...	naz·deek·ta·*reen* ...
nearest ...?	کجاست؟	*ko*·jaast
dentist	دندان پزشک	dan·daan pe·*zeshk*
doctor	دکتر	dok·*tor*
hospital	بیمارستان	bee·maa·res·*taan*
(night) pharmacist	داروخانه	daa·roo·khaa·ne·*ye*
	(شبانه)	(sha·baa·*ne*)

I need a doctor (who speaks English).

من یک دکتر لازم دارم
(که انگلیسی صحبت می کند).

man yek dok-tor laa-zem daa-ram
(kee een-gee-lee-see soh-bat mee-ko-ne)

Could I see a female doctor?

می توانم یک دکتر
خانم را ببینم.

mee-too-nam yek dok-to-re
khaa-nom ro be-bee-nam

I've run out of my medication.

داروهایم تمام شده است.

daa-roo-haam ta-moom sho-de

I'm sick.

من مریض هستم.

man ma-reez has-tam

It hurts here.

اینجا درد می کند.

een-jaa dard mee-ko-ne

I have (a) ...	من ... دارم.	man ... daa-ram
asthma	آسم	aasm
constipation	یبوست	yoo-boo-sat
diarrhoea	اسهال	es-haal
fever	تب	tab
headache	سردرد	sar-dard
heart condition	بیماری قلبی	bee-maa-ree-ye ghal-bee
nausea	تهوع	ta-hav-vo'
pain	درد	dard
sore throat	گلو درد	ga-loo-dard
toothache	دندان درد	dan-doon-dard

I'm allergic to ...	من به ...	man be ...
	حساسیت دارم.	has-saa-see-yat daa-ram
antibiotics	آنتی بیوتیک	aan-tee-bee-yoo-teek
anti-inflammatories	ضد التهاب	zed-de el-te-haab
aspirin	آسپرین	aas-pe-reen
bees	زنبور	zan-boor
codeine	کودئین	ko-de-'een
penicillin	پنی سیلین	pe-nee-see-leen

english–farsi dictionary

Words in this dictionary are marked as n (noun), a (adjective), v (verb), sg (singular) and pl (plural) where necessary.

A

accident تصادف ta-saa-*dof*
accommodation مسکن mas-*kan*
adaptor آداپتور aa-daap-*tor*
address n آدرس aad-*res*
Afghanistan افغانستان af-ghaa-nes-*taan*
after بعد ba'd
air-conditioned دارای تهویه مطبوع daa-raa-ye tah-vee-ye-ye mat-*boo'*
airplane هواپیما ha-vaa-pey-*maa*
airport فرودگاه foo-rood-*gaah*
alcohol الکل al-*kol*
all همه ha-*me*
allergy حساسیت has-saa-see-*yat*
ambulance آمبولانس aam-boo-*laans*
and و va
ankle مچ پا mo-che paa
arm بازو baa-*zoo*
ashtray زیر سیگاری zeer see-gaa-*ree*
ATM خودپرداز khod-par-*daaz*

B

baby نوزاد no-*zaad*
back (body) پشت posht
backpack کوله پشتی koo-le posh-*tee*
bad بد bad
bag کیف keef
baggage claim تحویل گرفتن بار tah-*veel* ge-ref-ta-ne baar
bank بانک bank
bathroom دستشویی dast-shoo-*yee*
battery باطری baat-*ree*
beautiful قشنگ gha-*shang*
bed تخت خواب takht khaab
before قبل ghabl
behind پشت posht
bicycle دوچرخه do-char-*khe*
big بزرگ bo-*zorg*
bill n صورت حساب soo-*rat* he-*saab*

black سیاه see-*yaah*
blanket پتو pa-*too*
blood group گروه خونی goo-roo-he khoo-*nee*
blue آبی aa-*bee*
boat کشتی kesh-*tee*
book (make a reservation) v رزرو کردن re-zerv kar-*dan*
bottle بطری bot-*ree*
bottle opener در باز کن dar baaz kon
boy پسر pe-*sar*
brakes (car) ترمز tor-*moz*
breakfast صبحانه sob-haa-*ne*
broken (faulty) خراب kha-*raab*
bus اتوبوس oo-too-*boos*
business تجارت te-jaa-*rat*
buy خرید kha-*reed*

C

café کافه kaaf-*fe*
camera دوربین door-*been*
camp site محل چادر زدن ma-hal-le chaa-dor za-dan
cancel کنسل کردن kan-*sel* kar-dan
can opener در باز کن dar baaz kon
car ماشین maa-*sheen*
cash n نقد naghd
cash (a cheque) v نقد کردن naghd kar-*dan*
cell phone تلفن همراه te-le-fo-ne ham-*raah*
centre n مرکز mar-*kaz*
change (money) v پول خرد کردن pool khord kar-*dan*
cheap ارزان ar-*zaan*
check (bill) صورت حساب soo-*rat* he-*saab*
check-in تحویل دادن tah-*veel* daa-dan
chest سینه see-*ne*
child بچه bach-*che*
cigarette سیگار see-*gaar*
city شهر shahr
clean a تمیز ta-*meez*
closed بسته bas-*te*
coffee قهوه ghah-*ve*

coins سکه sek-ke
cold a سرد sard
come آمدن aa-ma-dan
computer کامپیوتر kaam-pee-yoo-ter
condom کاندوم kaan-dom
contact lenses لنز کانتکت kaan-taakt lenz
cook v پختن pokh-tan
cost n خرج داشتن kharj dash-tan
credit card کارت اعتباری kar-te e'-te-baa-ree
cup فنجان fen-jaan
currency exchange تبدیل ارز tab-dee-le arz
customs (immigration) گمرک gom-rok

D

dangerous خطرناک kha-tar-naak
date (time) n تاریخ taa-reekh
day روز rooz
delay n تاخیر ta'-kheer
dentist دندان پزشک dan-daan pe-zeshk
depart حرکت کردن ha-re-kat kar-dan
diaper پوشک poo-shak
dictionary فرهنگ لغت far-han-ge lo-ghat
dinner شام shaam
direct a مستقیم mos-ta-gheem
dirty کثیف ka-seef
disabled معلول ma'-lool
discount n تخفیف takh-feef
doctor دکتر dok-tor
double bed تخت دو خوابه takh-te do-khaa-be
double room اتاق دو نفره o-taa-ghe do na-fa-re
drink v نوشیدنی noo-shee-da-nee
drive v راندن دنده کردن raa-nan-de-gee kar-dan
drivers licence گواهی رانندگی ga-vaa-hee-ye raa-nan-de-gee
drug (illicit) مواد مخدر ma-vaad-de mo-khad-der
dummy (pacifier) پستانک pes-taa-nak

E

ear گوش goosh
east شرق shargh
eat خوردن khor-dan
economy class عادی aa-dee
electricity برق bargh
elevator آسانسور aa-saan-sor
email n ایمیل ee-meyl
embassy سفارت se-faa-rat
emergency اضطراری ez-te-raa-ree

English (language) انگلیسی een-gee-lee-see
entrance ورودی voo-roo-dee
evening شب shab
exchange rate نرخ ارز ner-khe arz
exit n خروج khoo-rooj
expensive گران ge-raan
express mail پست اکسپرس pos-te eks-pe-res
eye چشم cheshm

F

far دور door
Farsi فارسی faar-see
fast تند tond
father پدر pe-dar
film (camera) فیلم feelm
finger انگشت an-gosht
first-aid kit جعبه کمک های اولیه ja'-be-ye ko-mak-haa-ye av-va-lee-ye
first class درجه یک da-ra-je-ye yek
fish ماهی maa-hee
food غذا gha-zaa
foot پا paa
fork چنگال chan-gaal
free (of charge) رایگان raay-gaan
friend دوست doost
fruit میوه mee-ve
full پر por
funny خنده دار khan-de daar

G

gift هدیه hed-ye
girl دختر dokh-tar
glass (drinking) لیوان lee-vaan
glasses (eyesight) عینک ey-nak
go رفتن raf-tan
good خوب khoob
green سبز sabz
guide n راهنما raah-na-maa

H

half n نصف nesf
hand دست dast
handbag کیف دستی kee-fe das-tee
happy خوشحال khosh-haal
have داشتن dash-tan
he او oo

head سر sar
heart قلب ghalb
heat n گرما gar-maa
heavy سنگین san-geen
help v کمک کردن ko-mak kar-dan
here اینجا een-jaa
high بلند bo-land
highway بزرگراه bo-zorg-raah
hike v کوهنوردی کردن kooh-na-var-dee kar-dan
holiday تعطیلی ta'-tee-lee
homosexual همجنس باز ham-jens baaz
hospital بیمارستان bee-maa-res-taan
hot داغ daagh
hotel هتل ho-tel
hungry گرسنه go-ros-ne
husband شوهر sho-har

I

I من man
identification (card) کارت شناسایی
  kar-te she-naa-saa-yee
ill مریض ma-reez
important مهم mo-hem
included شامل shaa-mel
injury زخم zakhm
Iran ایران i-raan
insurance بیمه bee-me
internet اینترنت een-ter-net
interpreter مترجم mo-tar-jem

J

jewellery جواهرات ja-vaa-he-raat
job شغل shoghl

K

key کلید kee-leed
kilogram کیلو گرم kee-lo ge-ram
kitchen آشپزخانه aash-paz-khaa-ne
knife چاقو chaa-ghoo

L

laundry (place) لباس شویی le-baas shoo-yee
lawyer وکیل va-keel
left (direction) چپ chap

left-luggage office دفتر بارهای جا مانده
  daf-ta-re baar-haa-ye jaa maan-de
leg ساق پا saa-ghe paa
lesbian همجنس باز زن ham-jens-baa-ze zan
less کمتر kam-tar
letter (mail) نامه naa-me
lift (elevator) آسانسور aa-saan-sor
light n لامپ laamp
like v دوست داشتن doost dash-tan
lock n قفل ghofl
long دراز de-raaz
lost گم شده gom sho-de
lost-property office دفتر اشیای گم شده
  daf-ta-re ash-yaa-ye gom sho-de
love v دوست داشتن doost dash-tan
luggage بار baar
lunch ناهار naa-haar

M

mail n نامه naa-me
man مرد mard
map نقشه nagh-she
market بازار baa-zaar
matches کبریت keb-reet
meat گوشت goosht
medicine دارو daa-roo
menu منو me-noo
message پیغام pey-ghaam
milk شیر sheer
minute دقیقه da-ghee-ghe
mobile phone تلفن همراه te-le-fo-ne ham-raah
money پول pool
month ماه maah
morning صبح sobh
mother مادر maa-dar
motorcycle موتور mo-tor
motorway اتوبان oo-too-baan
mouth دهان da-haan
music موسیقی moo-see-ghee

N

name n اسم esm
napkin دستمال dast-maal
nappy پوشک poo-shak
near adv نزدیک naz-deek
neck گردن gar-dan
new تازه taa-ze

news اخبار akh-*baar*
newspaper روزنامه rooz-naa-*me*
night شب shab
no نه na
noisy پر سروصدا por sa-ro-se-*daa*
nonsmoking غیر سیگاری ghey-re see-gaa-*ree*
north شمال sho-*maal*
nose بینی bee-*nee*
now حالا haa-*laa*
number شماره sho-maa-*re*

O

oil (engine) روغن ro-*ghan*
old کهنه koh-*ne*
one-way ticket بلیط یک سره be-lee-*te* yek sa-*re*
open n باز baaz
outside بیرون bee-*roon*

P

package بسته bas-*te*
paper کاغذ kaa-*ghaz*
park (car) v پارک کردن park kar-*dan*
passport گذرنامه go-zar naa-*me*
pay v پرداختن par-daakh-*tan*
pen خودکار khod-*kaar*
petrol بنزین ben-*zeen*
pharmacy دارو خانه daa-roo-khaa-*ne*
phone card کارت تلفن kar-*te* te-le-*fon*
photo عکس aks
plate (food) بشقاب bosh-*ghaab*
police پلیس po-*lees*
postcard کارت پستال kar-*te* pos-*taal*
post office اداره پست e-daa-re-ye post
pregnant حامله haa-me-*le*
price n قیمت ghey-*mat*

Q

quiet ساکت saa-*ket*

R

rain n باران baa-*raan*
razor تیغ teegh
receipt n رسید re-*seed*
red قرمز gher-*mez*
refund n پس دادن پول pas daa-da-*ne* pool
registered mail پست سفارشی pos-*te* se-faa-re-*shee*

rent v اجاره کردن e-jaa-re kar-*dan*
repair v تعمیر کردن ta'-*meer* kar-*dan*
reservation رزرو re-*zerv*
restaurant رستوران res-too-*raan*
return v برگشتن bar-gash-*tan*
return ticket بلیط رفت و برگشت be-lee-*te* raf-*to* bar-*ghasht*
right (direction) راست raast
road جاده jaa-*de*
room اتاق o-*taagh*

S

safe a امن amn
sanitary napkin نوار بهداشتی na-vaar beh-daash-*tee*
seat جا jaa
send v فرستادن fe-res-taa-*dan*
service station پمپ بنزین pom-*pe* ben-*zeen*
sex جنسیت jen-see-*yat*
shampoo شامپو shaam-*poo*
share (a dorm etc) هم اتاقی شدن ham o-taa-ghee sho-*dan*
shaving cream خمیر ریش kha-*meer* reesh
she او oo
sheet (bed) ملافه ma-laa-*fe*
shirt پیراهن pee-raa-*han*
shoes کفش kafsh
shop n مغازه ma-ghaa-*ze*
short شلوار کوتاه shal-*vaar* koo-*taah*
shower n دوش dosh
single room اتاق تکی o-*taagh* ta-*kee*
skin پوست poost
skirt دامن daa-*man*
sleep v خوابیدن khaa-bee-*dan*
slowly آهسته aa-hes-*te*
small کوچک koo-*chek*
smoke (cigarettes) v سیگار کشیدن see-*gaar* ke-shee-*dan*
soap صابون saa-*boon*
some مقداری megh-daa-*ree*
soon بزودی be-zoo-*dee*
south جنوب joo-*noob*
souvenir shop کادو فروشی kaa-*do* foo-roo-*shee*
speak صحبت کردن soh-*bat* kar-*dan*
spoon قاشق ghaa-*shogh*
stamp تمبر tamr
stand-by ticket بلیط لیست انتظار be-lee-*te* lees-*te* en-te-*zaar*
station (train) ایستگاه eest-*gaah*
stomach معده me'-*de*

stop v توقف کردن ta·vagh·ghof kar·dan
stop (bus) n ایستگاه eest·gaah
street خیابان khee·yaa·baan
student دانش آموز daa·nesh aa·mooz
sun آفتاب aaf·taab
ke·re·me zed·de aaf·taab
sunscreen کرم ضد آفتاب
ke·re·me zed·de aaf·taab
swim v شنا کردن she·naa kar·dan

T

Tajikistan تاجیکستان taa·jee·kes·taan
tampons تامپون taam·pon
taxi تاکسی taak·see
teaspoon قاشق چای خوری
ghaa·sho·ghe chaay kho·ree
teeth دندان dan·daan
telephone n تلفن te·le·fon
television تلویزیون te·le·vee·zee·yon
temperature (weather) دما da·maa
tent چادر chaa·dor
that (one) آن aan
they آنها aan·haa
thirsty تشنه tesh·ne
this (one) این een
throat گلو ga·loo
ticket بلیط be·leet
time n وقت vaght
tired خسته khas·te
tissues دستمال کاغذی
dast·maal kaa·gha·zee
today امروز em·rooz
toilet توالت too·vaa·let
tomorrow فردا far·daa
tonight امشب em·shab
toothbrush مسواک mes·vaak
toothpaste خمیر دندان
kha·meer dan·daan
torch (flashlight) چراغ قوه
che·raagh ghov·ve
tour n تور toor
tourist office اداره جهانگردی
e·daa·re·ye ja·haan·gar·dee
towel حوله ho·le
train قطار gha·taar
translate ترجمه کردن tar·jo·me kar·dan
travel agency آژانس مسافرتی
aa·zhaan·se mo·saa·fe·ra·tee
travellers cheque چک مسافرتی
che·ke mo·saa·fe·ra·tee

trousers شلوار shal·vaar
twin beds تخت دو خوابه takh·te do·khaa·be
tyre تایر taa·yer

U

underwear لباس زیر le·baa·se zeer
urgent اضطراری ez·te·raa·ree

V

vacant خالی khaa·lee
vacation تعطیلات ta'·tee·laat
vegetable n سبزی sab·zee
vegetarian a گیاه خوار gee·yaah·khaar
visa ویزا vee·zaa

W

waiter گارسن gaar·son
walk v پیاده رفتن pee·yaa·de raf·tan
wallet کیف keef
warm a گرم garm
wash (something) شستن shos·tan
watch n ساعت saa·'at
water آب aab
we ما maa
weekend آخر هفته aa·kha·re haf·te
west کمر ka·mar
wheelchair صندلی چرخدار
san·da·lee·ye charkh·daar
when کی key
where کجا ko·jaa
white سفید se·feed
who کی kee
why چرا che·raa
wife زن zan
window پنجره pan·ja·re
with با baa
without بدون be·doo·ne
woman زن zan
write نوشتن ne·vesh·tan

Y

yellow زرد zard
yes بله ba·le
yesterday دیروز dee·rooz
you sg تو to
you pl شما sho·maa

Hebrew

hebrew alphabet

א *a*·leph	ב bet	ב vet	ג *gi*·mel	ד *da*·let
ה heh	ו vav	ז *za*·yin	ח khet	ט tet
י yud	כ kaf	כ/ך khaf *	ל *la*·med	מ/ם mem *
נ/ן nun *	ס *sa*·mekh	ע *a*·yin	פ pe	פ/ף feh *
צ/ץ *tsa*·di *	ק kof	ר resh	ש shin	ש sin
ת tav				

*the second form of the letter (when read from right to left) is used when the letter appears at the end of a word

introduction

Few languages have as astonishing a history as Hebrew (עברית iv-*rit*). Some two millennia ago, as a result of the Jewish 'captivity in Babylon', Hebrew, one of the world's oldest tongues, ceased to be an everyday spoken language. It survived only as Biblical Hebrew, the language of the Jewish religion. Then, at the dawn of the 20th century, as Jews from around the world began to settle again in Palestine, Hebrew was revived as a spoken language. It's now the national language of Israel, with seven to eight million speakers worldwide.

This extraordinary feat of linguistic resurrection was largely due to the efforts of one man, Eliezer Ben-Yehuda, a European Jew who moved to Jerusalem in the late 1800s. Ben-Yehuda, together with the Language Committee that he founded, set about creating a contemporary form of spoken Hebrew with a vast store of new vocabulary for modern times. They delved into the language to discover words and constructions that could be reshaped to suit modern needs, and borrowed vocabulary from the closely related Arabic and Aramaic languages and from Greek and Latin. Modern Hebrew has become a creative new hybrid tongue as a result.

One of the driving forces behind the rebirth of Hebrew was the desire to unify Jews around the world. Until Hebrew was revived, Jewish spoken communication was divided between, on the one hand, the Ladino language of the Sephardic Jews living in North Africa, Spain, the Middle East and Turkey, and on the other, the Yiddish language of Ashkenazi Jews in Northern and Eastern Europe. Although the two languages were both written in the Hebrew alphabet, they were mutually unintelligible, with Ladino resembling Spanish and Yiddish related to German. By providing Jewish people with a common language, Hebrew has a powerful symbolic value.

Aside from its fascinating history, Hebrew has intriguing characteristics which make learning some well worth the effort. Like Arabic, it's written from right to left, using an elegant alphabet. It also has an interesting way of forming words: vowels are inserted between the three consonants that make up most word roots, allowing for subtle shifts in meaning. While it's still recognisably a member of the Semitic language family, Hebrew has been quick to adopt from other languages, and has been strongly influenced by Germanic and Slavic languages giving it a cosmopolitan flavour. Furthermore, it has donated numerous words to English and other languages – like *amen*, *cabal*, *cherub*, *goliath*, *jubilee*, *Messiah*, *leviathan*, *Satan* ... Hebrew's treasure trove of picturesque idioms is another perk of learning this amazing language.

pronunciation

vowel sounds

The Hebrew vowel system is pretty straightforward, as it consists of the five basic vowels and one diphthong (a combination of two vowel sounds). You might be surprised to learn that all letters in the Hebrew alphabet are consonants. The vowel sounds are represented with fixed symbols – dots and strokes – and a few combinations of both. These symbols can be written above, under or inside the word, but they can also be omitted. You don't need to worry about this, though, as the correct pronunciation of each word or phrase is always given in our coloured pronunciation guides, included next to the Hebrew script throughout this chapter.

symbol	english equivalent	hebrew example	transliteration
a	act	אבא	*a*·ba
ai	aisle	מתי	ma·*tai*
e	bet	עמק	*e*·mek
i	hit	איכר	i·*kar*
o	pot	אוזן	*o*·zen
u	put	עוגה	**u**·*ga*

consonant sounds

Most consonants in Hebrew sound the same as in English. They aren't always followed by a vowel, so listen carefully to the locals and follow their lead and it shouldn't be too hard to get the hang of this. You might also need some practice with the kh and the r – both are guttural sounds, pronounced at the back of the mouth. The glottal stop (represented in this chapter with an apostrophe) sounds like a catch in the throat, marking a break in the flow of speech. Note also that when you see the symbol t written twice, it should be pronounced as a stronger sound.

symbol	english equivalent	hebrew example	transliteration
b	**b**ed	בקבוק	bak·*buk*
ch	**ch**eat	צ'יפס	chips
d	**d**og	דף	daf
f	**f**un	עוף	of
g	**g**o	גל	gal
h	**h**at	הלילה	ha·*lay*·la
j	**j**ar	פריג'דר	fri·ji·*der*
k	**k**it	כד	kad
kh	as the 'ch' in the Scottish *loch*	חתול	kha·*tul*
l	**l**ot	לבן	la·*van*
m	**m**an	מפה	ma·*pa*
n	**n**ot	נהר	na·*har*
p	**p**et	פתוח	pa·*tu*·akh
r	**r**un (guttural, as the Parisian French 'r')	רשת	*re*·shet
s	**s**un	עשרים	es·*rim*
sh	**sh**ot	שבת	sha·*bat*
t	**t**op	שבת	sha·*bat*
ts	ha**ts**	צל	tsel
v	**v**ery	וריד	vrid
y	**y**es	ירוק	ya·*rok*
z	**z**ero	זמר	za·*mar*
'	glottal stop (like the pause in the middle of 'uh-oh')	האזנה	ha'·za·*na*

word stress

In Hebrew, stress usually falls on the last or the second-last syllable of a word. In words borrowed from other languages, stress is usually placed on the first syllable. In our coloured pronunciation guides the stressed syllable is always in italics.

language difficulties

Do you speak English?

| אתה מדבר אנגלית? | a·ta me·da·ber ang·lit m |
| את מדברת אנגלית? | at me·da·be·ret ang·lit f |

Do you understand?

| אתה מבין? | a·ta mi·vin m |
| את מבינה? | at mi·vi·na f |

I understand.

| אני מבין/מבינה. | a·ni mi·vin/mi·vi·na m/f |

I don't understand.

| אני לא מבין/מבינה. | a·ni lo mi·vin/mi·vi·na m/f |

Could you	...בבקשה? ...אתה יכול	a·ta ya·khol be·va·ka·sha ... m
please ...?	...בבקשה? ...את יכולה	at ye·kho·la be·va·ka·sha ... f
repeat that	לחזור על זה	la·kha·zor al ze
speak more slowly	לדבר לאט	le·da·ber le·at
write it down	לרשום את זה	ler·shom et ze

numbers

0	אפס	e·fes	20	עשרים	es·rim
1	אחת	a·khat	30	שלושים	shlo·shim
2	שתיים	shta·yem	40	ארבעים	ar·ba·im
3	שלוש	sha·losh	50	חמישים	kha·me·shim
4	ארבע	ar·ba	60	ששים	she·shim
5	חמש	kha·mesh	70	שבעים	she·vim
6	שש	shesh	80	שמונים	shmo·nim
7	שבע	she·va	90	תשעים	tesh·im
8	שמונה	shmo·ne	100	מאה	me·a
9	תשע	te·sha	1000	אלף	e·lef
10	עשר	e·ser	1,000,000	מליון	mil·yon

Note that English numerals are used in modern Hebrew text.

time & dates

What time is it?	?מה השעה	ma ha·sha·*a*
It's one o'clock.	.השעה אחת	ha·sha·*a* a·*khat*
It's (two) o'clock.	.(השעה (שתיים	ha·sha·*a* (shta·yem)
Quarter past (two).	.(שתיים) ורבע	(shta·yem) va·*re*·va
Half past (two).	.(שתיים) וחצי	(shta·yem) va·*khe*·tsi
Quarter to (two).	.(רבע ל(שתיים	*re*·va le·(shta·yem)
At what time ...?	?... באיזה שעה	be·*e*·ze sha·*a* ...
At ...	ב ...	be ...
am	לפני הצהריים	*lef*·ne ha·tso·ho·*ra*·yem
pm	אחרי הצהריים	a·kha·*re* ha·tso·ho·*ra*·yem
Monday	שני	she·*ni*
Tuesday	שלישי	shli·*shi*
Wednesday	רביעי	re·ve·*i*
Thursday	חמישי	kha·mɪ·*shɪ*
Friday	שישי	shi·*shi*
Saturday	שבת	sha·*bat*
Sunday	ראשון	re·*shon*
last/next ...	... האחרון/הבא	ha·a·kha·*ron*/ha·*ba* ...
night	לילה	*lai*·la
week	שבוע	sha·*vo*·a
month	חודש	*kho*·desh
year	שנה	sha·*na*
yesterday ...	... אתמול	et·*mol* ...
tomorrow ...	... מחר	ma·*khar* ...
morning	בוקר	*bo*·ker
afternoon	צהריים	tso·ho·*ra*·yem
evening	ערב	*e*·rev

What date is it today?

מה התאריך היום? — ma ha·ta·*rikh* ha·*yom*

It's (15 December).

היום הוא — ha·*yom* hu
(.החמש עשרה לדצמבר) — (ha·kha·*mesh* es·re le·de·*tsem*·ber)

border crossing

I'm here ...	... אני כאן	a·ni kan ...
in transit	בתחנת ביניים	be·ta·kha·*nat* bi·*na*·yim
on business	לעסקים	le·a·sa·kim
on holiday	בחופשה	be·khof·*sha*

I'm here for ...	... אני כאן ל	a·ni kan le ...
(10) days	(עשרה) ימים	(a·sa·*ra*) ya·*mim*
(three) weeks	(שלושה) שבועות	(shlo·*sha*) shvo·ot
(three) months	(שלושה) חודשים	(shlo·*sha*) kho·da·*shim*

I'm going to (Haifa).

אני נוסע ל(חיפה).   a·ni no·se·ya le·(khe·*fa*)

I'm staying at the (Dan Panorama).

אני שוהה ב(דן פנורמה).   a·ni sho·he/sho·ha be·(dan pa·no·ra·ma) m/f

I have nothing to declare.

אין לי על מה להצהיר.   en li al ma le·hats·*hir*

I have something to declare.

יש לי משהו להצהיר עליו.   yesh li ma·shi·hu le·hats·*hir* a·*lav*

That's (not) mine.

זה (לא) שלי.   ze (lo) she·*li*

tickets & luggage

Where can I buy a ticket?

איפה אפשר לקנות כרטיס?   e·fo ef·*shar* lek·*not* kar·*tis*

Do I need to book a seat?

אני צריך להזמין מושב מראש?   a·ni tsa·*rikh* le·haz·*min* mo·*shav* me·*rosh*

One ... ticket	... כרטיס אחד	kar·*tis* e·*khad* ...
(to Tel Aviv), please.	(לתל-אביב), בבקשה.	(le·tel·a·*viv*) be·va·ka·*sha*
one-way	לכיוון אחד	le·ki·*vun* e·*khad*
return	הלוך ושוב	ha·*lokh* va·*shov*

I'd like to ... my	אני רוצה ... את	a·ni ro·tse/ro·tsa ... et
ticket, please.	הכרטיס שלי,	ha·kar·tis she·li
	בבקשה.	be·va·ka·sha m/f
cancel	לבטל	le·va·tel
change	להחליף	le·hakh·lif
collect	לאסוף	le·sof

I'd like a ...	אני רוצה מושב,	a·ni ro·tse/ro·tsa mo·shav
seat, please.	... בבקשה.	... be·va·ka·sha m/f
nonsmoking	ללא עישון	le·lo i·shun
smoking	עם עישון	im i·shun

Is there air conditioning?

האם יש מיזוג אוויר?   ha·im yesh mi·zug a·vir

Is there a toilet?

האם יש שירותים?   ha·im yesh shi·ru·tim

How long does the trip take?

כמה זמן הנסיעה לוקחת?   ka·ma zman ha·ni·si·a lo·ka·khat

Is it a direct route?

האם זה מסלול ישיר?   ha·im ze mas·lul ya·shir

My luggage	המטען שלי ...	ha·mit·an she·li ...
has been ...		
damaged	ניזוק	ni·zok
lost	אבד	a·vad
stolen	נגנב	nig·nav

transport

Where does flight (VL245) arrive/depart?

איפה מגיעה/ממריאה טיסה   e·fo ma·gi·a/mam·ri·a ti·sa
(VL245)?   (vi el shta·yem ar·ba kha·mesh)

Is this the ...	האם זה/זאת ה ...	ha·im ze/zot ha ...
to (Haifa)?	ל(חיפה)?	le·(khe·fa) m/f
boat	אוניה	o·ni·ya f
bus	אוטובוס	o·to·bus m
plane	מטוס	ma·tos m
train	רכבת	ra·ke·vet f

What time's	באיזה שעה	be·e·ze sha·a
the ... bus?	האוטובוס ה ...?	ha·o·to·bus ha ...
first	ראשון	ri·shon
last	אחרון	a·kha·ron
next	בא	ba

How long will it be delayed?

כמה זמן זה הולך להתעכב?   *ka·ma zman ze ho·lekh le·hit·a·kev*

What station/stop is this?

איזה תחנה כאן?   *e·ze ta·kha·na kan*

Please tell me when we get to (Jerusalem).

תגיד לי מתי מגיעים	*ta·gid li ma·tai ma·gi·im*
(לירושלים), בבקשה.	*(le·yi·ru·sha·la·yim) be·va·ka·sha*

Is this seat available?

האם המושב הזה פנוי?   *ha·im ha·mo·shav ha·ze pa·nu·i*

That's my seat.

זה המושב שלי.   *ze ha·mo·shav she·li*

I'd like a taxi ...	אני צריך מונית ...	a·ni tsa·rikh mo·nit ...
at (9am)	ב(תשע בבוקר)	be·(te·sha ba·bo·ker)
now	עכשיו	akh·shav
tomorrow	מחר	ma·khar

How much is it to ...?

כמה זה ל ...?   *ka·ma ze le ...*

Please put the meter on.

תפעיל/תפעילי מונה בבקשה.   *taf·il/taf·i·li mo·ne be·va·ka·sha* m/f

Please take me to (this address).

תיקח/תיקחי אותי	*ti·kakh/tik·khi o·ti*
(לכתובת הזאת) בבקשה.	*(lak·to·vet ha·zot) be·va·ka·sha* m/f

Please stop here.

בבקשה תעצור/תעצרי כאן.   *be·va·ka·sha ta·tsor/ta·tsi·ri kan* m/f

Please wait here.

בבקשה תחכה/תחכי כאן.   *be·va·ka·sha ti·kha·ke/ti·kha·ki kan* m/f

I'd like to hire a ...	אני צריך/צריכה	a·ni tsa·rikh/tsri·kha
	לשכור ...	les·khor ... m/f
car	מכונית	mi·kho·nit
4WD	רכב שטח	re·khev she·takh

with ...	עם ...	im ...
a driver	נהג/נהגת	na·hag/na·he·get m/f
air conditioning	מזגן	maz·gan

How much for	כמה זה עולה	ka·ma ze o·le
... hire?	לשכור ל...?	les·khor le ...
daily	יום	yom
weekly	שבוע	sha·vu·a

I need a mechanic.
אני צריך/צריכה מכונאי. a·ni tsa·rikh/tsri·kha me·khu·nai m/f

I've run out of petrol.
נגמר לי הדלק. neg·mar li ha·de·lek

I have a flat tyre.
יש לי פנצ'ר. yesh li pan·cher

directions

Where's the ...?	איפה ה...?	e·fo ha ...
bank	בנק	bank
market	שוק	shuk

Where's the post office?
איפה סניף הדואר? e·fo snif ha·do·ar

Is this the road to (Hadera)?
האם הכביש הזה מוביל ha·im hak·vish ha·ze mo·vil
ל(חדרה)? le·(khe·de·ra)

Can you show me (on the map)?
אתה/את יכול להראות a·ta/at ya·khol le·har·ot
(לי על המפה)? (li al ha·ma·pa) m/f

What's the address?
מה הכתובת? ma hak·to·vet

How far is it?
כמה זה רחוק? ka·ma ze ra·khok

How do I get there?

איך אני יכול/יכולה	ekh a·ni ya·khol/ya·kho·la	
להגיע לשם?	le·ha·gi·a le·sham m/f	

Turn left/right.

תפנה שמאלה/ימינה.	tif·ne smo·la/yi·mi·na m
תפני שמאלה/ימינה.	tif·ni smo·la/yi·mi·na f

It's ...	... זה	ze ...
behind ...	... מאחורי	mi·a·kho·re ...
in front of ...	... לפני	lef·ne ...
near to ...	... קרוב ל	ka·rov le...
next to ...	... ליד	li·yad ...
on the corner	בפינה	ba·pi·na
opposite ...	... ממול	mi·mul ...
straight ahead	ישר קדימה	ya·shar ka·di·ma
there	שם	sham

north	צפון	tsa·fon
south	דרום	da·rom
east	מזרח	miz·rakh
west	מערב	ma·rav

signs

כניסה	kni·sa	Entrance
יציאה	yi·tsi·a	Exit
פתוח	pa·tu·akh	Open
סגור	sa·gur	Closed
מודיעין	mo·di·in	Information
תחנת משטרה	ta·kha·nat mish·ta·ra	Police Station
אסור	a·sur	Prohibited
שירותים	shi·ru·tim	Toilets
גברים	gva·rim	Men
נשים	na·shim	Women
חם	kham	Hot
קר	kar	Cold

accommodation

Where's a ...?	?... איפה	e·fo ...
camping ground	אתר הקמפינג	a·tar ha·kam·ping
guesthouse	בית ההארחה	bet ha·ha·'ra·kha
hotel	בית המלון	bet ma·lon
youth hostel	אכסניית הנוער	akh·san·yat no·ar

Can you recommend	אתה יכול	a·ta ya·khol
somewhere ...?	?... להמליץ על מקום	le·ham·lits al ma·kom ... m
	את יכולה	at ya·kho·la
	?... להמליץ על מקום	le·ham·lits al ma·kom ... f
cheap	זול	zol
good	טוב	tov
nearby	קרוב	ka·rov

Do you have a	יש לך	yesh le·kha/lakh
... room?	?... חדר	khe·der ... m/f
single	ליחיד	le·ya·khid
double	זוגי	zu·gi
twin	כפול	ka·ful

How much is it	כמה זה	ka·ma ze
per ...?	?... עולה ל	o·le le ...
night	לילה	lai·la
person	אדם	a·dam

I'd like to book a room, please.
אני רוצה להזמין חדר,
בבקשה.
a·ni ro·tse/ro·tsa le·haz·min khe·der
be·va·ka·sha m/f

I have a reservation.
יש לי הזמנה.
yesh li haz·ma·na

I'd like to stay for (two) nights.
אני רוצה להישאר ל(שתי)
לילות.
a·ni ro·tse/ro·tsa le·hi·sha·er le·(sh·te)
le·lot m/f

Am I allowed to camp here?
?האם זה מותר להקים אוהל כאן
ha·im ze mu·tar le·ha·kim o·hel kan

Could I have my key, please?
אפשר לקבל את המפתח שלי,
?בבקשה
if·shar le·ka·bel et ha·maf·te·yakh she·li
be·va·ka·sha

Can I get another (blanket)?

אפשר לקבל עוד (שמיכה)? ef·shar le·ka·bel od (smi·kha)

The (air conditioning) doesn't work.

(המזגן) לא עובד. (ha·maz·gan) lo o·ved

(This sheet) isn't clean.

(הסדין) הזה לא נקי. (ha·sa·din) ha·ze lo na·ki

Is there an elevator/a safe?

יש מעלית/כספת? yesh ma·a·lit/ka·se·fet

What time is checkout?

מתי צריכים לעזוב? ma·tai tsri·khim la·'zov

Could I have my	אני יכול/יכולה לקבל	a·ni ya·khol/ya·kho·la le·ka·bel
..., please?	את ה ... שלי,	et ha ... she·li
	בבקשה?	be·va·ka·sha m/f
deposit	פקדון	pi·ka·don
passport	דרכון	dar·kon
valuables	דברים יקרי ערך	dva·rim ya·ka·re e·rekh

banking & communications

Where's a/an ...?	איפה יש ...?	e·fo yesh ...
ATM	כספומט	kas·pu·mat
foreign exchange office	סניף החלפת מטבעות	snif hakh·la·fat mat·bi·ot

I'd like to ...	אני רוצה ...	a·ni ro·tse/ro·tsa ... m/f
arrange a transfer	לבצע העברה	le·va·tse·a haa'·va·ra
cash a cheque	לפדות צ'ק	lef·dot chek
change a travellers cheque	להמיר צ'ק מטיילים	le·ha·mir chek mi·tai·lim
change money	להחליף כסף	le·hakh·lif ke·sef
withdraw money	למשוך כסף	lem·shokh ke·sef

What's the ...?	מה ...?	ma ...
charge for that	העמלה עבור זה	ha·ma·la a·vur ze
exchange rate	שער החליפין	sha·ar ha·kha·li·fin

Where's the local internet café?

איפה האינטרנט קפה המקומי? | e·fo ha·*in*·tar·net ka·*fe* ha·mi·ku·*mi*

How much is it per hour?

כמה זה עולה לשעה? | *ka*·ma ze o·le la·sha·a

I'd like to ...	... אני רוצה	a·*ni* ro·tse/ro·tsa ... m/f
check my email	לבדוק את	lev·*dok* et
	האימייל שלי	ha·*i*·mel she·*li*
get internet access	להשתמש	le·hish·ta·*mesh*
	באינטרנט	ba·*in*·tar·net
use a printer	להשתמש	le·hish·ta·*mesh*
	במדפסת	ba·mad·*pe*·set
use a scanner	להשתמש בסורק	le·hish·ta·*mesh* ba·so·*rek*

I'd like a ... for hire.	אני רוצה	a·*ni* ro·tse/ro·tsa
	... לשכור	les·*khor* ... m/f
mobile/cell phone	טלפון נייד	te·le·fon na·*yad*
SIM card for your	כרטיס סים לרשת	kar·*tis* sim la·*re*·shet
network	שלך	shel·*kha*

What's your phone number?

מה מספר הטלפון שלך? | ma mis·*par* ha·te·le·fon shel·*kha*/she·lakh m/f

The number is ...

... המספר הוא | ha·mis·*par* hu ...

Where's the nearest public phone?

איפה הטלפון הציבורי הכי קרוב? | e·fo ha·te·le·fon ha·tsi·bu·*ri* ha·*khi* ka·*rov*

I'd like to buy a phonecard.

אני רוצה לקנות כרטיס לטלפון. | a·*ni* ro·tse/ro·tsa lek·*not* kar·*tis* la·te·le·fon m/f

How much does a (three)-minute call cost?

כמה עולה שיחת טלפון | *ka*·ma o·*la* si·*khat* te·le·fon
ל(שלוש) דקות? | le·(sha·*losh*) da·*kot*

What are the rates?

מה התעריפים? | ma ha·ta·ri·*fim*

I want to ...	... אני רוצה	a·*ni* ro·tse/ro·tsa ... m/f
call (Canada)	להתקשר ל(קנדה)	le·hit·ka·*sher* le·(*ka*·na·da)
make a local	לעשות שיחה	la·*sot* si·*kha*
call	מקומית	mi·ku·*mit*
reverse the charges	לחייב את היעד	le·kha·*yev* et ha·*ya*·ad

I want to send a ...	אני רוצה	a·ni ro·tse/ro·tsa
	לשלוח ...	lesh·lo·akh ... m/f
fax	פקס	faks
parcel	חבילה	kha·vi·la
I want to buy a/an ...	אני רוצה	a·ni ro·tse/ro·tsa
	לקנות ...	lek·not ... m/f
envelope	מעטפה	ma·ta·fa
stamp	בול	bul
Please send it	תשלח את זה	tish·lakh et ze
(to Australia)	(לאוסטרליה)	(le·ost·ral·ya)
by ...	בבקשה דרך ...	be·va·ka·sha de·rekh ...
airmail	הדואר האווירי	ha·do·ar ha·a·vi·ri
surface mail	דואר הים	do·ar ha·yam

sightseeing

What time does it open/close?

מתי פותחים/סוגרים?   ma·tai pot·khim/sog·rim

What's the admission charge?

כמה דמי הכניסה?   ka·ma dme hak·ni·sa

Is there a discount for students/children?

יש הנחה לסטודנטים   yesh ha·na·kha las·tu·den·tim/
ילדים?   yi·la·dim

I'd like a ...	אני רוצה ...	a·ni ro·tse/ro·tsa ... m/f
catalogue	קטלוג	ka·ta·log
guide	מדריך	mad·rikh
local map	מפה לאיזור	ma·pa la·i·zor
When's the next ...?	מתי ה ... הבא?	ma·tai ha ... ha·ba
day trip	טיול יום	ti·yul yom
tour	טיול	ti·yul

Is ... included?	?... האם זה כולל	ha·im ze ko·lel ...
accommodation	מגורים	mi·gu·rim
the admission charge	דמי הכניסה	dme ha·kni·sa
food	אוכל	o·khel
transport	תחבורה	takh·bu·ra

How long is the tour?

כמה זמן לוקח הטיול? *ka*·ma zman lo·ke·yakh ha·ti·*yul*

What time should we be back?

מתי חוזרים? ma·*tai* khoz·*rim*

I'd like to see ...

אני רוצה לראות ... a·*ni* ro·tse/ro·tsa ler·ot ... m/f

What's that?

מה זה? ma ze

Can I take a photo?

אפשר לצלם? if·*shar* le·tsa·*lem*

sightseeing

castle	טירה	ti·*ra* f
church	כנסיה	kni·si·*ya* f
main square	כיכר מרכזית	ki·*kar* mir·ka·*zit* f
mosque	מסגד	mis·*gad* m
old city	עיר עתיקה	ir a·ti·*ka* f
palace	ארמון	ar·*mon* m
pyramids	פירמידות	pi·ra·*mi*·dot f
ruins	עתיקות	a·ti·*kot* f
synagogue	בית כנסת	bet *kne*·set m

shopping

Where's a ...?	?... איפה	e·fo ...
bookshop	חנות הספרים	kha·*nut* has·fa·*rim*
camera shop	חנות הצילום	kha·*nut* ha·tsi·*lum*
department store	חנות הכל-בו	kha·*nut* ha·*kol*·bo
grocery store	המכולת	ha·ma·*ko*·let
newsagency	סוכנות החדשות	sokh·*nut* ha·kha·da·*shot*
souvenir shop	חנות המזכרות	kha·*nut* ha·miz·ka·*rot*
supermarket	סופרמרקט	su·per·*mar*·ket

I'm looking for ...

אני מחפש/מחפשת ...   a·ni mi·kha·*pes*/mi·kha·*pe*·set ... m/f

Can I look at it?

אפשר להסתכל על זה?   if·*shar* le·his·ta·*kel* al ze

Do you have any others?

יש לך אחרים?   yesh le·*kha* a·khe·*rim*

Does it have a guarantee?

יש על זה אחריות?   yesh al ze akh·ra·*yut*

Can I have it sent overseas?

אפשר לשלוח את זה לחו"ל?   if·*shar* lish·*lo*·akh et ze le·*khul*

Can I have my ... repaired?

אפשר לתקן את ה ... שלי?   if·*shar* le·ta·*ken* et ha ... she·*li*

It's faulty.

זה לא עובד.   ze lo o·*ved*

How much is it?

כמה זה עולה?   *ka*·ma ze o·*le*

Can you write down the price?

אתה יכול לכתוב את המחיר?   a·*ta* ya·*khol* lekh·*tov* et ha·mi·*khir* m

את יכולה לכתוב את המחיר?   at ya·kho·*la* lekh·*tov* et ha·mi·*khir* f

That's too expensive.

זה יקר מדי.   ze ya·*kar* mi·*dai*

What's your lowest price?

מה המחיר הסופי?   ma ha·mi·*khir* ha·so·*fi*

I'll give you (50 shekels).

אני משלם (חמשים שקלים).   a·*ni* mi·sha·*lem* (kha·me·*shim* shka·*lim*)

There's a mistake in the bill.

יש טעות בחשבון.   yesh ta·*ut* ba·khish·*bon*

I'd like ..., please.

אני רוצה ...,   a·*ni* ro·*tse*/ro·*tsa* ...

בבקשה.   be·va·ka·*sha* m/f

  a bag   תיק   tik

  a refund   החזר   hekh·*zer*

  to return this   להחזיר את זה   le·hakh·*zir* et ze

Do you accept ...?	? . . . אתם מקבלים	a·tem mi·kab·lim ...
credit cards	כרטיסי אשראי	kar·ti·se ash·rai
debit cards	כרטיסי חיוב	kar·ti·se khi·yuv
travellers cheques	צ'ק תיירים	chek ta·ya·rim
I'd like ..., please.	, . . . אני רוצה	a·ni ro·tse/ro·tsa ...
	בבקשה.	be·va·ka·sha m/f
my change	את העודף שלי	et ha·o·def she·li
a receipt	קבלה	ka·ba·la
I'd like ...	. . . אני רוצה	a·ni ro·tse/ro·tsa ... m/f
(100) grams	(מאה) גרם	(me·a) gram
(two) kilos	(שני) קילו	(shne) ki·lo
(three) pieces	(שלוש) חתיכות	(sha·losh) kha·ti·khot
(six) slices	(שש) פרוסות	(shesh) pru·sot
Less.	פחות.	pa·khot
Enough.	מספיק.	mas·pik
More.	יותר.	yo·ter

photography

Can you ...?	? . . . אתה יכול	a·ta ya·khol ... m
	? . . . את יכולה	at ya·kho·la ... f
burn a CD from	לצרוב מה שיש על	lets·rov ma she·yesh al
my memory	כרטיס הזכרון שלי	kar·tis ha·zi·ka·ron she·li
card	על גבי דיסק	al ga·be disk
develop this	לפתוח את הסרט	le·fa·te·yakh et ha·se·ret
film	הזה	ha·ze
load my film	לטעון את הסרט הזה	let·on et ha·se·ret ha·ze
I need a ... film	אני צריך/צריכה סרט	a·ni tsa·rikh/tsri·kha se·ret
for this camera.	. . . למצלמה הזאת.	... la·mats·li·ma ha·zot m/f
B&W	שחור/לבן	sha·khor/la·van
colour	צבעוני	tsiv·o·ni
slide	שקופיות	shku·fi·yot
(200) speed	מהירות (200)	mi·hi·rot (ma·ta·yim)
When will it be ready?	מתי זה יהיה מוכן?	ma·tai ze yeh·ye mo·khan

making conversation

Hello.	שלום.	sha·lom
Good night.	לילה טוב.	lai·la tov
Goodbye.	להתראות.	le·hit·ra·ot

Mr	מר	mar
Mrs/Miss	גברת	gi·ve·ret

How are you?

	מה נשמע?	ma nish·ma

Fine, thanks. And you?

	טוב, תודה.	tov to·da
	ואתה/ואת?	ve·a·ta/ve·at m/f

What's your name?

	איך קוראים לך?	ekh kor·im le·kha/lakh m/f

My name is ...

	שמי ...	shmi ...

I'm pleased to meet you.

	נעים מאוד.	na·im mi·od

This is my ...	זה ...	ze ...
brother	האח שלי	ha·akh she·li
daughter	הילדה שלי	ha·yal·da she·li
father	אבי	a·vi
friend	החבר שלי	ha·kha·ver she·li
husband	בעלי	baa'·li
mother	אמי	i·mi
sister	אחותי	a·kho·ti
son	הילד שלי	ha·ye·led she·li
wife	אשתי	ish·ti

Here's my ...	הנה ה ...	hi·ne ha ...
What's your ...?	מה ... שלך?	ma ... shel·kha/she·lakh m/f
address	הכתובת	hak·to·vet
email address	כתובת אימייל	kto·vet ha·e·mel
phone number	מספר הטלפון	mis·par ha·te·le·fon

What's your	במה אתה עוסק?	be·ma a·ta o·sek m
occupation?	במה את עוסקת?	be·ma at o·se·ket f

I'm a/an ...	... אני	a·ni ...
businessperson	איש/אשת עסקים	ish/i·shat a·sa·kim m/f
office worker	עובד/עובדת	o·ved/o·ve·det
	במשרד	ba·mis·rad m/f
tradesperson	בעל/בעלת מקצוע	ba·al/ba·a·lat mik·tso·a m/f

Where are you from?	מאיפה אתה/את?	mi·e·fo a·ta/at m/f

I'm from ...	... אני מ	a·ni me ...
Australia	אוסטרליה	ost·ra·lia
Canada	קנדה	ka·na·da
New Zealand	ניו זילנד	niyu zi·land
the UK	בריטניה	bri·tan·ya
the USA	ארצות הברית	ar·tsot hab·rit

Do you like ...?	אתה אוהב ...?	a·ta o·hev ... m
	את אוהבת ...?	at o·he·vet ... f
I (don't) like ...	אני (לא)	a·ni (lo)
	אוהב/אוהבת ...	o·hev/o·he·vet ... m/f
art	אמנות	a·ma·nut
movies	קולנוע	kol·no·a
music	מוזיקה	mu·zi·ka
reading	לקרוא	lek·ro
sport	ספורט	sport

eating out

Can you recommend a ...?	אתה יכול	a·ta ya·khol
	להמליץ על ...?	le·ham·lits al ... m
	את יכולה	at ya·kho·la
	להמליץ על ...?	le·ham·lits al ... f
bar	בר	bar
café	בית קפה	bet ka·fe
restaurant	מסעדה	mis·a·da

I'd like ..., please.	אני צריך/צריכה	a·ni tsa·rikh/tsri·kha
	..., בבקשה.	... be·va·ka·sha m/f
a table for (four)	שולחן ל(ארבעה)	shol·khan le·(ar·ba·a)
the (non)smoking section	אזור (ללא) עישון	i·zor (le·lo) i·shun

breakfast	ארוחת בוקר	a·ro·khat bo·ker f
lunch	ארוחת צהריים	a·ro·khat tso·ho·ra·yim f
dinner	ארוחת ערב	a·ro·khat e·rev f

I'd like (the) ..., please.	אני צריך/צריכה את ...., בבקשה.	a·ni tsa·rikh/tsri·kha et ... be·va·ka·sha m/f
bill	החשבון	ha·khish·bon
drink list	תפריט המשקאות	taf·rit ha·mish·ka·ot
menu	התפריט	ha·taf·rit
that dish	המאכל הזה	ha·ma·khal ha·ze

What would you recommend?

מה אתה ממליץ? — ma a·ta mam·lits m
מה את ממליצה? — ma at mam·li·tsa f

What's the local speciality?

מה המאכל המקומי? — ma ha·ma·khal ha·mi·ko·mi

What's that?

מה זה? — ma ze

drinks

(cup of) coffee ...	(ספל) קפה ...	(se·fel) ka·fe ...
(cup of) tea ...	(ספל) תה ...	(se·fel) te ...
with milk	עם חלב	em kha·lav
without sugar	ללא סוכר	le·lo su·kar

| (orange) juice | מיץ (תפוזים) | mits (ta·pu·zim) m |
| soft drink | משקה קל | mish·ke kal m |

... water	מים ...	ma·yim ... m
boiled	רותחים	rot·khim
mineral	מינרליים	mi·ni·ra·li·tim

I'll have ...

אני אקח ... — a·ni i·kakh ...

I'll buy you a drink.

אני אזמין לך משקה. — a·ni az·min le·kha/lakh mash·ke m/f

What would you like?

מה בא לך? — ma ba le·kha/lakh m/f

| a bottle/glass of beer | בקבוק/כוס בירה | bak·buk/kos bi·ra |
| a shot of (whisky) | כוסית (וויסקי) | ko·sit (wis·ki) |

a bottle/glass of	בקבוק/כוס	bak·buk/kos
... wine	יין ...	ya·yin ...
red	אדום	a·dom
sparkling	תוסס	to·ses
white	לבן	la·van

special diets & allergies

Is there a vegetarian restaurant near here?
האם יש מסעדה צמחונית באזור? ha·im yesh mis·a·da tsim·kho·nit ba·i·zor

Do you have ... food?	יש לכם אוכל ...?	yesh la·khem o·khel ...
halal	חלאל	ha·lal
kosher	כשר	ka·sher
vegetarian	צמחוני	tsim·kho·ni

Could you prepare a	אפשר להכין	if·shar le·ha·khin
meal without ...?	מנה בלי ...?	ma·na bli ...
butter	חמאה	khim·a
eggs	ביצים	bi·tsim
meat stock	ציר בשר	tsir ba·sar

I'm allergic to ...	אני רגיש/רגישה ל ...	a·ni ra·gish/ra·gi·sha le ... m/f
dairy produce	מוצרי חלב	mo·tsa·re kha·lav
gluten	גלוטן	glu·ten
nuts	אגוזים	e·go·zim
seafood	פירות ים	pi·rot yam

emergencies

Help!	הצילו!	ha·tsi·lu
Stop!	עצור!	a·tsor
Go away!	לך מפה!	lekh mi·po
Thief!	גנב!	ga·nav
Fire!	שריפה!	sri·fa
Watch out!	זהירות!	ze·hi·rut

Call ...!   !... תתקשר ל   tit·ka·*sher* le ...
- a doctor   רופא   ro·*fe*/ro·*fa* m/f
- an ambulance   אמבולנס   *am*·bu·lans
- the police   משטרה   mish·ta·*ra*

Could you help me, please?

אתה יכול לעזור לי בבקשה?   a·*ta* ya·*khol* la·*zor* li be·va·ka·*sha* m

את יכולה לעזור לי בבקשה?   at ya·kho·*la* la·*zor* li be·va·ka·*sha* f

I have to use the phone.

אני חייב/חייבת להשתמש   a·*ni* kha·*yav*/kha·*ye*·vet le·hish·ta·*mesh*

בטלפון.   ba·*te*·le·fon m/f

I'm lost.

אני אבוד/אבודה.   a·*ni* a·*vud*/a·vu·*da* m/f

Where are the toilets?

איפה השירותים?   e·fo ha·shi·ru·*tim*

Where's the police station?

איפה תחנת המשטרה?   e·fo ta·kha·*nat* ha·mish·ta·*ra*

I want to report an offence.

אני רוצה לדווח על עבירה.   a·*ni* ro·tse/ro·tsa le·da·ve·yakh al a·vi·*ra* m/f

I have insurance.

יש לי ביטוח.   yesh li bi·*tu*·akh

I want to contact my embassy.

אני רוצה להתקשר עם   a·*ni* ro·tse/ro·tsa le·hit·ka·*sher* em

השגרירות שלי.   ha·shag·ri·*rut* she·*li* m/f

I've been assaulted.   הותקפתי.   hot·*kaf*·ti
I've been raped.   נאנסתי.   ne·nas·*ti*
I've been robbed.   שדדו אותי.   sha·di·*du* o·ti

I've lost my ...   איבדתי את ה ... שלי.   i·ba·di·ti et ha ... she·*li*
- bag   תיק   tik
- credit card   כרטיס אשראי   kar·*tis* ash·*rai*
- money   כסף   *ke*·sef
- passport   דרכון   dar·*kon*
- travellers cheques   צ'קים לתיירים   *che*·kim la·ta·ya·*rim*

health

Where's the nearest ...?	איפה ה ... הכי קרוב?	e·fo ha ... ha·khi ka·rov
dentist	רופא/רופאת שיניים	ro·fe/ro·fat shi·na·yim m/f
doctor	רופא	ro·fe/ro·fa m/f
hospital	בית חולים	bet kho·lim
(night) pharmacist	בית מרקחת	bet mir·ka·khat

I need a doctor (who speaks English).

אני צריך רופא
(שמי·דא·בר אנגלית).

a·ni tsa·rikh ro·fe/ro·fa
(she·mi·da·ber ang·lit) m/f

Could I see a female doctor?

אפשר לבקר אצל רופא?

if·shar le·va·ker e·tsel ro·fa

I've run out of my medication.

נגמרו לי התרופות.

nig·mi·ru li hat·ru·fot

I'm sick.

אני חולה.

a·ni kho·le/kho·la m/f

It hurts here.

כואב לי כאן.

ko·ev li kan

I have (a) ...	... יש לי	yesh li ...
asthma	אסטמה	ast·ma
constipation	עצירות	a·tsi·rut
diarrhoea	שלשול	shil·shul
fever	חום	khom
headache	כאב ראש	ke·ev rosh
heart condition	מחלת לב	ma·kha·lat lev
nausea	בחילה	bkhi·la
pain	כאב	ke·ev
sore throat	גרון צרוד	ga·ron tsa·rud
toothache	כאב שיניים	ke·ev shi·na·yim

I'm allergic to ...	... אני רגיש ל	a·ni ra·gish le ...
antibiotics	אנטיביוטיקה	an·ti·bi·yo·ti·ka
anti-inflammatories	אנטי-דלקות	an·ti·da·la·kot
aspirin	אספירין	as·pi·rin
bees	דבורים	dvo·rim
codeine	קודיאין	ko·de·in
penicillin	פניצלין	pen·tsa·lin

english–hebrew dictionary

Words in this dictionary are marked as n (noun), a (adjective), v (verb), ⓜ (masculine), ⓕ (feminine),
sg (singular) and pl (plural) where necessary. Verbs are given in the present tense in the third-person
singular masculine form – for feminine forms, generally just add ה ah to the end of a verb. For exceptions
to this rule both masculine and feminine form of the verb are given.

A

accident תאונה te·u·na ⓜ
accommodation דיור di·yur ⓜ
adaptor שנאי sha·nai ⓜ
address כתובת kto·vet ⓕ
after אחרי a·kha·re
air-conditioned ממוזג־אויר mi·mu·zag a·vir
airplane מטוס ma·tos ⓜ
airport שדה־תעופה sde te·ofa ⓜ
alcohol אלכוהול al·ko·hol ⓜ
all כל kol
allergy רגישות re·gi·shut ⓕ
ambulance אמבולנס am·bu·lans ⓜ
and ו ve
ankle קרסול kar·sul ⓜ
arm זרוע zro·aa ⓕ
ashtray מאפרה ma'·fe·ra ⓕ
ATM כספומט kas·pu·mat ⓜ

B

baby תינוק ti·nok ⓜ
back (body) גב gav ⓜ
backpack תרמיל tar·mil ⓜ
bad רע/רעה ra/ra·aa ⓜ/ⓕ
bag תיק tik ⓜ
baggage claim מסוף מזוודות ma·sof miz·va·dot
bank בנק bank ⓜ
bar בר bar ⓜ
bathroom מקלחת mik·la·khat ⓕ
battery בטריה ba·ta·ri·ya ⓕ
beautiful יפה/יפה ya·fe/ya·fa ⓜ/ⓕ
bed מיטה mi·ta ⓕ
beer בירה bi·ra ⓕ
before לפני lif·ne
behind מאחורי mi·a·khu·re
bicycle אופניים o·fa·na·yem
big גדול/גדולה ga·dol/gdo·la ⓜ/ⓕ
bill חשבון khish·bon ⓜ
black שחור/שחורה sha·khor/sh'kho·ra ⓜ/ⓕ
blanket שמיכה smi·kha ⓕ

blood group סוג דם sug dam ⓜ
blue כחול/כחולה ka·khol/k'kho·la ⓜ/ⓕ
boat סירה si·ra ⓕ
book (make a reservation) v להזמין hiz·min
bottle בקבוק bak·buk ⓜ
bottle opener פותחן בקבוקים
   put·khan bak·bu·kim ⓜ
boy ילד ye·led ⓜ
brakes (car) בלמים ba·la·mim ⓜ
breakfast ארוחת בוקר a·ro·khat bo·ker ⓕ
broken (faulty) מקולקל/מקולקלת
   mi·kul·kal/mi·kul·ke·let ⓜ/ⓕ
bus אוטובוס o·to·bus ⓜ
business עסק e·sek ⓜ
buy לקנות lek·not

C

café בית קפה bet ka·fe ⓜ
camera מצלמה mats·le·ma ⓕ
camp site מחנה ma·kha·ne ⓜ
cancel ביטל bi·tel
can opener פותחן קופסאות put·khan kuf·sa·ot ⓜ
car מכונית mi·kho·nit ⓕ
cash n מזומן mi·zu·man ⓜ
cash (a cheque) v לפדות lef·dot
cell phone טלפון נייד te·le·fon na·yad ⓜ
centre n מרכז mir·kaz ⓜ
change (money) v להמיר le·ha·mir
cheap זול/זולה zol/zo·la ⓜ/ⓕ
check (bill) n חשבון khish·bon ⓜ
check-in n רישום ri·shum ⓜ
chest חזה kha·ze ⓜ
child ילד/ילדה ye·led/yal·da ⓜ/ⓕ
cigarette סיגריה si·gar·ya ⓕ
city עיר ir ⓕ
clean a נקי/נקיה na·ki/na·ki·ya ⓜ/ⓕ
closed סגור/סגורה sa·gur/sgu·ra ⓜ/ⓕ
coffee קפה ka·fe ⓜ
coins מטבעות mat·bi·ot ⓕ
cold a קר/קרה kar/ka·ra ⓜ/ⓕ
collect call שיחת גוביינה si·khat go·vai·na ⓕ

come בוא bo
computer מחשב makh·shev ⓜ
condom קונדום kon·dom ⓜ
contact lenses עדשות מגע ad·shot ma·ga ①
cook v לבשל le·va·shel
cost v עלות a·lut
credit card כרטיס אשראי kar·tis ash·rai ⓜ
cup ספל se·fel ⓜ
currency exchange המרת מטבעות
ha·ma·rat mat·be·ot ①
customs (immigration) מכס me·khes ⓜ

D

dangerous מסוכן/מסוכנת
mi·su·kan/mi·su·ke·net ⓜ/①
date (time) ה תאריך ta·rikh ⓜ
day יום yom ⓜ
delay ה עיקוב i·kuv ⓜ
dentist רופא/רופאת שיניים
ro·fe/ro·fat shi·na·yim
depart עוזב o·zev
diaper חיתול khi·tul ⓜ
dictionary מילון mi·lon ⓜ
dinner ארוחת ערב a·ro·khat e·rev ①
direct a ישיר/ישירה ya·shir/ya·shi·ra ⓜ/①
dirty מלוכלך/מלוכלכת
mi·lukh·lakh/mi·lukh·le·khet ⓜ/①
disabled נכה na·khe/na·kha
discount ה הנחה ha·na·kha ①
doctor רופא ro·fe/ro·fa
double bed מיטה זוגית mi·ta zu·git ①
double room חדר זוגי khe·der zu·gi ⓜ
drink ה משקה mish·ke
drive v נסע na·sa
drivers licence רישיון נהיגה ri·sha·yon ni·hi·ga ⓜ
drug (illicit) סמים sa·mim
dummy (pacifier) מוצץ mo·tsets

E

ear אוזן o·zen ①
east מזרח miz·rakh ⓜ
eat לאכול le·khol
economy class מחלקת תיירים
makh·le·ket ta·ya·rim ①
electricity חשמל khash·mal ⓜ
elevator מעלית ma·a·lit ①
email ה דואר אלקטרוני do·ar e·lekt·ro·ni ⓜ
embassy שגרירות shag·ri·rut ①
emergency חירום khi·rum ⓜ

English (language) אנגלית ang·lit ①
entrance כניסה kni·sa ①
evening ה ערב e·rev ⓜ
exchange rate שער חליפין sha·ar kha·li·fin ⓜ
exit ה יציאה yi·tsi·a ①
expensive יקר/יקרה ya·kar/ya·ka·ra ⓜ/①
express mail דואר מהיר do·ar ma·hir ⓜ
eye עין a·yin ①

F

far רחוק ra·khok
fast מהר ma·her
father אב av ⓜ
film (camera) סרט se·ret ⓜ
finger אצבע ets·ba ①
first-aid kit ציוד עזרה ראשונית
tsi·yud iz·ra ri·shu·na ⓜ
first class מחלקה ראשונה
makh·la·ka ri·shu·na ①
fish ה דג dag ⓜ
food אוכל o·khel ⓜ
foot רגל re·gel ①
fork מזלג maz·leg ⓜ
free (of charge) חופשי/חופשית
khof·shi/khof·shit ⓜ/①
friend חבר/חברה kha·ver/kha·ve·ra ⓜ/①
fruit פרי pri ⓜ
full מלא/מלאה ma·le/m'li·aa ⓜ/①
funny מצחיק/מצחיקה
mats·khik/mats·khi·ka ⓜ/①

G

gift מתנה ma·ta·na ①
girl ילדה yal·da ①
glass (drinking) כוס kos ①
glasses (eyesight) משקפיים mish·ka·fa·yem ①
go לך lekh
good טוב/טובה tov/to·va ⓜ/①
green ירוק/ירוקה ya·rok/ye·ro·ka ⓜ/①
guide מדריך/מדריכה
mad·rikh/mad·ri·kha ⓜ/①

H

half חצי khe·tsi ⓜ
hand יד yad ①
handbag תיק יד tik yad ⓜ
happy שמח/שמחה sa·me·yakh/s'me·kha ⓜ/①

DICTIONARY

I

have יש לו/לה yesh lo/la ⓜ/ⓕ

he הוא hu

head ראש rosh ⓜ

heart לב lev ⓜ

heat n חום khom

heavy כבד/כבדה ka-ved/kve-da ⓜ/ⓕ

Hebrew עברית iv-rit

help עזרה iz-ra

here כאן kan

high גבוה/גבוהה ga-voh/gvo-ha ⓜ/ⓕ

highway כביש ראשי kvish ra-shi ⓜ

hike v צעד tsa-ad

holiday חופש kho-fesh

homosexual n הומוסקסואל ho-mo-sek-su-al ⓜ

hospital בית חולים bet kho-lim ⓜ

hot חם/חמה kham/kha-ma ⓜ/ⓕ

hotel בית מלון bet ma-lon ⓜ

hungry רעב/רעבה ra-ev/ra-e-va ⓜ/ⓕ

husband בעל ba-al ⓜ

I

I אני a-ni

identification (card) זהוי zi-hu-i ⓜ

ill חולה/חולה kho-le/kho-la ⓜ/ⓕ

important חשוב/חשובה
kha-shuv/kha-shu-va ⓜ/ⓕ

included כלול/כלולה ka-lul/klu-la ⓜ/ⓕ

injury פגיעה p'gi-a ⓕ

insurance ביטוח bi-tu-akh ⓜ

internet אינטרנט in-tar-net ⓜ

interpreter מתורגמן mi-tur-gi-man ⓜ

Israel ישראל yis-ra-el

J

jewellery תכשיטים takh-shi-tim ⓜ

job עבודה a-vo-da ⓕ

K

key מפתח maf-te-yakh ⓜ

kilogram קילוגרם ki-lu-gram ⓜ

kitchen מטבח mit-bakh ⓜ

knife סכין sa-kin ⓜ

L

laundry (place) מכבסה makh-bi-sa ⓕ

lawyer עורך דין o-rekh din ⓜ

left (direction) שמאלה smo-la

left-luggage office מחלקת כבודה שאבדה
makh-le-ket kvu-da she-av-da ⓕ

leg רגל re-gel ⓜ

lesbian n לסבית les-bit ⓕ

less פחות pa-khot

letter (mail) מכתב mikh-tav ⓜ

lift (elevator) מעלית ma-a-lit ⓕ

light n אור or ⓜ

like v מחבב/מחבבת
mi-kha-vev/mi-kha-ve-vet ⓜ/ⓕ

lock n מנעול man-ul ⓜ

long ארוך/ארוכה a-rokh/a-ro-ka ⓜ/ⓕ

lost אבוד/אבודה a-vud/a-vu-da ⓜ/ⓕ

lost-property office מחלקת אבידות
makh-le-ket a-vi-dot ⓕ

love v אוהב/אוהבת o-hev/o-he-vet ⓜ/ⓕ

luggage מטען mit-an ⓜ

lunch ארוחת צהריים a-ro-khat tso-ho-ra-yim ⓕ

M

mail n דואר do-ar ⓜ

man גבר ge-ver ⓜ

map מפה ma-pa ⓕ

market שוק shuk ⓜ

matches גפרורים gaf-ru-rim ⓜ

meat בשר ba-sar ⓜ

medicine תרופה tru-fa ⓕ

menu תפריט taf-rit ⓜ

message הודעה hu-da-a ⓕ

milk חלב kha-lav ⓜ

minute דקה da-ka ⓕ

mobile phone טלפון נייד te-le-fon na-yad ⓜ

money כסף ke-sef ⓜ

month חודש kho-desh ⓜ

morning בוקר bo-ker ⓜ

mother אם em ⓕ

motorcycle אופנוע o-fa-no-aa' ⓜ

motorway כביש מהיר kvish ma-hir ⓜ

mouth פה pe ⓜ

music מוסיקה mu-zi-ka ⓕ

N

name שם shem ⓜ

napkin מפית-סעודה ma-pit se-u-da ⓕ

nappy חיתול khi-tul ⓜ

near קרוב ka-rov

neck צואר tsa-var ⓜ

new חדש kha-dash ⓜ & ⓕ

news חדשות kha-da-shot ⓕ

newspaper עיתון i-ton ⓜ

night לילה lai-la ⓕ
no לא lo
noisy רועש ro-esh ⓜ & ⓕ
nonsmoking לא עישון le-lo i-shun
north צפון tsa-fon ⓜ
nose אף af ⓜ
now עכשיו akh-shav
number מספר mis-par ⓜ

O

oil (engine) שמן מנוע 'she-men ma-no-u-aa ⓜ
old ישן/ישנה ya-shan/ya-sha-na ⓜ/ⓕ
one way ticket כרטיס לכיוון אחד kar-tis la-ki-vun i-khad ⓜ
open a פתוח/פתוחה pa-tu-akh/p'tu-kha ⓜ/ⓕ
outside בחוץ ba-khuts

P

package חבילה kha-vi-la ⓕ
paper נייר ni-yar ⓜ
park (car) v החנה hikh-na
passport דרכון dar-kon ⓜ
pay v לשלם li-sha-lem
pen עט et ⓜ
petrol דלק de-lek ⓜ
pharmacy בית מרקחת bet mir-ka-khat ⓜ
phone card כרטיס טלפון kar-tis te-le-fon ⓜ
photo תמונה tmu-na ⓕ
plate צלחת tsa-la-khat ⓕ
police משטרה mish-ta-ra ⓕ
postcard גלויה glu-ya ⓕ
post office סניף דואר snif do-ar ⓜ
pregnant הרה ha-ra ⓕ
price מחיר mi-khir ⓜ

Q

quiet שקט/שקטה sha-ket/sh'ke-ta ⓜ/ⓕ

R

rain n גשם ge-shem ⓜ
razor סכין גילוח sa-kin gi-lu-akh ⓜ
receipt n קבלה ka-ba-la ⓕ
red אדום/אדומה a-dom/a-do-ma ⓜ/ⓕ
refund n החזר hekh-zer ⓜ
registered mail דואר רשום do-ar ra-shum ⓜ
rent v השכיר hes-khir

repair v תקן ti-ken
reservation הזמנת מקום מראש haz-ma-nat ma-kom mi-rosh ⓕ
restaurant מסעדה mis-a-da ⓕ
return v חזר kha-zar
return ticket כרטיס הלוך ושוב kar-tis ha-lokh ve-shov ⓜ
right (direction) ימינה yi-mi-na
road כביש kvish
room חדר khe-der ⓜ

S

safe a בטוח ba-tu-akh ⓜ & ⓕ
sanitary napkin תחבושת היגיינית takh-bo-shet hig-ye-nit ⓕ
seat מושב mu-shav ⓜ
send שלח sha-lakh
service station תחנת דלק ta-kha-nat de-lek ⓕ
sex מין min ⓜ
shampoo שמפו sham-pu ⓜ
share (a dorm etc) לחלוק lekh-lok
shaving cream קרם גילוח krem gi-lu-akh ⓜ
she היא hi
sheet (bed) סדין sa-din ⓜ
shirt חולצה khul-tsa ⓕ
shoes נעליים naa'-la-yem ⓕ
shop n חנות kha-nut ⓕ
short קצר/קצרה ka-tsar/k'tsa-ra ⓜ/ⓕ
shower n מקלחת mik-la-khat ⓕ
single room חדר ליחיד khe-der le-ya-khid ⓜ
skin עור or ⓜ
skirt חצאית kha-tsa-it ⓕ
sleep v ישן ya-shan
slowly לאט le-at
small קטן/קטנה ka-tan/kta-na ⓜ/ⓕ
smoke (cigarettes) v לעשן le-a'a-shen
soap n סבון sa-bon ⓜ
some מעט mi-at
soon בקרוב be-ka-rov
south דרום da-rom ⓜ
souvenir shop חנות מזכרות kha-nut miz-ka-rot ⓕ
speak לדבר le-da-ber
spoon כף kaf ⓕ
stamp בול bul ⓜ
stand-by ticket כרטיס בהמתנה kar-tis be-ham-ta-na ⓜ
station (train) תחנת רכבת ta-kha-nat ra-ke-vet ⓕ
stomach בטן be-ten ⓕ
stop v עצור a-tsor

stop (bus) n תחנת אוטובוס ta-kha-*nat* o-to-bus ⓕ

street רחוב re-*khov*

student סטודנט stu-*dent* ⓜ

sun שמש she-*mesh* ⓕ

sunscreen קרם הגנה krem ha-ga-*na* ⓜ

swim v שחה sa-*kha*

T

tampons טמפונים tam-*po*-nim ⓜ

taxi מונית mo-*nit* ⓕ

teaspoon כפית ka-*pit* ⓕ

teeth שיניים shi-*na*-yem ⓜ

telephone n טלפון te-le-*fon* ⓜ

television טלוויזיה te-le-*viz*-ya ⓕ

temperature (weather) טמפרטורה tem-pe-ra-*tu*-ra ⓕ

tent אוהל o-*hel* ⓜ

that (one) הוא/היא hu/hi ⓜ/ⓕ

they הם/הן hem/hen ⓜ/ⓕ

thirsty צמא/צמאה tsa-*me*/tsme-*aa* ⓜ/ⓕ

this (one) זה/זאת ze/zot ⓜ/ⓕ

throat גרון ga-*ron* ⓜ

ticket כרטיס kar-*tis* ⓜ

time זמן zman ⓜ

tired עייף/עייפה a-*yef*/a-ye-*fa* ⓜ/ⓕ

tissues ממחטת נייר mem-khe-tet ni-*yar* ⓕ

today היום ha-*yom*

toilet שירותים shi-ru-*tim* ⓜ

tomorrow מחר ma-*khar*

tonight הלילה ha-*lai*-la

toothbrush מברשת שיניים miv-re-*shet* shi-*na*-yim ⓕ

toothpaste משחת שיניים mish-*khat* shi-*na*-yim ⓕ

torch (flashlight) פנס יד pa-*nas* yad ⓜ

tour n טיול ti-*yul* ⓜ

tourist office משרד לתיירים mis-*rad* la-ta-ya-*rim* ⓜ

towel מגבת ma-ge-*vet* ⓕ

train רכבת ra-*ke*-vet ⓕ

translate תרגם tir-*gem*

travel agency משרד נסיעות mis-*rad* ne-si-*ot* ⓜ

travellers cheque שיק מטיילים shek mi-tai-*lim*

trousers מכנסיים mikh-na-*sa*-yim ⓜ

twin beds מיטה זוגית mi-*ta* zu-*git* ⓕ

tyre צמיג tsa-*mig* ⓜ

U

underwear תחתונים takh-tu-*nim* ⓜ

urgent דחוף da-*khuf* ⓜ&ⓕ

V

vacant פנוי pa-*nu*-i ⓜ&ⓕ

vacation חופשה khuf-*sha* ⓕ

vegetable n ירק ye-*rek* ⓜ

vegetarian צמחוני/צמחונית tsim-khu-*ni*/tsim-khu-*ni* ⓜ/ⓕ

visa אשרת כניסה ash-*rat* kni-sa ⓕ

W

waiter מלצר mil-*tsar* ⓜ

walk v הלך ha-*lakh*

wallet ארנק ar-*nak* ⓜ

warm a חמים kha-*mim* ⓜ&ⓕ

wash (something) רחץ ra-*khats*

watch n שעון sha-*on* ⓜ

water מים *ma*-yim ⓜ

we אנחנו a-*nakh*-nu

weekend סוף שבוע sof sha-vu-*a* ⓜ

west מערב ma-*rav* ⓜ

wheelchair כסא גלגלים ki-se gal-ga-*lim* ⓜ

when מתי ma-*tai*

where איפה e-*fo*

white לבן/לבנה la-*van*/le-va-*na* ⓜ/ⓕ

who מי mi

why למה *la*-ma

wife אשה i-*sha* ⓕ

window חלון khlon ⓜ

wine יין *ya*-yin ⓜ

with עם im

without ללא le-*lo*

woman אשה i-*sha* ⓕ

write כתב ka-*tav*

Y

yellow צהוב/צהובה tsa-*hov*/tse-hu-*ba* ⓜ/ⓕ

yes כן ken

yesterday אתמול it-*mol*

you sg אתה/את a-ta/at ⓜ/ⓕ

you pl אתם/אתן a-*tem*/a-*ten* ⓜ/ⓕ

Turkish

turkish alphabet

A a a	*B b* be	*C c* je	*Ç ç* che	*D d* de
E e e	*F f* fe	*G g* ge	*Ğ ğ* yu-*moo*-shak ge	*H h* he
I ı uh	*İ i* ee	*J j* zhe	*K k* ke	*L l* le
M m me	*N n* ne	*O o* o	*Ö ö* er	*P p* pe
R r re	*S s* se	*Ş ş* she	*T t* te	*U u* oo
Ü ü ew	*V v* ve	*Y y* ye	*Z z* ze	

TURKISH
türkçe

introduction

Turkish (*Türkçe* tewrk·che) traces its roots as far back as 3500 BC, has travelled through Central Asia, Persia, North Africa and Europe and been written in both Arabic and Latin script – and has left us words like *yogurt*, *horde*, *sequin* and *bridge* (game) along the way. But how did it transform itself from a nomad's tongue spoken in Mongolia into the language of modern Turkey, with a prestigious interlude as the diplomatic language of the Ottoman Empire?

The first evidence of the Turkish language, which is a member of the Ural-Altaic language family, was found on stone monuments from the 8th century BC in what's now Outer Mongolia. In the 11th century, the Seljuq clan invaded Asia Minor (Anatolia) and imposed their language on the peoples they ruled. Over time, Arabic and Persian vocabulary was adopted to express artistic and philosophical concepts and Arabic script began to be used. By the 14th century, another clan – the Ottomans – was busy establishing the empire that was to control Eurasia for centuries. In their wake, they left the Turkish language. There were then two levels of Turkish – ornate Ottoman Turkish, with flowery Persian phrases and Arabic honorifics (words showing respect), used for diplomacy, business and art, and the language of the common Turks, which still used 'native' Turkish vocabulary and structures.

When the Ottoman Empire fell in 1922, the military hero, amateur linguist and historian Kemal Atatürk came to power and led the new Republic of Turkey. With the backing of a strong language reform movement, he devised a phonetic Latin script that reflected Turkish sounds more accurately than Arabic script. On 1 November 1928, the new writing system was unveiled: within two months, it was illegal to write Turkish in the old script. In 1932 Atatürk created the *Türk Dil Kurumu* (Turkish Language Society) and gave it the brief of simplifying the Turkish language to its 'pure' form of centuries before. The vocabulary and structure was completely overhauled. As a consequence, Turkish has changed so drastically that even Atatürk's own speeches are barely comprehensible to today's speakers of *öztürkçe* ('pure Turkish').

With 70 million speakers worldwide, Turkish is the official language of Turkey and the Turkish Republic of Northern Cyprus (recognised as a nation only by the Turkish government). Elsewhere, the language is also called *Osmanlı* os·man·luh, and is spoken by large populations in Europe and the '-stans' of Central Asia. Start practising and you might soon be complimented with *Ağzına sağlık!* a·zuh·na sa·luhk 'Well said!'.

pronunciation

vowel sounds

Most Turkish vowel sounds can be found in English, although in Turkish they're generally shorter and slightly harsher. When you see a double vowel, such as *saat* sa·*at* (hour), you need to pronounce both vowels.

symbol	english equivalent	turkish example	transliteration
a	run	*abide*	a·bee·*de*
ai	aisle	*hayvan*	hai·*van*
ay	say	*ney*	nay
e	bet	*ekmek*	ek·*mek*
ee	see	*ile*	ee·*le*
eu	nurse	*özel*	eu·*zel*
ew	ee pronounced with rounded lips	*üye*	ew·*ye*
o	pot	*oda*	o·*da*
oo	zoo	*uçak*	oo·*chak*
uh	ago	*ıslak*	uhs·*lak*

word stress

In Turkish, the stress generally falls on the last syllable of the word. Most two-syllable place names, however, are stressed on the first syllable (eg *Kıbrıs* kuhb·ruhs), and in three-syllable place names the stress is usually on the second syllable (eg *İstanbul* ees·*tan*·bool). Another common exception occurs when a verb has a form of the negative marker *me* (*me* me, *ma* ma, *mı* muh, *mi* mee, *mu* moo, or *mü* mew) added to it. In such cases, the stress goes onto the syllable before the marker – eg *gelmiyorlar* gel·mee·yor·lar (they're not coming). You don't need to worry too much about this, as the stressed syllable is always in italics in our coloured pronunciation guides.

consonant sounds

Most Turkish consonant sounds are the same as in English, so they're straightforward to pronounce. The exception is the Turkish sound r, which is always rolled. Note also that the written ğ is a silent letter which extends the vowel before it – it acts like the 'gh' combination in 'weigh', and is never pronounced.

symbol	english equivalent	turkish example	transliteration
b	bed	*bira*	*bee-ra*
ch	cheat	*çanta*	*chan-ta*
d	dog	*deniz*	*de-neez*
f	fat	*fabrika*	*fab-ree-ka*
g	go	*gar*	*gar*
h	hat	*hala*	*ha-la*
j	joke	*cadde*	*jad-de*
k	kit	*kadın*	*ka-duhn*
l	lot	*lider*	*lee-der*
m	man	*maç*	*mach*
n	not	*nefis*	*ne-fees*
p	pet	*paket*	*pa-ket*
r	red (rolled)	*rehber*	*reh-ber*
s	sun	*saat*	*sa-at*
sh	shot	*şarkı*	*shar-kuh*
t	top	*tas*	*tas*
v	van (but softer, between a 'v' and a 'w')	*vadi*	*va-dee*
y	yes	*yarım*	*ya-ruhm*
z	zero	*zarf*	*zarf*
zh	pleasure	*jambon*	*zham-bon*

language difficulties

Do you speak English?
*İngilizce konuşuyor
musunuz?*
een-gee-*leez*-je ko-noo-*shoo*-yor
moo-soo-*nooz*

Do you understand?
Anlıyor musun?
an-*luh*-yor moo-*soon*

I understand.
Anlıyorum.
an-*luh*-yo-room

I don't understand.
Anlamıyorum.
an-*la*-muh-yo-room

Could you please …?   *Lütfen …?*   *lewt*-fen …
  repeat that   *tekrarlar mısınız*   tek-*rar*-lar muh-suh-*nuhz*
  speak more   *daha yavaş*   da-*ha* ya-*vash*
  slowly   *konuşur musunuz*   ko-noo-*shoor* moo-soo-*nooz*
  write it down   *yazar mısınız*   ya-*zar* muh-suh-*nuhz*

numbers

0	*sıfır*	suh-*fuhr*	20	*yirmi*	yeer-*mee*
1	*bir*	beer	30	*otuz*	o-*tooz*
2	*iki*	ee-*kee*	40	*kırk*	kuhrk
3	*üç*	ewch	50	*elli*	el-*lee*
4	*dört*	deurt	60	*altmış*	alt-*muhsh*
5	*beş*	besh	70	*yetmiş*	yet-*meesh*
6	*altı*	al-*tuh*	80	*seksen*	sek-*sen*
7	*yedi*	ye-*dee*	90	*doksan*	dok-*san*
8	*sekiz*	se-*keez*	100	*yüz*	yewz
9	*dokuz*	do-*kooz*	1000	*bin*	been
10	*on*	on	1,000,000	*bir milyon*	beer meel-*yon*

time & dates

What time is it?	Saat kaç?	sa-at kach
It's one o'clock.	Saat bir.	sa-at beer
It's (10) o'clock.	Saat (on).	sa-at (on)
Quarter past (10).	(Onu) çeyrek geçiyor.	(o-noo) chay-rek ge-chee-yor
Half past (10).	(On) buçuk.	(on) boo-chook
Quarter to (11).	(Onbire) çeyrek var.	(on-bee-re) chay-rek var
At what time …?	Saat kaçta …?	sa-at kach-ta …
At …	Saat …	sa-at …

am (midnight–noon)	sabah	sa-bah
am (breakfast–lunch)	öğleden evvel	er-le-den ev-vel
pm (after lunch)	öğleden sonra	er-le-den son-ra
pm (6pm–8pm)	akşam	ak-sham
pm (after 8pm)	gece	ge-je

Monday	Pazartesi	pa-zar-te-see
Tuesday	Salı	sa-luh
Wednesday	Çarşamba	char-sham-ba
Thursday	Perşembe	per-shem-be
Friday	Cuma	joo-ma
Saturday	Cumartesi	joo-mar-te-see
Sunday	Pazar	pa-zar

last/next …	geçen/gelecek …	ge-chen/ge-le-jek …
night	gece	ge-je
week	hafta	haf-ta
month	ay	ai
year	yıl	yuhl

yesterday/tomorrow …	dün/yarın …	dewn/ya-ruhn …
morning	sabah	sa-bah
afternoon	öğleden sonra	eu-le-den son-ra
evening	akşam	ak-sham

What date is it today?
Bugün ayın kaçı?   boo-gewn a-yuhn ka-chuh

It's (18 October).
(Onsekiz Ekim).   (on-se-keez e-keem)

border crossing

I'm here ...	Ben ...	ben ...
in transit	transit yolcuyum	tran-*seet* yol-*joo*-yoom
on business	iş gezisindeyim	eesh ge-zee-seen-*de*-yeem
on holiday	tatildeyim	ta-teel-*de*-yeem

I'm here for ...	Ben ... buradayım.	ben ... boo-ra-*da*-yuhm
(10) days	(on) günlüğüne	(on) gewn-lew-ew-*ne*
(three) weeks	(üç) haftalığına	(ewch) haf-ta-luh-uh-*na*
(two) months	(iki) aylığına	(ee-*kee*) ai-luh-uh-*na*

I'm going to (Sarıyer).
(Sarıyer'e) gidiyorum.
(sa-*ruh*-ye-re) gee-dee-*yo*-room

I'm staying at the (Divan).
(Divan'da) kalıyorum.
(*dee*-van-da) ka-luh-*yo*-room

I have nothing to declare.
Beyan edecek hiçbir şeyim yok.
be-*yan* e-de-*jek* heech-beer she-*yeem* yok

I have something to declare.
Beyan edecek bir şeyim var.
be-*yan* e-de-*jek* beer she-*yeem* var

That's (not) mine.
Bu benim (değil).
boo be-*neem* (de-*eel*)

tickets & luggage

Where can I buy a ticket?
Nereden bilet alabilirim?
ne-re-den bee-*let* a-*la*-bee-lee-reem

Do I need to book a seat?
Yer ayırtmam gerekli mi?
yer a-*yuhrt*-mam ge-rek-*lee* mee

One ... ticket to	(Bostancı'ya) ...	(bos-*tan*-juh-ya) ...
(Bostancı), please.	lütfen.	*lewt*-fen
one-way	bir gidiş bileti	beer gee-*deesh* bee-le-*tee*
return	gidiş-dönüş	gee-deesh-deu-*newsh*
	bir bilet	beer bee-*let*

I'd like to ... my	Biletimi ...	bee-le-tee-*mee* ...
ticket, please.	istiyorum.	ees-*tee*-yo-room
cancel	iptal ettirmek	eep-*tal* et-teer-*mek*
change	değiştirmek	de-eesh-teer-*mek*

I'd like a ... seat, please.	... bir yer istiyorum.	... beer yer ees·tee·yo·room
nonsmoking	Sigara içilmeyen kısımda	see·ga·ra ee·cheel·me·yen kuh·suhm·da
smoking	Sigara içilen kısımda	see·ga·ra ee·chee·len kuh·suhm·da

Is there air conditioning?
Klima var mı?   klee·ma var muh

Is there a toilet?
Tuvalet var mı?   too·va·let var muh

How long does the trip take?
Yolculuk ne kadar sürer?   yol·joo·look ne ka·dar sew·rer

Is it a direct route?
Direk güzergah mı?   dee·rek gew·zer·gah muh

My luggage has been ...	Bagajım ...	ba·ga·zhuhm ...
damaged	zarar gördü	za·rar geu·dew
lost	kayboldu	kai·bol·doo
stolen	çalındı	cha luhn duh

transport

Where does flight (TK0060) arrive?
(TK0060) sefer sayılı uçak nereye iniyor?   (te·ka suh·fuhr suh·fuhr alt·muhsh) se·fer sa·yuh·luh oo·chak ne·re·ye ee·nee·yor

Where does flight (TK0060) depart?
(TK0060) sefer sayılı uçak nereden kalkıyor?   (te·ka suh·fuhr suh·fuhr alt·muhsh) se·fer sa·yuh·luh oo·chak ne·re·den kal·kuh·yor

Is this the ... to (Sirkeci)?	(Sirkeci'ye) giden ... bu mu?	(seer·ke·jee·ye) gee·den ... boo moo
boat	vapur	va·poor
bus	otobüs	o·to·bews
plane	uçak	oo·chak
train	tren	tren

What time's the	... otobüs	... o·to·*bews*
... bus?	*ne zaman?*	ne za·*man*
first	*İlk*	eelk
last	*Son*	son
next	*Sonraki*	son·ra·*kee*

How long will it be delayed?
Ne kadar gecikecek?　　　　ne ka·*dar* ge·jee·ke·*jek*

What station/stop is this?
Bu hangi istasyon/durak?　boo *han*·gee ees·tas·*yon*/doo·*rak*

Please tell me when we get to (Beşiktaş).
(Beşiktaş'a) vardığımızda　(be·*sheek*·ta·sha) var·duh·uh·muhz·*da*
lütfen bana söyleyin.　　　*lewt*·fen ba·*na* say·*le*·yeen

Is this seat available?
Bu koltuk boş mu?　　　　boo kol·*took* bosh moo

That's my seat.
Burası benim yerim.　　　boo·ra·*suh* be·*neem* ye·*reem*

I'd like a taxi ...	... bir taksi istiyorum.	... beer tak·*see* ees·*tee*·yo·room
at (9am)	*(Sabah dokuzda)*	(sa·*bah* do·kooz·*da*)
now	*Hemen*	*he*·men
tomorrow	*Yarın*	*ya*·ruhn

How much is it to ...?
... ne kadar?　　　　　　... ne ka·*dar*

Please put the meter on.
Lütfen taksimetreyi　　　*lewt*·fen tak·*see*·met·re·yee
çalıştırın.　　　　　　　cha·luhsh·*tuh*·ruhn

Please take me to (this address).
Lütfen beni (bu adrese)　*lewt*·fen be·*nee* (boo ad·re·*se*)
götürün.　　　　　　　geu·*tew*·rewn

Please ...	*Lütfen ...*	*lewt*·fen ...
stop here	*burada durun*	boo·ra·*da* doo·roon
wait here	*burada bekleyin*	boo·ra·*da* bek·*le*·yeen

I'd like to	*Bir ... kiralamak*	beer ... kee·ra·la·*mak*
hire a ...	*istiyorum.*	ees·*tee*·yo·room
car	*araba*	a·ra·*ba*
4WD	*dört çeker*	deut che·*ker*

with …		
a driver	*şoförlü*	sho·feur·*lew*
air conditioning	*klimalı*	klee·ma·*luh*

How much	*… kirası ne*	*… kee·ra·suh* ne
for … hire?	*kadar?*	ka·*dar*
daily	*Günlük*	gewn·*lewk*
weekly	*Haftalık*	haf·ta·*luhk*

I need a mechanic.
Tamirciye ihtiyacım var.　　ta·meer·jee·ye eeh·tee·ya·*juhm* var

I've run out of petrol.
Benzinim bitti.　　ben·zee·*neem* beet·*tee*

I have a flat tyre.
Lastiğim patladı.　　las·tee·*eem* pat·la·*duh*

directions

Where's the …?	*… nerede?*	*… ne·re·de*
bank	*Banka*	*ban·ka*
market	*Pazar yeri*	pa·*zar* ye·*ree*
post office	*Postane*	pos·*ta·ne*

Is this the road to (Taksim)?
(Taksim'e) giden yol bu mu?　　(tak·see·me) gee·*den* yol boo moo

Can you show me (on the map)?
Bana (haritada)　　ba·*na* (ha·ree·ta·*da*)
gösterebilir misiniz?　　geus·te·re·bee·leer mee·seen·*neez*

What's the address?
Adresi nedir?　　ad·re·*see* ne·deer

How far is it?
Ne kadar uzakta?　　ne ka·*dar* oo·zak·*ta*

How do I get there?
Oraya nasıl gidebilirim?　　o·ra·*ya* na·*suhl* gee·*de·*bee·lee·reem

Turn left/right.
Sola/Sağa dön.　　so·*la*/sa·*a* deun

It's ...

behind ...	... arkasında.	... ar·ka·suhn·da
here	Burada.	boo·ra·da
in front of ...	... önünde.	... eu·newn·de
near ...	... yakınında.	... ya·kuh·nuhn·da
next to ...	... yanında.	... ya·nuhn·da
on the corner	Köşede.	keu·she·de
opposite ...	... karşısında.	... kar·shuh·suhn·da
straight ahead	Tam karşıda.	tam kar·shuh·da
there	Şurada.	shoo·ra·da

north	kuzey	koo·zay
south	güney	gew·nay
east	doğu	do·oo
west	batı	ba·tuh

signs

Giriş/Çıkış	gee·reesh/chuh·kuhsh	**Entrance/Exit**
Açık/Kapalı	a·chuhk/ka·pa·luh	**Open/Closed**
Danışma	da·nuhsh·ma	**Information**
Polis Karakolu	po·lees ka·ra·ko·loo	**Police Station**
Yasak	ya·sak	**Prohibited**
Tuvaletler	too·va·let·ler	**Toilets**
Erkek	er·kek	**Men**
Kadın	ka·duhn	**Women**
Sıcak/Soğuk	suh·jak/so·ook	**Hot/Cold**

accommodation

Where's a ...?	Buralarda nerede ... var?	boo·ra·lar·da ne·re·de ... var
camping ground	kamp yeri	kamp ye·ree
guesthouse	misafirhane	mee·sa·feer·ha·ne
hotel	otel	o·tel
tree house	ağaç ev	a·ach ev
youth hostel	gençlik hosteli	gench·leek hos·te·lee

Can you recommend somewhere ...?	... bir yer tavsiye edebilir misiniz?	... beer yer tav·see·ye e·de·bee·leer mee·see·neez
cheap	Ucuz	oo·jooz
good	İyi	ee·yee
nearby	Yakın	ya·kuhn

Do you have a ... room?	... odanız var mı?	... o·da·nuhz var muh
single	Tek kişilik	tek kee·shee·leek
double	İki kişilik	ee·kee kee·shee·leek
twin	Çift yataklı	cheeft ya·tak·luh

How much is it per ...?	... ne kadar?	... ne ka·dar
night	Geceliği	ge·je·lee·ee
person	Kişi başına	kee·shee ba·shuh·na

I'd like to book a room, please.
Bir oda ayırtmak
istiyorum lütfen.
beer o·da a·yuhrt·mak
ees·tee·yo·room lewt·fen

I have a reservation.
Rezervasyonum var.
re·zer·vas·yo·noom var

I'd like to stay for (three) nights.
Kalmak istiyorum (üç) geceliğine.
kal·mak ees·tee·yo·room (ewch) ge·je·lee·ee·ne

Am I allowed to camp here?
Burada kamp yapabilir miyim?
boo·ra·da kamp ya·pa·bee·leer mee·yeem

Is there an elevator/a safe?
Asansör/Kasanız var mı?
a·san·seur/ka·sa·nuhz var muh

Could I have my key, please?
Anahtarımı alabilir miyim?
a·nah·ta·ruh·muh a·la·bee·leer mee·yeem

Can I get another (blanket)?
Başka bir (battaniye)
alabilir miyim?
bash·ka beer (bat·ta·nee·ye)
a·la·bee·leer mee·yeem

The (air conditioning) doesn't work.
(Klima) çalışmıyor.
(klee·ma) cha·luhsh·muh·yor

This (sheet) isn't clean.
Bu (çarşaf) temiz değil.
boo (char·shaf) te·meez de·eel

What time is checkout?
Çıkış ne zaman?
chuh·kuhsh ne za·man

Could I have	... alabilir	... a·*la*·bee·leer
my ..., please?	miyim lütfen?	mee·*yeem* lewt·fen
deposit	Depozitomu	de·po·zee·to·*moo*
passport	Pasaportumu	pa·sa·por·too·*moo*
valuables	Değerli eşyalarımı	de·er·*lee* esh·ya·la·ruh·*muh*

banking & communications

Where's a/an ...?	... nerede var?	... ne·re·de var
ATM	Bankamatik	ban·ka·ma·*teek*
foreign exchange office	Döviz bürosu	deu·veez bew·ro·*soo*

I'd like to ...	... istiyorum.	... ees·*tee*·yo·room
cash a cheque	Çek bozdurmak	chek boz·door·*mak*
change a travellers cheque	Seyahat çeki bozdurmak	se·ya·*hat* che·*kee* boz·door·*mak*
change money	Para bozdurmak	pa·ra boz·door·*mak*
withdraw money	Para çekmek	pa·ra chek·*mek*

What's the ...?	... nedir?	... ne·deer
charge for that	Ücreti	ewj·re·*tee*
exchange rate	Döviz kuru	deu·veez koo·*roo*

Where's the local internet café?
En yakın internet kafe nerede?   en ya·*kuhn* een·ter·*net* ka·*fe* ne·re·de

How much is it per hour?
Saati ne kadar?   sa·a·*tee* ne ka·*dar*

I'd like to ...	... istiyorum.	... ees·*tee*·yo·room
check my email	E-postama bakmak	e·pos·ta·ma bak·*mak*
get internet access	İnternete girmek	een·ter·ne·*te* geer·*mek*
use a printer	Printeri kullanmak	preen·te·*ree* kool·lan·*mak*
use a scanner	Tarayıcıyı	ta·ra·yuh·juh·*yuh*

I'd like a ...	... istiyorum.	... ees·*tee*·yo·room
mobile/cell phone for hire	Cep telefonu kiralamak	jep te·le·fo·*noo* kee·ra·la·*mak*
SIM card for your network	Buradaki şebeke için SİM kart	boo·ra·da·*kee* she·be·*ke* ee·*cheen* seem kart

What's your phone number?
Telefon numaranız nedir? te·le·*fon* noo·ma·ra·*nuhz* ne·deer

The number is ...
Telefon numarası ... te·le·*fon* noo·ma·ra·*suh* ...

Where's the nearest public phone?
En yakın telefon en ya·*kuhn* te·le·*fon*
kulübesi nerede? koo·lew·be·*see* ne·re·de

I'd like to buy a phonecard.
Telefon kartı almak te·le·*fon* kar·*tuh* al·*mak*
istiyorum. ees·*tee*·yo·room

How much does a (three)-minute call cost?
(Üç) dakikalık konuşma (ewch) da·kee·ka·*luhk* ko·noosh·ma
ne kadar eder? ne ka·*dar* e·der

What are the rates?
Ucret tarifesi nedir? ewj·*ret* tà·ree·fe·*see* ne·deer

I want to ...	*... istiyorum.*	*... ees·tee·yo·room*
call (Singapore)	*(Singapur'u)*	*(seen·ga·poo·roo)*
	aramak	a·ra·*mak*
make a local	*Yerel bir görüşme*	ye·*rel* beer geu·rewsh·me
call	*yapmak*	yap·*mak*
reverse the	*Ödemeli görüşme*	eu·de·me·*lee* ger rewsh·me
charges	*yapmak*	yap·*mak*

I want to send a ...	*Bir ... göndermek*	beer ... geun·der·*mek*
	istiyorum.	ees·*tee*·yo·room
fax	*faks*	faks
parcel	*paket*	pa·*ket*

I want to buy a/an ...	*... satın almak*	*... sa·tuhn al·mak*
	istiyorum.	ees·*tee*·yo·room
envelope	*Zarf*	zarf
stamp	*Pul*	pool

Please send it	*Lütfen ...*	*lewt·fen ...*
(to Australia) by ...	*(Avustralya'ya)*	(a·voos·*tral*·ya·ya)
	gönderin.	geun·*de*·reen
airmail	*hava yoluyla*	ha·*va* yo·*looy*·la
surface mail	*deniz yoluyla*	de·*neez* yo·*looy*·la

sightseeing

What time does it open/close?
Saat kaçta açılır/kapanır?
sa·*at* kach·*ta* a·chuh·*luhr*/ka·pa·*nuhr*

What's the admission charge?
Giriş ücreti nedir?
gee·*reesh* ewj·re·*tee* ne·*deer*

Is there a discount for children/students?
Çocuk/Öğrenci indirimi
cho·*jook*/eu·ren·*jee* een·dee·ree·*mee*
var mı?
var muh

I'd like to see ...
... görmek istiyorum.
... geur·*mek* ees·*tee*·yo·room

I'd like a ...	*... istiyorum.*	... ees·*tee*·yo·room
catalogue	*Katalog*	ka·ta·*log*
guide	*Rehber*	reh·*ber*
local map	*Yerel harita*	ye·*rel* ha·ree·*ta*

When's the next ...?	*Sonraki ... ne zaman?*	son·ra·*kee* ... ne za·*man*
day trip	*gündüz turu*	gewn·*dewz* too·*roo*
tour	*tur*	toor

Is ... included?	*... dahil mi?*	... da·*heel* mee
accommodation	*Kalacak yer*	ka·la·*jak* yer
the admission charge	*Giriş*	gee·*reesh*
food	*Yemek*	ye·*mek*
transport	*Ulaşım*	oo·la·*shuhm*

How long is the tour?
Tur ne kadar sürer?
toor ne ka·*dar* sew·*rer*

What time should we be back?
Saat kaçta dönmeliyiz?
sa·*at* kach·*ta* deun·me·*lee*·yeez

What's that?
Bu nedir?
boo ne·*deer*

Can I take a photo?
Bir fotoğrafınızı
beer fo·to·ra·fuh·nuh·*zuh*
çekebilir miyim?
che·*ke*·bee·leer mee·*yeem*

castle	*kale*	ka·*le*
church	*kilise*	kee·lee·*se*
main square	*meydan*	may·*dan*
mosque	*cami*	ja·*mee*
old city	*eski şehir*	es·kee she·*heer*
palace	*saray*	sa·*rai*
ruins	*harabeler*	ha·ra·be·*ler*
Turkish bath	*hamam*	ha·*mam*

shopping

Where's a ...?	*... nerede?*	*... ne·re·de*
bookshop	*Kitapçı*	kee·tap·*chuh*
camera shop	*Fotoğrafçı*	fo·to·raf·*chuh*
department store	*Büyük mağaza*	bew·*yewk* ma·a·*za*
grocery store	*Bakkal*	bɑk·*kul*
newsagency	*Gazete bayii*	ga·ze·te ba·yee·*ee*
souvenir shop	*Hediyelik eşya dükkanı*	he·dee·ye·*leek* esh·*ya* dewk·ka·*nuh*
supermarket	*Süpermarket*	sew·per·mar·ket

I'm looking for ...
... istiyorum.   *... ees·tee·yo·room*

Can I look at it?
Bakabilir miyim?   ba·ka·bee·leer mee·*yeem*

Do you have any others?
Başka var mı?   bash·*ka* var muh

Does it have a guarantee?
Garantisi var mı?   ga·ran·tee·*see* var muh

Can I have it sent overseas?
Yurt dışına gönderebilir misiniz?   yoort duh·shuh·*na* geun·de·*re*·bee·leer mee·see·*neez*

Can I have my ... repaired?
... burada tamir ettirebilir miyim?   *... boo·ra·da* ta·*meer* et·tee·*re*·bee·leer mee·*yeem*

It's faulty.
Arızalı.   a·ruh·za·*luh*

How much is it?
Ne kadar? · ne ka-*dar*

Can you write down the price?
Fiyatı yazabilir misiniz? · fee-ya-*tuh* ya-*za*-bee-leer mee-see-*neez*

That's too expensive.
Bu çok pahalı. · boo chok pa-ha-*luh*

Is that your lowest price?
Son fiyatınız bu mu? · son fee-ya-tuh-*nuhz* boo moo

I'll give you (30) lira.
(Otuz) lira veririm. · (o-*tooz*) lee-*ra* ve-ree-reem

There's a mistake in the bill.
Hesapta bir yanlışlık var. · he-sap-*ta* beer yan-luhsh-*luhk* var

Do you accept ...?	... kabul ediyor musunuz?	... ka-*bool* e-*dee*-yor moo-soo-*nooz*
credit cards	*Kredi kartı*	*kre*-dee kar-*tuh*
debit cards	*Banka kartı*	*ban*-ka kar-*tuh*
travellers cheques	*Seyahat çeki*	se-ya-*hat* che-*kee*

I'd like ..., please.	... istiyorum lütfen.	... ees-*tee*-yo-room *lewt*-fen
a bag	*Çanta*	chan-*ta*
my change	*Paramın üstünü*	pa-ra-*muhn* ews-tew-*new*
a receipt	*Makbuz*	mak-*booz*
a refund	*Para iadesi*	pa-*ra* ee-a-de-*see*
to return this	*Bunu iade etmek*	boo-*noo* ee-a-de et-mek

I'd like ...	... istiyorum.	... ees-*tee*-yo-room
(200) grams	*(İkiyüz) gram*	(ee-kee-*yewz*) gram
(two) kilos	*(İki) kilo*	(ee-*kee*) kee-*lo*
(three) pieces	*(Üç) parça*	(ewch) par-*cha*
(six) slices	*(Altı) dilim*	(al-*tuh*) dee-*leem*

Less.	*Daha az.*	da-*ha* az
Enough.	*Yeterli.*	ye-ter-*lee*
More.	*Daha fazla.*	da-*ha* faz-*la*

photography

Can you ...?	... misiniz?	... mee·see·neez
develop this film	Bu filmi basabilir	boo feel·mee ba·sa·bee·leer
load my film	Filmi makineye	feel·mee ma·kee·ne·ye
	takabilir	ta·ka·bee·leer
transfer photos	Kameramdaki	ka·me·ram·da·kee
from my	fotoğrafları	fo·to·raf·la·ruh
camera to CD	CD'ye aktarabilir	see·dee·ye ak·ta·ra·bee·leer

I need a/an ... film	Bu kamera için ...	boo ka·me·ra ee·cheen ...
for this camera.	film istiyorum.	feelm ees·tee·yo·room
APS	APS	a·pe·se
B&W	siyah-beyaz	see·yah·be·yaz
colour	renkli	renk·lee
slide	slayt	slayt
(200) speed	(ikiyüz) hızlı	(ee·kee·yewz) huhz·luh

When will it be ready?	Ne zaman hazır olur?	ne za·man ha·zuhr o·loor

making conversation

Hello.	Merhaba.	mer·ha·ba
Good night.	İyi geceler.	ee·yee ge·je·ler
Goodbye.	Hoşçakal. inf	hosh·cha·kal
(by person leaving)	Hoşçakalın. pol	hosh·cha·ka·luhn
Goodbye.	Güle güle.	gew·le gew·le
(by person staying)		

Mr	Bay	bai
Mrs/Miss	Bayan	ba·yan

How are you?	Nasılsın? inf	na·suhl·suhn
	Nasılsınız? pol	na·suhl·suh·nuhz
Fine.	İyiyim.	ee·yee·yeem
And you?	Ya sen/siz? inf/pol	ya sen/seez
What's your name?	Adınız ne? inf	a·duh·nuhz ne
	Adınız nedir? pol	a·duh·nuhz ne·deer

My name is ...	Benim adım ...	be-*neem* a-*duhm* ...
I'm pleased to meet you.	Tanıştığımıza sevindim.	ta-nuhsh-tuh-uh-muh-*za* se-veen-*deem*
This is my ...	Bu benim ...	boo be-*neem* ...
brother	kardeşim	kar-de-*sheem*
daughter	kızım	kuh-*zuhm*
father	babayım	ba-ba-*yuhm*
friend	arkadaşım	ar-ka-da-*shuhm*
husband	kocam	ko-*jam*
mother	anneyim	an-ne-*yeem*
sister	kız kardeşim	kuhz kar-de-*sheem*
son	oğlum	o-*loom*
wife	karım	ka-*ruhm*
Here's my ...	İşte benim ...	eesh-te be-*neem* ...
address	adresiniz	ad-re-see-*neez*
email address	e-posta adresiniz	e-pos-ta ad-re-see-*neez*
phone number	telefon numaram	te-le-*fon* noo-ma-*ram*
What's your ...?	Sizin ... nedir?	see-*zeen* ... ne-deer
address	adresiniz	ad-re-see-*neez*
email address	e-posta adresiniz	e-pos-ta ad-re-see-*neez*
phone number	telefon numaranız	te-le-*fon* noo-ma-ra-*nuhz*
Where are you from?	Nerelisin? inf	ne-re-lee-seen
	Nerelisiniz? pol	ne-re-lee-see-neez
I'm from ...	Ben ...	ben ...
Australia	Avustralya'lıyım	a-voos-*tral*-ya-luh-yuhm
Canada	Kanada'lıyım	ka-*na*-da-luh-yuhm
the UK	İngiltere'liyim	een-*geel*-*te*-re-lee-yeem
the USA	Amerika'lıyım	a-*me*-ree-ka-luh-yuhm
What's your occupation?	Mesleğin nedir? inf	mes-le-*een* ne-deer
	Mesleğiniz nedir? pol	mes-le-ee-*neez* ne-deer
I'm a/an ...	Ben ...	ben ...
business person	iş adamıyım m	ish a-da-*muh*-yuhm
	kadınıyım f	ka-duh-*nuh*-yuhm
manual worker	işçiyim m&f	eesh-*chee*-yeem
office worker	memurum m&f	me-*moo*-room

Do you like ...?	... sever misin?	... se-ver mee-seen
I like ...	... seviyorum.	... se-vee-yo-room
I don't like ...	... sevmiyorum.	... sev-mee-yo-room
art	Sanat	sa-nat
movies	Sinemaya gitmeyi	see-ne-ma-ya geet-me-yee
music	Müzik	mew-zeek
reading	Okumayı	o-koo-ma-yuh
sport	Sporu	spo-roo

eating out

Can you	İyi bir ... tavsiye	ee-yee beer ... tav-see-ye
recommend a ...?	edebilir misiniz?	e-de-bee-leer mee-see-neez
bar	bar	bar
café	kafe	ka-fe
restaurant	restoran	res-to-ran
I'd like ..., please.	... istiyorum.	... ees-tee-yo-room
a table for (five)	(Beş) kişilik	(besh) kee-shee-leek
	bir masa	beer ma-sa
the nonsmoking	Sigara içilmeyen	see-ga-ra ee-cheel-me-yen
section	bir yer	beer yer
the smoking	Sigara içilen	see-ga-ra ee-chee-len
section	bir yer	beer yer
breakfast	kahvaltı	kah-val-tuh
lunch	öğle yemeği	eu-le ye-me-ee
dinner	akşam yemeği	ak-sham ye-me-ee

What would you recommend?
Ne tavsiye edersiniz?   ne tav-see-ye e-der-see-neez

What's the local speciality?
Bu yöreye has yiyecekler neler?   boo yeu-re-ye has yee-ye-jek-ler ne-ler

What's that?	Bu nedir?	boo ne·deer
I'd like (the)...	... istiyorum.	... ees·tee·yo·room
bill	Hesabı	he·sa·buh
drink list	İçecek listesini	ee·che·jek lees·te·see·nee
menu	Menüyü	me·new·yew
that dish	Şu yemeği	shoo ye·me·ee

drinks

(cup of) coffee ...	(fincan) kahve ...	(feen·jan) kah·ve ...
(cup of) tea ...	(fincan) çay ...	(feen·jan) chai ...
with milk	sütlü	sewt·lew
without sugar	şekersiz	she·ker·seez
(orange) juice	(portakal) suyu	(por·ta·kal) soo·yoo
soft drink	alkolsüz içecek	al·kol·sewz ee·che·jek
sparkling mineral water	maden sodası	ma·den so·da·suh
still mineral water	maden suyu	ma·den soo·yoo
(hot) water	(sıcak) su	(suh·jak) soo
a bottle/glass of beer	bir şişe/bardak bira	beer shee·she/bar·dak bee·ra
a shot of (whisky)	bir tek (viski)	beer tek (vees·kee)
a bottle/glass of ... wine	bir şişe/bardak ... şarap	beer shee·she/bar·dak ... sha·rap
red	kırmızı	kuhr·muh·zuh
sparkling	köpüklü	keu·pewk·lew
white	beyaz	be·yaz
I'll have ...	... alayım.	... a·la·yuhm
I'll buy you a drink.	Sana içecek alayım.	sa·na ee·che·jek a·la·yuhm
What would you like?	Ne alırsınız?	ne a·luhr·suh·nuhz

special diets & allergies

Where's a vegetarian restaurant?
Buralarda vejeteryan restoran var mı?
boo·ra·lar·da ve·zhe·ter·yan res·to·ran var muh

Do you have ... food?	... yiyecekleriniz var mı?	... yee·ye·jek·le·ree·neez var muh
halal	helal	he·lal
kosher	koşer	ko·sher
vegetarian	vejeteryan	ve·zhe·ter·yan

Is it cooked with ...?	İçinde ... var mı?	ee·cheen·de ... var muh
butter	tereyağ	te·re·ya
eggs	yumurta	yoo·moor·ta
meat stock	et suyu	et soo·yoo

I'm allergic to ...	... alerjim var.	... a·ler·zheem var
dairy produce	Süt ürünlerine	sewt ew·rewn·le·ree·ne
gluten	Glutene	gloo·te·ne
nuts	Çerezlere	che·rez·le·re
seafood	Deniz ürünlerine	de·neez ew·rewn·le·ree·ne

emergencies

Help!	İmdat!	eem·dat
Stop!	Dur!	door
Go away!	Git burdan!	geet boor·dan
Thief!	Hırsız var!	huhr·suhz var
Fire!	Yangın var!	yan·guhn var
Watch out!	Dikkat et!	deek·kat et

Call ...!	... çağırın!	... cha·uh·ruhn
a doctor	Doktor	dok·tor
an ambulance	Ambulans	am·boo·lans
the police	Polis	po·lees

Could you help me, please?
Yardım edebilir misiniz lütfen?
yar·duhm e·de·bee·leer mee·see·neez lewt·fen

Can I use your phone?
Telefonunuzu kullanabilir miyim?
te·le·fe·noo·noo·*zoo* kool·la·*na*·bee·leer mee·*yeem*

I'm lost.
Kayboldum.
kai·bol·*doom*

Where are the toilets?
Tuvaletler nerede?
too·va·let·*ler* ne·re·de

Where's the police station?
Polis karakolu nerede?
po·*lees* ka·ra·ko·*loo* ne·re·de

I want to report an offence.
Şikayette bulunmak istiyorum.
shee·ka·yet·*te* boo·loon·*mak* ees·*tee*·yo·room

I have insurance.
Sigortam var.
see·gor·*tam* var

I want to contact my embassy.
Elçilikle görüşmek istiyorum.
el·chee·*leek*·le geu·rewsh·*mek* ees·*tee*·yo·room

I've been ...	*Ben ...*	ben ...
assaulted	*saldırıya uğradım*	sal·duh·ruh·*ya* oo·ra·*duhm*
raped	*tecavüze uğradım*	te·ja·vew·*ze* oo·ra·*duhm*
robbed	*soyuldum*	so·yool·*doom*

I've lost my ...	*... kayıp.*	... ka·*yuhp*
My ... was/were stolen.	*... çalındı.*	... cha·luhn·*duh*
bags	*Çantalar*	chan·ta·*lar*
credit card	*Kredi kartı*	kre·dee kar·*tuh*
money	*Para*	pa·*ra*
papers	*Evraklar*	ev·rak·*lar*
passport	*Pasaport*	pa·sa·*port*
travellers cheques	*Seyahat çekleri*	se·ya·*hat* chek·le·*ree*

health

Where's the nearest ...?	En yakın ... nerede?	en ya·*kuhn* ... ne·re·de
dentist	dişçi	deesh·*chee*
doctor	doktor	dok·*tor*
hospital	hastane	has·*ta*·ne
(night) pharmacist	(nöbetçi) eczane	(neu·bet·*chee*) ej·*za*·ne

I need a doctor (who speaks English).
(İngilizce konuşan)   (een·gee·*leez*·je ko·noo·*shan*)
Bir doktora ihtiyacım var.   beer dok·to·*ra* eeh·tee·ya·*juhm* var

Could I see a female doctor?
Bayan doktora   ba·*yan* dok·to·*ra*
görünebilir miyim?   geu·rew·*ne*·bee·leer mee·*yeem*

I've run out of my medication.
İlacım bitti.   ee·la·*juhm* beet·*tee*

I'm sick.	Hastayım.	has·ta yuhm
It hurts here.	Burası ağrıyor.	boo·ra·*suh* a·*ruh*·yor
I have a toothache.	Dişim ağrıyor.	dee·*sheem* a·*ruh*·yor
I have (a) ...	Bende ... var.	ben·*de* ... var

asthma	astım	as·*tuhm*
constipation	kabızlık	ka·buhz·*luhk*
diarrhoea	ishal	ees·*hal*
fever	ateş	a·*tesh*
headache	baş ağrısı	bash a·ruh·*suh*
heart condition	kalp rahatsızlığı	kalp ra·hat·suhz·luh·*uh*
nausea	bulantı	boo·lan·*tuh*
pain	ağrı	a·*ruh*
sore throat	boğaz ağrısı	bo·*az* a·ruh·*suh*

I'm allergic to ...	... alerjim var.	... a·ler·*zheem* var
antibiotics	Antibiyotiklere	an·tee·bee·yo·teek·le·*re*
anti-	Anti-	an·*tee*·
inflammatories	emflamatuarlara	em·fla·ma·too·ar·la·ra
aspirin	Aspirine	as·pee·ree·*ne*
bees	Arılara	a·ruh·la·*ra*
codeine	Kodeine	ko·de·ee·*ne*
penicillin	Penisiline	pe·nee·see·lee·*ne*

english–turkish dictionary

Words in this dictionary are marked as a (adjective), n (noun), v (verb), sg (singular), pl (plural), inf (informal) and pol (polite) where necessary.

A

accident *kaza* ka-*za*
accommodation *kalacak yer* ka-la-*jak* yer
adaptor *adaptör* a-dap-*teur*
address n *adres* ad-*res*
after *sonra* son-*ra*
air conditioning *klima* klee-ma
airplane *uçak* oo-*chak*
airport *havaalanı* ha-va-a-la-nuh
alcohol *alkol* al-*kol*
all *hepsi* hep-*see*
allergy *alerji* a-ler-*zhee*
ambulance *ambulans* am-boo-*lans*
and *ve* ve
ankle *ayak bileği* a-*yak* bee-le-*ee*
arm *kol* kol
ashtray *kül tablası* kewl tab-la-*suh*
ATM *bankamatik* ban-ka-ma-*teek*

B

baby *bebek* be-*bek*
back (body) *sırt* suhrt
backpack *sırt çantası* suhrt chan-ta-*suh*
bad *kötü* keu-*tew*
bag *çanta* chan-ta
baggage claim *bagaj konveyörü* ba-*gazh* kon-ve-yeu-*rew*
bank *banka* ban-ka
bar *bar* bar
bathroom *banyo* ban-yo
battery *pil* peel
beautiful *güzel* gew-*zel*
bed *yatak* ya-*tak*
beer *bira* bee-ra
before *önce* eun-*je*
behind *arkasında* ar-ka-suhn-*da*
bicycle *bisiklet* bee-seek-*let*
big *büyük* bew-*yewk*
bill *hesap* he-*sap*
black *siyah* see-*yah*
blanket *battaniye* bat-*ta*-nee-ye

blood group *kan grubu* kan goo-roo-*boo*
blue *mavi* ma-vee
boat *vapur* va-*poor*
book (make a reservation) v *yer ayırtmak* yer a-yuhrt-*mak*
bottle *şişe* shee-she
bottle opener *şişe açacağı* shee-she a-cha-ja-*uh*
boy *oğlan* o-*lan*
brakes (car) *fren* fren
breakfast *kahvaltı* kah-val-*tuh*
broken (faulty) *bozuk* bo-*zook*
bus *otobüs* o-to-*bews*
business *iş* eesh
buy *satın almak* sa-tuhn al-*mak*

C

café *kafe* ka-*fe*
camera *kamera* ka-me-ra
camp site *kamp yeri* kamp ye-*ree*
cancel *iptal etmek* eep-*tal* et-*mek*
can opener *konserve açacağı* kon-ser-ve a-cha-ja-*uh*
car *araba* a-ra-ba
cash n *nakit* na-*keet*
cash (a cheque) v *(çek) bozdurmak* (chek) boz-door-*mak*
cell phone *cep telefonu* jep te-le-fo-*noo*
centre n *merkez* mer-*kez*
change (money) v *bozdurmak* boz-door-*mak*
cheap *ucuz* oo-*jooz*
check (hill) n *fatura* fa-*too*-ra
check-in n *giriş* gee-*reesh*
chest *göğüs* geu-*ews*
child *çocuk* cho-*jook*
cigarette *sigara* see-*ga*-ra
city *şehir* she-*heer*
clean a *temiz* te-*meez*
closed *kapalı* ka-pa-*luh*
coffee *kahve* kah-*ve*
coins *madeni para* ma-de-nee pa-*ra*
cold a *soğuk* so-*ook*
collect call *ödemeli telefon* eu-de-me-*lee* te-le-*fon*
come *gelmek* gel-*mek*

computer *bilgisayar* beel-gee-sa-*yar*
condom *prezervatif* pre-zer-va-*teef*
contact lenses *kontak lens* kon-*tak* lens
cook ∨ *pişirmek* pee-sheer-*mek*
cost n *fiyat* fee-*yat*
credit card *kredi kartı* kre-dee kar-*tuh*
cup *fincan* feen-*jan*
currency exchange *döviz kuru* deu-veez koo-*roo*
customs (immigration) *gümrük* gewm-*rewk*

D

dangerous *tehlikeli* teh-lee-ke-*lee*
date (time) *tarih* ta-*reeh*
day *gün* gewn
delay n *gecikme* ge-jeek-*me*
dentist *dişçi* deesh-*chee*
depart *ayrılmak* ai-ruhl-*mak*
diaper *bebek bezi* be-*bek* be-*zee*
dictionary *sözlük* seuz-*lewk*
dinner *akşam yemeği* ak-*sham* ye-me-*ee*
direct *direk* dee-*rek*
dirty *kirli* keer-*lee*
disabled *özürlü* eu-zewr-*lew*
discount n *indirim* een-dee-*reem*
doctor *doktor* dok-*tor*
double bed *iki kişilik yatak* ee-kee kee-shee-*leek* ya-*tak*
double room *iki kişilik oda* ee-kee kee-shee-*leek* o-*da*
drink n *içecek* ee-che-*jek*
drive ∨ *sürmek* sewr-*mek*
drivers licence *ehliyet* eh-lee-*yet*
drugs (illicit) *uyuşturucu* oo-yoosh-too-roo-*joo*
dummy (pacifier) *emzik* em-*zeek*

E

ear *kulak* koo-*lak*
east *doğu* do-*oo*
eat *yemek* ye-*mek*
economy class *ekonomi sınıfı* e-ko-no-mee suh-nuh-*fuh*
electricity *elektrik* e-lek-*treek*
elevator *asansör* a-san-*seur*
email n *e-posta* e-pos-*ta*
embassy *elçilik* el-chee-*leek*
emergency *acil durum* a-jeel doo-*room*
English (language) *İngilizce* een-gee-*leez*-je
entrance *giriş* gee-*reesh*
evening *akşam* ak-*sham*
exchange rate *döviz kuru* deu-veez koo-*roo*
exit n *çıkış* chuh-*kuhsh*

expensive *pahalı* pa-ha-*luh*
express mail *ekspres posta* eks-*pres* pos-*ta*
eye *göz* geuz

F

far *uzak* oo-*zak*
fast *hızlı* huhz-*luh*
father *baba* ba-*ba*
film (camera) *film* feelm
finger *parmak* par-*mak*
first-aid kit *ilk yardım çantası* eelk yar-*duhm* chan-ta-*suh*
first class *birinci sınıf* bee-reen-*jee* suh-*nuhf*
fish n *balık* ba-*luhk*
food *yiyecek* yee-ye-*jek*
foot *ayak* a-*yak*
fork *çatal* cha-*tal*
free (of charge) *ücretsiz* ewj-ret-*seez*
friend *arkadaş* ar-ka-*dash*
fruit *meyve* may-*ve*
full *dolu* do-*loo*
funny *komik* ko-*meek*

G

gift *hediye* he-dee-*ye*
girl *kız* kuhz
glass (drinking) *bardak* bar-*dak*
glasses (eyesight) *gözlük* geuz-*lewk*
go *gitmek* geet-*mek*
good *iyi* ee-*yee*
green *yeşil* ye-*sheel*
guide n *rehber* reh-*ber*

H

half n *yarım* ya-*ruhm*
hand *el* el
handbag *el çantası* el chan-ta-*suh*
happy *mutlu* moot-*loo*
have *sahip olmak* sa-*heep* ol-*mak*
he *o* o
head *baş* bash
heart *kalp* kalp
heat n *ısı* uh-*suh*
heavy *ağır* a-*uhr*
help ∨ *yardım etmek* yar-*duhm* et-*mek*
here *burada* boo-ra-*da*
high *yüksek* yewk-*sek*

highway *otoyol* o-to-yol
hike v *uzun yürüyüşe çıkmak* oo-zoon yew-rew-yew-she chuhk-mak
holiday *tatil* ta-teel
homosexual *homoseksüel* ho-mo-sek-sew-el
hospital *hastane* has-ta-ne
hot *sıcak* suh-jak
hotel *otel* o-tel
hungry *aç* ach
husband *koca* ko-ja

I

I *ben* ben
identification (card) *kimlik kartı* keem-leek kar-tuh
ill *hasta* has-ta
important *önemli* eu-nem-lee
included *dahil* da-heel
injury *yara* ya-ra
insurance *sigorta* see-gor-ta
internet *internet* een-ter-net
interpreter *tercüman* ter-jew-man

J

jewellery *mücevherler* mew-jev-her-ler
job *meslek* mes-lek

K

key *anahtar* a-nah-tar
kilogram *kilogram* kee-lo-gram
kitchen *mutfak* moot-fak
knife *bıçak* buh-chak

L

laundry (place) *çamaşırlık* cha-ma-shuhr-luhk
lawyer *avukat* a-voo-kat
left (direction) *sol* sol
left-luggage office *emanet bürosu* e-ma-net bew-ro-soo
leg *bacak* ba-jak
lesbian *lezbiyen* lez-bee-yen
less *daha az* da-ha az
letter (mail) *mektup* mek-toop
lift (elevator) *asansör* a-san-seur
light n *ışık* uh-shuhk
like v *sevmek* sev-mek
lock n *kilit* kee-leet
long *uzun* oo-zoon

lost *kayıp* ka-yuhp
lost-property office *kayıp eşya bürosu* ka-yuhp esh-ya bew-ro-soo
love v *aşık olmak* a-shuhk ol-mak
luggage *bagaj* ba-gazh
lunch *öğle yemeği* eu-le ye-me-ee

M

mail n *mektup* mek-toop
man *adam* a-dam
map *harita* ha-ree-ta
market *pazar* pa-zar
matches *kibrit* keeb-reet
meat *et* et
medicine *ilaç* ee-lach
menu *yemek listesi* ye-mek lees-te-see
message *mesaj* me-sazh
milk *süt* sewt
minute *dakika* da-kee-ka
mobile phone *cep telefonu* jep te-le-fo-noo
money *para* pa-ra
month *ay* ai
morning *sabah* sa-bah
mother *anne* an-ne
motorcycle *motosiklet* mo-to-seek-let
motorway *paralı yol* pa-ra-luh yol
mouth *ağız* a-uhz
music *müzik* mew-zeek

N

name *ad* ad
napkin *peçete* pe-che-te
nappy *bebek bezi* be-bek be-zee
near *yakında* ya-kuhn-da
neck *boyun* bo-yoon
new *yeni* ye-nee
news *haberler* ha-ber-ler
newspaper *gazete* ga-ze-te
night *gece* ge-je
no *hayır* ha-yuhr
noisy *gürültülü* gew-rewl-tew-lew
nonsmoking *sigara içilmeyen* see-ga-ra ee-cheel-me-yen
north *kuzey* koo-zay
nose *burun* boo-roon
now *şimdi* sheem-dee
number *sayı* sa-yuh

O

oil (engine) *jağ* ya
old (object/person) *eski/yaşlı* es-kee/yash-luh
one-way ticket *gidiş bilet* gee-deesh bee-let
open a *açık* a-chuhk
outside *dışarıda* duh-sha-ruh-da

P

package *ambalaj* am-ba-lazh
paper *kağıt* ka-uht
park (car) v *park etmek* park et-mek
passport *pasaport* pa-sa-port
pay v *ödemek* eu-de-mek
pen *tükenmez kalem* tew-ken-mez ka-lem
petrol *benzin* ben-zeen
pharmacy *eczane* ej-za-ne
phonecard *telefon kartı* te-le-fon kar-tuh
photo *fotoğraf* fo-to-raf
plate *tabak* ta-hak
police *polis* po-lees
postcard *kartpostal* kart-pos-tal
post office *postane* pos-ta-ne
pregnant *hamile* ha-mee-le
price *fiyat* fee-yat

Q

quiet *sakin* sa-keen

R

rain n *yağmur* ya-moor
razor *traş makinesi* trash ma-kee-ne-see
receipt n *makbuz* mak-booz
red *kırmızı* kuhr-muh-zuh
refund n *para iadesi* pa-ra ee-a-de-see
registered mail *taahhütlü posta* ta-ah-hewt-lew pos-ta
rent v *kiralamak* kee-ra-la-mak
repair v *tamir etmek* ta-meer et-mek
reservation *rezervasyon* re-zer-vas-yon
restaurant *restoran* res-to-ran
return v *geri dönmek* ge-ree deun-mek
return ticket *gidiş-dönüş bilet* gee-deesh-deu-newsh bee-let
right (direction) *doğru yön* do-roo yeun

road *yol* yol
room *oda* o-da

S

safe a *emniyetli* em-nee-yet-lee
sanitary napkin *hijyenik kadın bağı* heezh-ye-neek ka-duhn ba-uh
seat *yer* yer
send *göndermek* geun-der-mek
service station *benzin istasyonu* ben-zeen ees-tas-yo-noo
sex *seks* seks
shampoo *şampuan* sham-poo-an
share (a dorm) *paylaşmak* pai-lash-mak
shaving cream *tıraş kremi* tuh-rash kre-mee
she *o* o
sheet (bed) *çarşaf* char-shaf
shirt *gömlek* geum-lek
shoes *ayakkabılar* a-yak-ka-buh-lar
shop n *dükkan* dewk-kan
short *kısa* kuh-sa
shower n *duş* doosh
single room *tek kişilik oda* tek kee-shee-leek o-da
skin *cilt* jeelt
skirt *etek* e-tek
sleep v *uyumak* oo-yoo-mak
slowly *yavaşça* ya-vash-cha
small *küçük* kew-chewk
smoke (cigarettes) v *sigara içmek* see-ga-ra eech-mek
soap *sabun* sa-boon
some *biraz* bee-raz
soon *yakında* ya-kuhn-da
south *güney* gew-nay
souvenir shop *hediyelik eşya dükkanı* he-dee-ye-leek esh-ya dewk-ka-nuh
speak *konuşmak* ko-noosh-mak
spoon *kaşık* ka-shuhk
stamp n *pul* pool
stand-by ticket *açık bilet* a-chuhk bee-let
station (train) *istasyon* ees-tas-yon
stomach *mide* mee-de
stop v *durmak* door-mak
stop (bus) n *durağı* doo-ra-uh
street *sokak* so-kak
student *öğrenci* eu-ren-jee
sun *güneş* gew-nesh

sunscreen *güneşten koruma kremi*
gew-nesh-*ten* ko-roo-ma kre-*mee*
swim v *yüzmek* yewz-mek

T

tampons *tamponlar* tam-pon-*lar*
taxi *taksi* tak-*see*
teaspoon *çay kaşığı* chai ka-shuh-*uh*
teeth *dişler* deesh-*ler*
telephone n *telefon* te-le-fon
television *televizyon* te-le-veez-yon
temperature (weather) *derece* de-re-je
tent *çadır* cha-*duhr*
that (one) *şunu* shoo-*noo*
they *onlar* on-*lar*
thirsty *susamış* soo-sa-*muhsh*
this (one) *bunu* boo-*noo*
throat *boğaz* bo-*az*
ticket *bilet* bee-*let*
time *zaman* za-*man*
tired *yorgun* yor-*goon*
tissues *kağıt mendil* ka-*uht* men-*deel*
today *bugün* boo-*gewn*
toilet *tuvalet* too-va-*let*
tomorrow *yarın* ya-*ruhn*
tonight *bu gece* boo ge-*je*
toothbrush *diş fırçası* deesh fuhr-cha-*suh*
toothpaste *diş macunu* deesh ma-joo-*noo*
torch (flashlight) *el feneri* el fe-ne-*ree*
tour n *tur* toor
tourist office *turizm bürosu* too-reezm bew-ro-*soo*
towel *havlu* hav-*loo*
train *tren* tren
translate *çevirmek* che-veer-*mek*
travel agency *seyahat acentesi* se-ya-hat a-jen-te-*see*
travellers cheque *seyahat çeki* se-ya-hat che-*kee*
trousers *pantolon* pan-to-*lon*
Turkey *Türkiye* tewr-kee-ye
Turkish (language) *Türkçe* tewrk-che
Turkish Republic of Northern Cyprus (TRNC)
Kuzey Kıbrıs Türk Cumhuriyeti (KKTC) koo-*zay*
kuhb-*ruhs* tewrk joom-hoo-ree-ye-*tee* (ka-ka-*te*-je)
twin beds *çift yatak* cheeft ya-*tak*
tyre *lastik* las-*teek*

U

underwear *iç çamaşırı* eech cha-ma-shuh-*ruh*
urgent *acil* a-*jeel*

V

vacant *boş* bosh
vacation *tatil* ta-teel
vegetable n *sebze* seb-ze
vegetarian a *vejeteryan* ve-zhe-ter-*yan*
visa *vize* vee-ze

W

waiter *garson* gar-*son*
walk v *yürümek* yew-rew-*mek*
wallet *cüzdan* jewz-*dan*
warm a *ılık* uh-*luhk*
wash (something) *yıkamak* yuh-ka-*mak*
watch n *saat* sa-*at*
water n *su* soo
we *biz* beez
weekend *hafta sonu* haf-*ta* so-*noo*
west *batı* ba-*tuh*
wheelchair *tekerlekli sandalye*
te-ker-lek-*lee* san-*dal*-ye
when *ne zaman* ne za-man
where *nerede* ne-re-de
white *beyaz* be-*yaz*
who *kim* keem
why *neden* ne-den
wife *karı* ka-*ruh*
window *pencere* pen-je-*re*
wine *şarap* sha-*rap*
with *ile* ee-le
without *-sız/-siz/-suz/-süz* -*suhz*/-seez/-*sooz*/-*sewz*
woman *kadın* ka-*duhn*
write *yazı yazmak* ya-zuh yaz-*mak*

Y

yellow *sarı* sa-*ruh*
yes *evet* e-*vet*
yesterday *dün* dewn
you sg inf *sen* sen
you sg pol & pl *siz* seez

Culture

The glory of the Middle East is the sheer diversity of its myriad cultures – from rich **histories** and varied **cuisines** to colourful **festivals**, the Middle East has it all. Here we present you with a cultural snapshot of the region and give you the tools to communicate and travel in an exciting, respectful and **sustainable** way.

history timeline

Take a wander through the rich history of the Middle East . . .

c 5000 BC	The Al-Ubaid culture first appears in Mesopotamia (ancient Iraq).
c 3100 BC	King Menes unifies the kingdoms of Upper and Lower Egypt, ushering in 3000 years of Pharaonic rule.
4000–2350 BC	The Sumerians, credited with inventing the world's first writing system, rule Mesopotamia.
2700 BC	The Epic of Gilgamesh – the story of a Sumerian king and one of the first works of world literature – is written.
2700–2600 BC	Pharaoh Zoser and his chief architect build what is considered Egypt's first pyramid, the Step Pyramid at Saqqara.
2700–2500 BC	The Pyramids of Giza (Egypt), the only ancient wonder to survive in the modern world, are built.
1750–1180 BC	Babylonians rule the Tigris–Euphrates region from the capital of Babylon, one of the great centres of the ancient world.
1600–609 BC	The Assyrian Empire conquers territories far and wide, including parts of Mesopotamia and Egypt.
900 BC–AD 500	The Garamante Empire, based in Libya's Wadi al-Hayat, controls the Saharan trade routes connecting central Africa to the Mediterranean coast.
6th–4th centuries BC	The Persian Empire founded by Cyrus the Great rules from India to the Aegean Sea.
3rd century BC	The amazing city of Petra is carved out of stone in Jordan.
334 BC	Alexander the Great of Macedonia begins a series of conquests that eventually wins him most of Asia Minor, the Middle East, Persia and northern India
c 300 BC	The oldest known Persian carpet, the exceptional Pazyryk carpet, is woven (according to radiocarbon testing performed after the carpet's discovery in AD 1949).
290 BC	The Library of Alexandria, which is regarded as the greatest of all classical institutions, is founded in Alexandria, Egypt.
188–31 BC	Romans conquer most of Asia Minor, Syria, Palestine, the North African territories of Carthage and Libya, and Egypt.

c 6 BC	Jesus – regarded as the Messiah by Christians and one of God's most beloved and important prophets by Muslims – is born in Jerusalem.
AD 66–70	The Jews of Jerusalem stage a revolt against their Roman rulers which results in the Jews being sent into exile.
331	Emperor Constantine declares Christianity the official religion of the Holy Roman (Byzantine) Empire, with the newly renamed Constantinople as its capital.
537	Construction of the Aya Sofya church in Istanbul is completed. Commissioned by Emperor Justinian, it is the best example of the more fluid architecture based on arches, vaults and domes that developed under the Byzantines in Constantinople.
570	The Prophet Mohammed is born in Mecca.
610	Mohammed retreats into the desert and begins to receive divine revelations from Allah via the archangel Gabriel.
622	The first year of the Islamic calendar (1 AH). Mohammed and his followers flee to Medina, marking the birth of Islam.
632–56	Following Mohammed's death, Arab tribes conquer all of Arabia, Libya, Egypt, Syria, Palestine, Iraq, Iran and Afghanistan.
634–44	Two of Mohammed's relatives – his father-in-law Abu Bakr and his cousin and son-in-law Ali – compete for the leadership of Islam. Abu Bakr initially triumphs, but power shifts to Ali when Abu Bakar's successor is assassinated.
680	The Umayyads, the first great Muslim dynasty, defeat Ali's successor, marking the start of Sunni Islam. Those who continue to support Ali's descendents become known as Shiites.
691	The gold-plated Dome of the Rock, the focus of the Temple Mount, is built over the site of Judaism's First and Second Temples, which were destroyed in 587 BC and AD 70 respectively.
705	The Umayyad Mosque is built in Damascus, Syria. It features Byzantine-style golden mosaics that cover the courtyard walls.
750	The Umayyads are toppled by the Abbasids, whose early rule is regarded as the golden age of Islamic culture.
c 950	Turkish guards imprison Abbasid caliphs, and the Seljuk dynasty begins.
1095	Pope Urban II calls for a 'crusade' to liberate Jerusalem. The city falls to the Crusaders four years later.

1187	The Muslim leader Salah ad-Din al-Ayyoub removes the Crusaders from Jerusalem with the help of the Mamluks.
1250–1517	The Mamluks rule Egypt, Syria, Palestine and western Arabia.
1258	Osman (Othman), the founder of the Ottoman Empire, is born in western Anatolia, Turkey.
End of the 14th century	The Ottomans have succeeded in conquering parts of Eastern Europe and most of present-day Turkey.
1453	In their greatest victory, the Ottomans take Constantinople.
1517	The Ottomans take the whole of the eastern Mediterranean, including Egypt and coastal Libya, from the Mamluks. The empire reaches its peak during the subsequent rule of Süleyman the Magnificent.
1557	Mimar Sinan, the master builder of the Ottoman Empire, builds his grandest mosque, Süleymaniye Camii, in Istanbul.
1571	The Ottoman navy is defeated at the Battle of Lepanto, costing the Ottomans control over the western Mediterranean.
1638	The Imam Mosque is built in Esfahan, Iran. It's almost entirely covered in turquoise-blue tiles, and has a 51-metre-high dome.
1798	Napoleon invades Egypt, in the first step of his plan to build a French empire in the Middle East and India. He is forced out by the British three years later.
1909	Tel Aviv, the first modern Jewish city, is founded in what the Ottomans refer to as *Arz-i Filistin* (the 'Land of Palestine').
1911	The Italians gain control of Tripoli and Cyrenaica, Libya.
1914	At the outbreak of WWI, the Ottomans side with Germany and declare a *jihad* (holy war) against Britain, France and Russia.
1916	The British secure Arabic help against the Ottoman Empire, and sign the secret Sykes–Picot Agreement with France, detailing how they'll carve up the Ottoman Empire after its defeat.
1917	British foreign secretary Arthur Balfour issues a declaration that promises that a Jewish homeland will be established in Palestine.
1923	The Ottoman monarchy is overthrown, and Mustafa Kemal 'Atatürk' becomes the first president of the Turkish Republic. Reza Khan sets up a secular republic in Persia.
1947	A UN vote to partition Palestine is rejected by the Arabs .

1948	David Ben-Gurion declares the creation of the Jewish State of Israel. War breaks out between the Arabs and the Jews.
1956	Fighting over the Suez Canal begins between the newly created republic of Egypt on one side, and Britain, France and Israel on the other.
1967	The Palestine Liberation Organisation (PLO) is formed. Egyptian forces move into Sinai, and Israel retaliates with an attack that sparks the Six-Day War.
1973	Israel is caught unawares when Egypt and Syria attack on Yom Kippur, the holiest day of the Jewish calendar.
1979	Egypt signs a peace treaty with Israel at Camp David in the USA. Ayatollah Khomeini establishes an Islamic republic in Iran.
1980	Iraq invades Iran, beginning a war that lasts until 1988, when the two countries grudgingly agree to a cease-fire.
1982	Israel invades Lebanon to force out the PLO, which has been using the country as a base to attack Israel.
1987	The popular Palestine uprising known as the *Intifada* begins.
1988	Egypt's Naguib Mahfouz wins the Nobel Prize for Literature.
1990	Iraq invades Kuwait and King Fahd of Saudi Arabia requests US help. The resulting US-led coalition drives Iraq out of Kuwait.
1993	The 'Oslo Accord' is cemented with a historic handshake between Yasser Arafat and Israeli prime minister Yitzhak Rabin.
1995	The Arab–Israeli peace process is derailed when the hardline Binyamin Netanyahu replaces an assassinated Rabin.
1997	Iran's pre-eminent film-maker Abbas Kiarostami wins the Palme d'Or at the Cannes Film Festival for *The Taste of Cherry*.
2001	The US-led invasion of Afghanistan begins.
2003	The US-led invasion of Iraq starts, ousting Saddam Hussein from power.
2006	Saddam Hussein, captured by US forces in 2003, is put on trial under the Iraqi interim government and executed by hanging. Israel is involved in two separate conflicts with Hamas militants in Israel and with Hezbollah in southern Lebanon. Turkish author Orhan Pamuk wins the Nobel Prize for Literature.

arabic food

Arabic cuisine began humbly as 'tent cookery', when staples such as rice and dates were transported with the help of animals like sheep and camels. As their caravans travelled through the Middle East, however, the Bedouins discovered other ingredients and absorbed new culinary influences. The Lebanese are credited with helping to spread this style of cooking throughout the world. Still, you may wonder, 'Is there more to the Middle East cuisine than *felafel* فلافل fe-*laa*-fel, *shawarma* شاورمة sha-*waar*-ma, *hummus* حمص *hum*-mus and *kebabs* كباب ka-*baab*?' The answer, obviously, is yes, so delve into some of the less-known dishes common across the Middle East.

In Egypt, look out for shops sporting large covered metal dishes in their windows, as they specialise in *kushari* كشاري ku-*shaa*-ree, a concoction that's inexpensive yet filling. Each tureen holds one of the ingredients – pasta, rice, black lentils, chick peas, dried onions and garlic – and as people place their orders, the '*kushari* man' dips his metal spoon into each tureen, scooping the contents into a bowl. It takes about five seconds to prepare and it's the spicy chilli sauce that makes the dish memorable.

Particularly common in Palestine, *makluba* مقلوبة mak-*loo*-beh is an upside-down rice dish prepared in a mould and turned out when firm, giving it the appearance of a cake. The dish has two versions – with or without tomatoes – and can be prepared with lamb or boneless chicken pieces and vegetables like potatoes or cauliflower. The Palestinian version is made with braised lamb, eggplant and tomatoes.

An amazing ceremonial dish, *khouzi* خوزي khoo-zee, is served at important Bedouin feasts. The Saudi version is considered the best in all the Gulf states. It consists of a whole lamb stuffed with a whole chicken, which in turn has been stuffed with hard-boiled eggs and a mixture of rice, nuts, onion, sultanas and spices. The lamb is cooked until the meat comes away from the bones. The stuffing is removed and spread over a serving dish, and the lamb is placed on top surrounded by salads, grapes and yogurt.

Less extravagant, but also delicious, Tunisian *brik* بريك brik are deep-fried pastries containing a whole egg with tuna, potato and flat leaf parsley. Eat them carefully if you don't want to end up with egg on your face! *Chakchouka* شكشوكة shak-*shoo*-ka is another egg dish that's popular in Tunisia, as well as in Algeria and Israel. Eaten for breakfast with crusty bread or rice, it's prepared by breaking eggs into a colourful stew of sautéed onions and garlic, tomatoes and red and green peppers.

Vegetarians will be pleased to hear about *fuul* فول fool, one of the most popular Middle Eastern snack foods. Its main ingredient is fava beans, slow-cooked in garlic and garnished with parsley, olive oil, lemon, salt, black pepper and cumin. Thought to contain the souls of dead people, fava beans were once condemned, but today *fuul* is everywhere, ladled into pita bread for a snack on the run. Another widely available vegetarian dish is *fattoush* فتوش fat-*toosh*, a toasted bread salad with tomatoes, onions and mint leaves, sometimes served with tangy pomegranate syrup.

hebrew food

Visit Israel during *Pesahk* פסח pe·sakh (the Feast of Passover, a week-long celebration of the time Moses led the Hebrew people from Egypt) and you'll notice that huge plastic tarps cover large sections of supermarkets, hiding all kinds of bread products, from pretzels to wheat grain. The bread that comes with *falafel* פלאפל fa·la·fel has been replaced with soft *matsa* מצה ma·tsa (unleavened bread), and even McDonald's uses buns made from mashed potatoes. According to *kashrut* כשרות kash·rut (the kosher rules that dictate what may be eaten) Jews can't touch leavened bread during *Pesahk*, nor anything that has touched leavened bread. This commemorates the haste of the Israelites, who fled Egypt so quickly they didn't have time to let their bread rise.

The Friday night dinner that marks the start of *Shabat* שבת sha·bat (the Jewish holy day and day of rest) is another example of how the Jewish faith influences the diet of its followers. All Jewish meals are considered a religious rite and begin with a blessing for bread. For *Shabat*, this is done over two loaves of specially baked *khala* חלה kha·la, a sweet braid-shaped egg bread that has a long history. In ancient times, it was customary for Jewish women to set aside a small piece of dough (called *khala*) for the temple priest whenever they made bread – over time the term came to refer to the whole bread. It's also become a *Shabat* tradition to eat *khamin* חמין kha·min, a slow-cooked stew often made of beef and beans. While no work of any kind, including cooking, may be carried out on *Shabat*, cooking *khamin* begins before the start of *Shabat* and it can be kept warm or reheated later.

Many of the kosher foods associated with Hebrew cuisine have Eastern European origins. These include *gefilte fish* גפלטעפיש ge·fel·ti·fish (a blend of a boned kosher fish, usually shaped into balls), *kugel* קוגל ku·gel (a baked potato pudding), *kreplach* קריפלך kre·pa·lakh (meat-filled dumplings often served in chicken soup), *latkes* לטקעס lat·keks (fried potato pancakes) and *blintzes* בלינטסיס blin·tsis (heavy pancakes typically with a savoury filling like mushrooms or cheese). And there are the ever-popular *beigel* בייגל bei·gel (bagels), which are generally crisp and dry in Israel (a softer style is produced in Tel Aviv). A traditional way to end a night out is to visit the bagel factory and pick up a hot bagel or two.

Israel is one of the world's oldest wine-producing regions, but most Israelis only drink wine on holidays such as *Shabat*, *Pesahk* and *Purim* פורים pu·rim – a holiday that recognises the foiling, by a man named Mordechai, of a 6th-century BC plot by the Persian noble Haman to kill the Jews of Persia. The Torah states that during *Purim* people are supposed to drink until they can't distinguish between the phrases *Arur Haman* ארור המן a·rur ha·man ('Cursed is Haman') and *Baruch Mordechai* ברוך מרדכי ba·rukh mor·di·khai ('Blessed is Mordechai'). Wine also features in some of the desserts prepared for these holidays. But for most of the time, Israelis content themselves with *kafe* קפה ka·fe (coffee) and *te* תה te (tea), Israel's most popular beverages.

persian food

Long before the advent of Weight Watchers, ancient Persian physicians warned that a diet high in fats, red meat, starch and alcohol transformed people into selfish brutes. While the ever-present *kebab* کباب ka·*baab* suggests that modern Iran has ignored this counsel, Iranians do strive to eat a balanced diet that achieves a harmony between 'hot' foods (eg meats and sweet desserts) and 'cold' foods (eg yogurt, cheese and radishes).

Persian cuisine centres around bread, rice and meat, but the inventive use of fresh fruits and vegetables, nuts, herbs and spices ensures that Persian dishes are healthy, colourful and fragrant. For example, the classic *fesenjun* فسنجان fe·sen·*joon* is a wonderfully aromatic *khoresht* خورشت kho·*resht* (stew) of pomegranate juice, walnuts, eggplant and cardamom served over roast chicken and rice. It's quite an honour to be served *fesenjun* in an Iranian home – so if you're lucky enough to be invited for a home-cooked meal, you're guaranteed a memorable experience.

The centrepiece of a family meal is the *sofreh* سفره sof·*re*, a tablecloth which is generally embroidered with traditional prayers and/or poetry, spread over a Persian carpet or table and laden with a colourful and elaborate array of staple ingredients and condiments. There's *naan-o-panir* نان و پنیر naan o pa·*neer* (fresh herbs and feta cheese with Persian bread), fresh cucumbers, butter with honey or sugar, nuts, raisins or *keshmesh* کشمش kesh·*mesh* (dried fruit), yogurt, *maast* ماست mast (Persian pickles and relishes), various *maze* مزه ma·*ze* (dips), sweetened *kharboze* خربزه khar·bo·*ze* (melon) slices, and *laboo* لبو la·*boo* (peeled, steamed beets).

Naan نان naan (bread) is dirt cheap in Iran and is either flat and paper-thin (*lavash* لواش la·*vaash* and *taftun* تافتون taaf·*toon*) or thick and oval-shaped (*barbari* بربری bar·ba·*ree* and *sangak* سنگک san·*gak*). Baked on a bed of stones, *sangak* is decorated elaborately and shared with guests after a *Sofreh Aghd* سفره عقد sof·re·*ye* aghd (Persian wedding ceremony), to bring the new couple happiness and prosperity. Iranians also consume copious amounts of *chelo* چلو che·*lo* (rice) at every meal, particularly lunch. The rice can be simply flavoured and coloured with saffron, or cooked with ingredients like nuts, spices or barberries.

With pomegranates, peaches, watermelons, grapefruits, oranges and mandarins on offer, you'll happily tuck into the bowl of *mive* میوه mee·*ve* (fruit) usually served for dessert. However, if you enjoy having an alcoholic drink with your meal, you'll be disappointed – in Iran, alcohol is prohibited by Islamic law. Drinking usually means *chay* چای chaay (tea): a host is honour-bound to offer a guest at least one cup, which the guest, in turn, is honour-bound to drink. The tea tray is always set with a bowl of *ghand* قند ghand (sugar cubes). Before drinking the tea, it's customary to 'clean' it by dipping a *ghand* into it, then to place the cube between your front teeth or on your tongue and suck the brew through it. A novice will probably find that the sugar dissolves in just seconds. An Iranian can make a cube last for a whole cup, or longer.

turkish food

As you'd expect from a people who've written love songs to yogurt, ballads about fish sandwiches and poems that imagine battles between pastry and pilav, the Turks are passionate about food. For the average Turk, food is much more than fuel – and with an abundance of fresh produce and recipes from all corners of the once-mighty Ottoman Empire, it's no wonder that Turkish cuisine is among the world's greatest.

Wherever you go, you'll find meal tables piled with delicious soups, stews, assorted *kebap* ke·*bap*, *köfte* keuf·*te* (meatballs) and, of course, bread. Unleavened sourdough bread (*ekmek* ek·*mek*) is ubiquitous, but you'll also find *pide* pee·*de* (flat bread that's also a base for *lahmacun* la·ma·*joon*, a type of pizza commonly topped with ground meat, onion, chilli and parsley), *lavaş* la·*vash* (thin, crispy bread) and *simit* see·*meet* (a small bread ring sprinkled with sesame seeds, whose popularity has inspired the design of multi-storey *simit* palaces in big cities).

Çorba chor·*ba* (soup) is served for breakfast, lunch and dinner. Turkey's most famous soup is even eaten late at night – but proceed with caution. While locals swear it's perfect for warding off a hangover, be prepared if someone suggests you go for *işkembe çorbası* eesh·kem·*be* chor·ba·*suh* as you roll out of a bar after too much *rakı* ra·*kuh* (a strong spirit made of grapes and infused with aniseed). The Turks love this soup made with tripe (lamb's stomach).

Many Westerners will be familiar with *döner kebap* deu·ner ke·*bap* – meat (usually lamb, but also beef and chicken) grilled on a vertical skewer and then shaved off. There are, however, many varieties of *kebap* named after their place of origin and distinguished by their preparation and ingredients. Two famous *kebaps* are the spicy hot *Adana kebap* a·da·na ke·*bap* with red pepper, and *Urfa kebap* oor·fa ke·*bap*, which comes with lashings of onion and black pepper.

While Turkey is a meat-lover's paradise, there's lots to tempt vegetarians. With 900 recorded ways to cook it, *patlıcan* pat·luh·*jan* (eggplant) is the most favoured vegetable. Turks also love *dolma* dol·*ma* (peppers, tomatoes, cabbage and vine leaves stuffed with rice, currants and pine nuts). Vegetarians also have a plethora of choices among *meze* me·*ze* –small, tasty appetisers similar to Spanish tapas.

If you can manage it after indulging in a feast of soups, starters and mains, don't forget the heavenly Turkish desserts, the most famous being *lokum* lo·*koom* (Turkish delight) – smooth, translucent, jellied dreams. Also worth sampling is *dondurma* don·door·*ma*, a thick ice cream traditionally made from goat's milk, sugar and *salep* sa·*lep* (an allegedly aphrodisiac powder of tapioca root). You may find the long, hard (but entirely rewarding) work required to eat *dondurma* quells any aphrodisiac effects! If you're still curious, you can always try the hot drink that's made with *salep* – it has a mild, slightly nutty taste and can be bought in the winter from street vendors and the occasional restaurant or *pastane* pas·ta·*ne* (pastry shop).

festivals

Ascension of Ramses II (Abu Simbel, Egypt)

In the Sacred Sanctuary of the Great Temple of Ramses II, statues representing the four gods of the *ma'*·bad معبد (temple) sit on their thrones and wait for dawn. One of them is the long-serving fa·ra·*'on* فرعون (pharaoh) Ramses II, who ordered that the temple be aligned so that on the dates of his ascension to the throne (22 February) and his birthday (22 October), the rising sun would illuminate the ta·ma·*seel* تماسيل (statues). Late last century, the construction of the Aswan High Dam threatened the temple's existence, but engineers managed to move it to a new location nearby. Today, crowds gather in the temple's chapel before sunrise on 22 February and 22 October each year to marvel at the sun's rays. Only the statue of Ptah, who ironically was the god of darkness, remains unlit. The crowd then proceeds outside for music, dancing, eating, drinking and markets.

Bosra Festival (Bosra, Syria)

A vast, steeply terraced hillside of stone seating, the magnificent 2nd-century Roman mu·*dar*·raj مدرّج (amphitheatre) in Bosra (the former capital of the Roman province of Arabia) is a wonderful site to explore at any time, but in September or October of every odd-numbered year, these atmospheric ruins turn electric when the site – one of the most well-preserved from the ancient world – hosts the Bosra Festival. A 10-day showcase of international music, dance and theatre from countries the Syrian government has invited, the festival's aim is to encourage cultural exchange and promote Syria's archaeological heritage.

Camel Wrestling Festival (Selçuk, Turkey)

This festival is so popular in Turkey that the 1994 event holds the Guinness World Record for 'Largest Audience at a Camel Wrestling Festival' (20,000 people, for the record). Despite the camel owner's pre-race bravado – as he parades his prize camel around the village, he boasts that the animal will destroy anyone silly enough to take him on – the actual 'fight' is more slapstick comedy than blood sport. The festival takes place in early January during mating season, when male camels normally jostle for the available female. In the arena this translates to the two *beserek* be·se·*rek* (male camels, literally 'bulls') vying for the affection of the young *maya* ma·*ya* (female camel, literally 'cow') led out, by half-heartedly butting and leaning on each other until one of them gives in and runs away. Just be careful not to stand too close to the action – the fleeing bull has been known to charge off towards the crowd, with the conquering bull in pursuit.

Dead Sea Ultra Marathon (Jordan)

On the second Friday of April each year, The Dead Sea Ultra Marathon brings runners back down to earth – to the lowest point on Earth that's not covered by water that is. The 50km course starts in Amman and finishes on the shores of the Dead Sea, around 400m below sea level. With temperatures in Jordan in the mid-thirties (Celsius) and over during April, the race is not for the faint-hearted. Still, all that sweat is helping to raise funds to provide lifesaving neurological surgery for those unable to afford it. As well as the full marathon – 42km, there's the junior marathon – 4.2km, the fun run – 10km and the half marathon – 21km.

Eid al-Adha (across the Middle East)

Celebrated on the 10th day of *Dhu al-Hijjah* الحجة ذو dhoo al-*hij*-jah (the last month of the Muslim year), Eid al-Adha – the most important feast of the Muslim calendar – commemorates the Prophet Ibrahim's obedience to Allah. During his lifetime Ibrahim survived many tests of his faith, but the greatest came when he was ordered to take his son Ismail to the mountains and kill him. With sorrow in his heart but an unwavering faith, Ibrahim proceeded to carry out Allah's order – but when he arrived at the appointed place, Allah ordered him to sacrifice a lamb instead. Today Muslims mark this day by sacrificing an animal (usually a sheep, but sometimes a goat or cow) and sharing the meat with needy people and older relatives. Clothes and money are sometimes given, too.

Holy Week (Jerusalem, Israel)

Celebrated first by the Protestants and Roman Catholics, and about two weeks later by the Orthodox Church, khag ha-*pas*-kha חג הפסחא (Easter) means absolute chaos in Jerusalem's Old City. Along with yom ri-*shon* shel ha-*pas*-kha יום ראשון של הפסחא (Easter Sunday), sha-*vu*-aa' ha-*ko*-desh שבוע הקודש (Holy Week) is the most important event in the Christian calendar, and pilgrims from across the world converge on the Old City for services and processions commemorating and re-enacting the last week of Jesus Christ's life. The week begins with a procession from Mount Olive to Jerusalem on yom ri-*shons* shel ka-*pot* hat-ma-*rim* יום ראשון של כפות התמרים (Palm Sunday) , but perhaps the biggest event occurs on yom shi-*shi* ha-*tov* יום שישי הטוב (Good Friday). Pilgrims clog the Via Dolorosa ('Way of Sorrows', which is said to be the route Jesus took as he carried his cross to Calvary), staking out their places for the procession that re-traces Christ's steps. It culminates at the Church of the Holy Sepulchre, the site of the chapel marking Calvary.

Jenadriyah National Festival (Jenadriyah, Saudi Arabia)

An annual two-week celebration of Saudi Arabia's cultural heritage takes place in late February or early March, at a special site northeast of central Riyadh. The festival kicks off with the King's Cup – run over a 12-mile track and attracting up to 2000 participants, it's Saudi Arabia's most prestigious camel race. The programme also includes the performance of traditional songs, poetry competitions and dances, pottery, woodwork and weaving demonstrations, and falconry from around the kingdom. The festival is one of the few places to witness the thrilling spectacle of Saudi Arabia's national dance, *al-ardha* العارضة al-*'aar*-dha, too – during this dance, sword-bearing men stand shoulder-to-shoulder, swaying in unison to a drumbeat and tossing their swords into the air, where they tremble and spin before dropping back into their hands.

Khareef Festival (Salalah, Oman)

If you're visiting the Arabian Peninsula between mid-June and mid-September, Salalah is the place to be. As the rest of the peninsula swelters through the worst of the summer heat, Salalah embraces the summer monsoon, and this small corner of the sultanate is transformed from dusty yellow to lush green. Known locally as the *khareef* خريف kha-*reef* (meaning 'wind of plenty'), the monsoon sweeps west from India. By the time it reaches Salalah, the heavy thunderstorms have diffused into a misty, wet breeze that covers the mountains and valleys in an enchanting haze, and creates a wonderful oasis of streams and waterfalls. Tourists flock to Salalah at this time, and the government celebrates the season with a 48-day festival of folk dances and cultural extravaganzas.

Mevlana Festival (Konya, Turkey)

The annual Mevlana Festival that runs from 10 to 17 December is an ideal introduction to the *sema* se-*ma*, the ritual dance of the Mevlevi Order, better known as the *semazenler* se-ma-*zen*-ler (Whirling Dervishes). The order was founded in the 13th century in honour of the great mystic philosopher Celaleddin Rumi, who later became known as *Mevlana* mev-*la*-na (Our Guide). Witnessing the *sema* can be an evocative and unforgettable experience: building slowly, it culminates in an ecstatic expression of the dervishes' mystical union with God. With their full skirts swooping up and down, the dancers whirl with their right arms held up to receive the blessing of heaven and their left arms turned down to give these blessings to the earth. The festival ends with *Şeb-i Arus* sheb-ee a-*roos* ('Nuptial Night') on 17 December, the anniversary of Mevlana's death and his union, or 'wedding night', with Allah.

No Ruz (throughout Iran)

When the New-Year hangovers and resolutions of Westerners are forgotten, the people of Iran are just gearing up for No Ruz نوروز, no·rooz, their New Year. Iranians prepare for this time of hope and renewal by spring-cleaning their houses and lighting bonfires that people can jump over to rid themselves of all their illnesses and misfortunes. The New Year is announced on the spring equinox (around 21 March), beginning 13 days of festivities. The last day is called Sizdah Bedar سیزده بدر, siz·dah be·dar which means 'getting rid of the omen of the 13th day' – Iranians go for picnics in the countryside with close relatives and friends, and enjoy traditional foods, music, dancing, games and sports. Unmarried girls can also wish for a husband by going into the fields and tying a knot between green shoots, symbolising a marriage knot.

Qasr Festival (Kabaw, Libya)

In April every year the Qasr Festival celebrates the unique heritage of the Berber people in Libya's Jebel Nafusa region. Berbers are essentially rural people who farm barley, corn, wheat and rye. The landscape of Jebel Nafusa is dotted with the architectural evidence: looking like something out of a Star Wars set, qasrs قصور ku·soor are fortified granary stores built from the 12th century, which provided protection for the crops necessary for the community's survival. While government policy has been to integrate the Berbers into the Arabic community and suppress their language and culture, they remain proud of their identity. The festivities emphasise Berber folklore and incorporate re-enactments of important local ceremonies – such as u·ru·saat عرسات (weddings), jun·naaz جناز (funerals) and has·saa·'id حصائد (harvests) – by people in traditional dress.

Tel Aviv Love Parade (Tel Aviv, Israel)

A festival where scantily clad if not nude revellers (decked out in body paint, silly hats and plastic clothes) dance in streets awash with pulsing techno beats probably isn't the first thing that comes to mind when you say 'the Middle East'. But since the year 2000, up to 250,000 people gather on the streets of Tel Aviv in October each year to shout a message of peace, love and tolerance – and have a good time too, of course! The Tel Aviv Love Parade is the only street party of its kind in the Middle East, and belongs to a series of parties intended to be calls for peace and international understanding through music – the first was held in Berlin four months before the demolition of the Berlin Wall. The Tel Aviv festival culminates with Friday's Parade Day, which features outrageously decorated floats pumping out trance and techno music at the masses on the streets.

sustainable travel & responsible tourism

As the climate change debate heats up, the matter of sustainability becomes an important part of the travel vernacular. In practical terms, this means assessing our impact on the environment and local cultures and economies – and acting to make that impact as positive as possible. Here are some basic phrases in Arabic (Modern Standard) ⓐ, Farsi ⓕ, Hebrew ⓗ and Turkish ⓣ to get you on your way ...

communication

I'd like to learn some (Arabic/Farsi/Hebrew/Turkish).

أريد أن أتعلَّم قليلا
من (اللغة العربية).

'u·ree·du an 'at·ta·'al·la·ma ka·lee·lan
min (al·lu·gha·til 'a·ra·bee·ya) ⓐ

من می خواهم کمی
(فارسی) یاد بگیرم.

man mee·khaam ka·mee
(faar·see) yaad be·gee·ram ⓕ

אני רוצה ללמוד (עברית).

a·ni rot·se/rot·sa lel·mod (iv·rit) m/f ⓗ

Biraz (Türkçe) öğrenmek
istiyorum.

bee·raz (tewrk·che) eu·ren·mek
ees·tee·yo·room ⓣ

What's this called in (Arabic/Farsi/Hebrew/Turkish)?

ما اسم هذا
(باللغة العربية)؟

maa 'is·mu haa·dhaa
(bil·lu·gha·til 'a·ra·bee·ya) ⓐ

این را در (فارسی) چی می گویند؟

een ro dar (faar·see) chee mee·gan ⓕ

איך קוראים לזה ב(עברית)?

ekh kor·im le·ze be·(iv·rit) ⓗ

Buna (Türkçe)'de ne denir?

boo·na (tewrk·che)·de ne de·neer ⓣ

Would you like me to teach you some English?

هل تريد أن أعلمك قليل
من اللغة الإنجليزية؟

hal tu·ree·du an 'u'·li·ma·ka ka·lee·lan
min al·lu·gha·til 'inj·lee·zee·ya ⓐ

می خواهید من به شما
کمی انگلیسی یاد بدهم؟

mee·khaa·heen man be sho·maa
ka·mee een·gee·lee·see yaad be·dam ⓕ

אתה/את רוצה שאלמד אותך קצת
אנגלית?

a·ta/at rot·se/rot·sa she·i·la·med ot·kha ktsat
ang·lit m/f ⓗ

Sana biraz İngilizce
öğretmemi ister misin?

sa·na bee·raz een·gee·leez·je
eu·ret·me·mee ees·ter mee·seen ⓣ

cultural differences

I respect your beliefs.

أنا أحترم إيمانك.

'a·naa 'ah·ta·ri·mu 'ee·maa·na·ka ⓐ

من به عقاید شما
احترام می گزارم.

man be a·ghaa·ye·de sho·maa
eh·te·raam mee·zaa·ram ⓕ

אני מכבד/מכבדת את	a·*ni* mi·kha·*bed*/mi·kha·*be*·det et
האמונה שלך.	ha·i·mu·*na* shel·*kha*/she·*lakh* m/f ⓗ
İnançlarına saygı	ee·nanch·la·ruh·*na* sai·*guh*
duyuyorum.	doo·*yoo*·yo·room ⓣ

I didn't mean to do/say anything wrong.

ما رغبت بفعل/بقول	maa ra·*ghib*·tu bi·fi·*'·li*/bi·*kaw*·li
أي شيء سيء.	*'ay*·yee shay·in *say*·yi ⓐ
من نمی خواستم چیز	man *ne*·mee·khaas·tam chee·*ze*
اشتباهی بکنم/بگویم.	esh·te·baa·*hee* be·ko·nam/be·*gam* ⓕ
לא התכוונתי לומר/לעשות	lo hit·ka·*van*·ti lo·*mar*/la·*sot*
משהו לא בסדר.	*ma*·shi·hu lo be·se·*der* ⓗ
Yanlış birşey yapmak/	yan·*luhsh* beer·shay yap·*mak*/
söylemek istemedim.	say·le·*mek* ees·te·me·deem ⓣ

Is this a local or national custom?

هل هذا تقليد محلي	'hal haa·*dhaa* tak·*leed* ma·ha·lee
أو وطني؟	aw wa·ta·nee ⓐ
این رسم محلی هست یا ملی؟	een ras·*me* ma·hal·*lee* hast yaa mel·*lee* ⓕ
האם זה מנהג מקומי?	ha·*im* ze min·*hag* mi·ko·mi ⓗ
Bu yerel mi yoksa	boo ye·*rel* mee yok·sa
ulusal bir gelenek mi?	oo·loo·*sal* beer ge·le·*nek* mee ⓣ

---

transport

Let's walk there.

فلنتمشى إلى هناك.	fal·na·ta·*mash*·sha *'i*·laa hu·*naak* ⓐ
تا آنجا پیاده برویم.	taa oon·*jaa* pee·yaa·*de* be·*reem* ⓕ
בוא/בואי נלך לשם.	bo/*bo*·i ni·*lekh* li·*sham* m/f ⓗ
Oraya yürüyelim.	o·ra·ya yew·rew·ye·*leem* ⓣ

Can we get there by public transport?

هل يمكننا أن نصل إلى	hal yum·*ki*·nu·naa 'an *na*·si·lu *'i*·laa
هناك بالمواصلات المشتركة؟	hu·*naak* bil·mu·wa·sa·*laat* al·*mush*·ta·rak ⓐ
می توانیم آنجا با وسایل	mee·*too*·neem oon·*jaa* baa va·saa·ye·*le*
نقلیه عمومی برویم؟	nagh·lee·ye·ye oo·*moo*·mee be·*reem* ⓕ
אפשר להגיע לשם בתחבורה	if·*shar* le·ha·gi·a le·*sham* ba·takh·bu·*ra*
ציבורית?	tsi·bu·*rit* ⓗ
Oraya toplu taşım aracı	o·ra·ya top·*loo* ta·*shuhm* a·ra·*juh*
ile gidebilir miyiz?	ee·le gee·de·bee·*leer* mee·*yeez* ⓣ

accommodation

I'd like to stay at a locally run hotel.

أريد أن أقيم في فندق وأصاحبه من هذه المنطقة.	'u·ree·du 'an 'u·kee·ma fee fun·duk·wa saa·hi·bu·hu min haa·dhi·hil man·ta·ka·a (a)
من می خواهم در یک مسافرخانه بمانم.	man mee·khaam dar yek mo·saa·fer·khoo·ne be·moo·nam (f)
אני רוצה להישאר בבית מלון שמנוהל על ידי מקומיים.	a·ni rot·se/rot·sa le·hi·sha·er be·bet ma·lon she·mi·nu·hal al ya·de mi·ko·mi·yim m/f (h)
Yerel çalıştırılan bir otelde kalmak istiyorum.	ye·rel cha·luhsh·tuh·ruh·lan bir o·tel·de kal·mak ees·tee·yo·room (i)

Can I open the window?

هل من الممكن أن افتح الشباك؟	hal min al·mum·kin 'an 'af·ta·ha ash·shub·baak (a)
می توانم پنجره را باز کنم؟	mee·too·nam pan·ja·re ro baaz ko·nam (f)
אני יכול/יכולה לפתוח את החלון?	a·ni ya·khol/ya·kho·la lef·to·akh kha·lon m/f (h)
Pencereyi açabilir miyim?	pen·je·re·yee a·cha·bee·leer mee·yeem (i)

I don't need a fresh towel.

لا أحتاج إلى منشفة جديدة.	laa 'ah·taa·ju 'i·laa man·sha·fa·tin ja·dee·da (a)
من حوله تازه لازم ندارم.	man ho·le·ye taa·ze laa·zem na·daa·ram (f)
אני לא צריך/צריכה מגבת חדשה.	a·ni lo tsa·rikh/tsri·kha ma·ge·vet kha·da·sha m/f (h)
Yeni havluya ihtiyacım yok.	ye·nee hav·loo·ya eeh·tee·ya·juhm yok (i)

shopping

Where can I buy locally produced (goods/souvenirs)?

من أين أشتري صناعات محلي؟	min 'ay·na 'ash·ta·ree si·naa·'aat ma·ha·lee (a)
من از کجا می توانم (کالاها/سوغاتی) های محلی بخرم؟	man az ko·jaa mee·too·nam (kaa·laa·haa/so·ghaa·tee·haa·yee) yee ma·hal·lee be·kha·ram (f)
האם אני יכול/יכולה לקנות (דברים/ מזכרות) מתוצרת מקומית?	ha·im a·ni ya·khol/ya·kho·la lek·not (dva·rim/ miz·ka·rot) mi·tot·se·ret mi·ko·mit m/f (h)
Bu yöreye ait (ürünler/hediyelik) eşyalar nereden alabilirim?	boo yeu·re·ye a·eet (ew·rewn·ler/he·dee·ye·leek) esh·ya·lar ne·re·den a·la·bee·lee·reem (i)

What's this made from?

هذا مصنوع من ما؟	haa·dhaa mas·noo·'un min maa (a)
این از چی ساخته شده؟	een az chee saakh·te sho·de (f)
ממה זה עשוי?	me·ma ze a·sui (h)
Bu neden yapılmış?	boo ne·den ya·puhl·muhsh (i)

food

Where can I find the health-food section?

أين أجد قسم الطعام الصحي؟	*'ay·na 'a·ji·du kis·mi at·ta·'aa·mi as·sah·hee* ⓐ
کجا می توانم قسمت	*ko·jaa mee·too·nam ghes·ma·te*
غذاهای سالم را پیدا کنم؟	*gha·zaa·haa·ye saa·lem ro pey·daa ko·nam* ⓕ
איפה מחלקת המזון הבריא?	*e·fo makh·le·ket ha·ma·zon ha·ba·ri* ⓗ
Sağlıklı gıda bölümü nerede?	*sa·luhk·luh guh·da beu·lew·mew ne·re·de* ⓣ

Do you sell organic produce?

هل تبيع غلال عضوية؟	*hal ta·bee·'u ghi·laal 'ud·wee·ya* ⓐ
شما تولیدات ارگانیکی	*sho·maa to·lee·daa·te or·gaa·nee·kee*
می فروشید؟	*mee·foo·roo·sheen* ⓕ
האם אתם מוכרים מוצרים	*ha·im a·tem mokh·rim mot·sa·rim*
אורגניים?	*or·ga·ni·yim* ⓗ
Organik ürünler satıyor musunuz?	*or·ga·neek ew·rewn·ler sa·tuh·yor moo·soo·nooz* ⓣ

sightseeing

I'd like to hire a local guide.

أريد دليل من هذه المنطقة.	*'u·ree·du da·leel min haa·dhi·hil man·ta·ka* ⓐ
من می خواهم یک	*man mee·khaam yek*
راهنمای محلی بگیرم.	*raah·na·maa·ye ma·hal·lee be·gee·ram* ⓕ
אני רוצה לשכור מדריך	*a·ni rot·se/rot·sa les·khor mad·rikh*
מקומי.	*mi·ko·mi* m/f ⓗ
Yerel bir rehber kiralamak istiyorum.	*ye·rel beer reh·ber kee·ra·la·mak ees·tee·yo·room* ⓣ

I'd like to go somewhere off the beaten track.

أريد أن أذهب إلى	*'u·ree·du 'an 'adh·ha·ba 'i·laa*
مكان غير معروف.	*ma·kaan ghay·ri ma·'roof* ⓐ
من می خواهم از یک جای	*man mee·kham az jaa·yee*
خارج از راه اصلی بروم .	*khaa·rej az raa·he as·lee be·ram* ⓕ
אני רוצה ללכת למקום לא	*a·ni rot·se/rot·sa la·le·khet le·ma·kom lo*
שיגרתי.	*shig·ra·ti* m/f ⓗ
Alışılmadık bir yere gitmek istiyorum.	*a·luh·shuhl·ma·duhk beer ye·re geet·mek ees·tee·yo·room* ⓣ

work

I'd like to do some volunteer work (for your organisation).

أريد أن أعمل كمتطوع/
كمتطوعة
(لمنظمتكم).

'u·ree·du an 'a'·ma·la ka·mu·ta·taw·wi'/
ka·mu·ta·taw·wi·'a
(li·mu·nadh·dhi·ma·ti·kum) m/f ⓐ

من می خواهم مقداری
کار داوطلبانه (برای
سازمان شما) بکنم.

man mee·khaam megh·daa·ree
kaa·re daav·ta·la·baa·ne (ba·raa·ye
saa·ze·maa·ne sho·maa) be·ko·nam ⓕ

אני רוצה להתנדב
(לארגון שלך).

a·ni rot·se/rot·sa le·hit·na·dev
(la·ir·gun shel·kha/she·lakh) m/f ⓗ

(Sizin kurumunuz için)
gönüllü olarak çalışmak
istiyorum.

(see·zeen koo·roo·moo·nooz ee·cheen)
geu·newl·lew o·la·rak cha·luhsh·mak
ees·tee·yo·room ⓘ

I'm a (doctor). Can I volunteer my skills?

أنا (طبيب/طبيبة).
هل يمكنني أن أتطوع
مساعدتي؟

'a·naa (ta·beeb/ta·bee·ba)
hal yum·ki·nu·nee an 'a·ta·taw·wa·'a
mu·saa·'a·da·tee m/f ⓐ

من یک (دکتر) هستم. من
می توانم مهارتم را
داوطلبا نه در اختیار
شما بگذارم؟

man yek (dok·tor) has·tam man
mee·too·nam ma·haa·ra·tam ro
daav·ta·la·baa·ne dar ekh·tee·yaa·re
sho·maa be·zaa·ram ⓕ

אני (רופא). האם אני יכול
להתנדב עם המומחיות שלי?

a·ni (ro·fe/ro·fa) ha·im a·ni ya·khol/ya·kho·la
le·hit·na·dev em ha·mom·kho·yut she·li m/f ⓗ

Ben (doktor)um. Gönüllü olarak
hizmet verebilir miyim?

ben (dok·tor)·oom geu·newl·lew o·la·rak
heez·met ve·re·bee·leer mee·yeem ⓘ

Is there a need for volunteer (English teachers)?

هل تحتاج إلى متطوع/
متطوعة (لتدريس
اللغة الإنجليزية)؟

hal tah·taa·ju 'i·laa mu·ta·taw·wi'/
mu·ta·taw·wi·'a (bi·tad·ree·sil
lu·gha·til 'inj·lee·zee·ya) m/f ⓐ

به (معلم های انگلیسی)
‌ ‌ نیاز دارید؟

be (mo·'al·lem·haa·ye een·gee·lee·see)
ye daav·ta·lab nee·yaaz daa·reen ⓕ

אתם צריכים מתנדבים/מתנדבות
(מורים/מורות לאנגלית)?

a·tem tsri·khim mit·nad·vim/mit·nad·vot
(mo·rim/mo·rot la·ang·lit) m/f ⓗ

Gönüllü (İngilizce
öğretmenleri)ne ihtiyaç var mı?

geu·newl·lew (een·gee·leez·je
er·ret·men·le·ree)·ne eeh·tee·yach var muh ⓘ

	MSA	Egy	Glf	Lev	Tun	Far	Heb	Tur
A								
accommodation	21	46	72	98	124	154	185	214
address	18, 20, 28	45, 54	70, 71, 80	96, 97, 106	122, 123, 132	152, 153, 162	182, 183, 192	212, 213, 222
addressing people	27	53	79	106	118, 131	161	192	221
admission (sightseeing)	24	49	76	102	128	158	188	218
airport	17	43	69	95	121	151	181	211
alcoholic drinks	30	56	82	108	134	–	195	224
allergies	31, 33	57, 59	83, 85	109, 111	135, 137	164, 167	195, 197	225, 227
alphabet	9, 12	9, 12	9, 12	9, 12	9, 12	144, 145	174, 175	204, 205
ambulance	31	57	83	110	135	165	196	225
amounts	27	52	78	105	130	160	191	220
art & architecture					234			
assault	32	58	84	110	136	166	196	226
B								
baggage	16, 32	42, 58	68, 84	94, 110	120, 136	150, 166	180, 196	210, 226
bank	19	45	71	97	123	153	183	213
banking	22	48	74	100	126	156	186	216
bar	29	55	81	107	133	–	193	223
bargaining	26	52	78	104	130	160	190	220
bill (restaurant)	30	56	82	108	134	164	194	224
bill (shopping)	26	52	78	104	130	160	190	220
boat	17	43	69	95	121	151	181	211
booking (accommodation)	21	47	73	99	125	155	185	215
booking (restaurant)	29	55	81	107	133	163	193	223
booking (tickets)	16	42	68	94	120	150	180	210
books	29	55	81	107	133	163	193	223
border crossing	16	42	68	94	120	150	180	210
bus	17	43	69	95	121	151	181	211
business	16	42	68	94	120	150	180	210
C								
café	29	55	81	107	133	163	193	223
camera	27	53	79	105	131	161	191	221
camping	21	46, 47	72, 73	98, 99	124, 125	154, 155	185	214, 215
car	19	44	71	96	122	152	183	212
cell phone	23	48	75	101	126	156	187	216
changing money	22	48	74	100	126	156	186	216
checking out	22	47	73	100	125	155	186	215
cinema	29	55	81	107	133	163	193	223

What kind of traveller are you?

A. You're eating chicken for dinner *again* because it's the only word you know.

B. When no one understands what you say, you step closer and shout louder.

C. When the barman doesn't understand your order, you point frantically at the beer.

D. You're surrounded by locals, swapping jokes, email addresses and experiences – other travellers want to borrow your phrasebook or audio guide.

If you answered A, B, or C, you NEED Lonely Planet's language products ...

- **Lonely Planet Phrasebooks** – for every phrase you need in every language you want
- **Lonely Planet Language & Culture** – get behind the scenes of English as it's spoken around the world – learn and laugh
- **Lonely Planet Fast Talk & Fast Talk Audio** – essential phrases for short trips and weekends away – read, listen and talk like a local
- **Lonely Planet Small Talk** – 10 essential languages for city breaks
- **Lonely Planet Real Talk** – downloadable language audio guides from lonelyplanet.com to your MP3 player

... and this is why

- **Talk to everyone everywhere**
  Over 120 languages, more than any other publisher
- **The right words at the right time**
  Quick-reference colour sections, two-way dictionary, easy pronunciation, every possible subject – and audio to support it

Lonely Planet Offices

Australia
90 Maribyrnong St, Footscray,
Victoria 3011
☎ 03 8379 8000
fax 03 8379 8111
✉ talk2us@lonelyplanet.com.au

USA
150 Linden St, Oakland,
CA 94607
☎ 510 893 8555
fax 510 893 8572
✉ info@lonelyplanet.com

UK
72-82 Rosebery Ave,
London EC1R 4RW
☎ 020 7841 9000
fax 020 7841 9001
✉ go@lonelyplanet.co.uk

lonelyplanet.com